TWELVE CITIES

Former Home Secretary, Chancellor of the Exchequer and President of the European Commission, Roy Jenkins was also Chancellor of Oxford University and President of the Royal Society of Literature. He was awarded the Wolfson History Prize 2001 for his contribution to historical writing, won the Whitbread Biography Prize for his study of Gladstone and was nominated for the Samuel Johnson Prize for Non-Fiction for his bestselling biography of Churchill, which also won the British Book Awards Biography of the Year. Hailed as the best literary politician since Churchill, Lord Jenkins died in January 2003, aged 82.

ALSO BY ROY JENKINS

Roy Jenkins

TWELVE CITIES

A Memoir

PAN BOOKS

First published 2002 by Macmillan

This edition published 2004 by Pan Books
an imprint of Pan Macmillan Ltd
Pan Macmillan, 20 New Wharf Road, London N1 9RR
Basingstoke and Oxford
Associated companies throughout the world
www.panmacmillan.com

ISBN 0 330 49333 7

1 3 5 7 9 8 6 4 2

A CIP catalogue record for this book is available from
the British Library.

Typeset by SetSystems Ltd, Saffron Walden, Essex
Printed and Bound in Great Britain by
Mackays of Chatham plc, Chatham, Kent

Contents

v

List of Illustrations

NAPLES

NEW YORK

BONN

CHICAGO

BARCELONA

BERLIN

Preface

THIS LITTLE BOOK IS intended partly as a relief for those who found *Churchill* heavy to hold and long to read, and partly as a form of reminiscent self-indulgence for myself after the rigours of writing that long life. The cities about which I have chosen to write these short essays are mostly those which in one form or another have been intertwined with my life. An unfriendly critic might, I suppose, say that I have used them as an excuse for having a second go at autobiography. As such, I believe that should never be done. One navel-gazing is wholly permissible. Two would point to self-obsession. Yet there are undoubtedly autobiographical – as well as anecdotal – elements in these essays. But there are also topographical, historical and architectural ones.

Broadly – and I suppose this brings out the semi-autobiographical side – the cities are arranged according to the chronology of their imprint upon my life. But not rigidly so. I thought, for instance, that Paris, which I first saw in 1931 and only got to know in 1938 and 1939, might make a more enticing opening than Cardiff, the (small) metropolis of my childhood, of which my experience therefore extended back into the 1920s as well as the 1930s. But Cardiff comes in second and Birmingham, another of the only three British cities in the list, comes in third. Birmingham, which displaced

Manchester as England's major manufacturing city in the early twentieth century when motor cars became more important than cotton, has in the last two decades survived the collapse of almost any form of manufacturing in Britain, particularly motor cars, and has emerged, semi-triumphant, as a warehousing and distribution, exhibition, convention and indeed artistic centre, rather like a smaller Chicago. I got to know it only at the end of the Second World War, but soon afterwards began a period of twenty-seven years as one of its dozen representatives in the House of Commons. It sustained the core of my parliamentary career.

For my fourth essay I have gone about as far from landlocked and down-to-earth (although now musically distinguished) 'Brum' as it is easy to imagine – to Naples. I wanted to have one Italian city, and Naples seemed to me to have more hidden depth, as well as being less written about, than Venice, Florence or Rome. My first visit was in 1949, followed by a gap but then by many increasingly enthusiastic returns in the last thirty-five years. I do not want to see Naples and die, but I regard it as one of the most rewarding although more recently under-appreciated medium-sized cities in the world, although that under-appreciation was not there in the nineteenth century.

New York, the ultimate metropolis, although, alas for the bloated aggregations of 10 million to 25 million which have outpaced it in this respect, by no means any longer the largest city in the world. It is, with Chicago, one of my only two American essays. New York I have known since 1953, at the beginning of the Eisenhower presidency. I have never lived there, but have paid many visits and been a consistent fan for nearly fifty years. Chicago I know less well (starting in 1960) but have been fascinated by its brief and concen-trated history, and particularly by the architectural aspects of this. I count it, paired with Barcelona, as one of the two greatest non-capital cities of the world – giving New York, as it clearly deserves in all but a purely political sense, capital-city status.

The Chicago essay is at once the longest and most impersonal one in the book, containing more objective economic and architectural history, and less reminiscence. Its main companion in this respect, as in the other already noted one, is appropriately Barcelona, which comes much later in my order. This is probably because they are the two which have been least intertwined in my life, although I have been to Chicago at least a dozen times, but Barcelona only half as often, though for longer visits. They both make up for this, however, by their inherent urban interest.

Then there are the two German capitals of the past half-century, Bonn and Berlin. From one point of view Bonn does not qualify: it is a small Rhineland town and not a *Großstadt*. But it played a crucial role in the brilliantly successful political history of the forty years of the West German Federal Republic and may therefore be allowed to leap out of its strictly civic capacity. Berlin, by contrast, is overwhelmingly a *Großstadt*, indeed a *Weltstadt*, which it was Kaiser Wilhelm II's ambition to make it, and in which he succeeded to the extent of getting it up to sixth place in the world by 1913. But he also sowed some of the seeds of the city's unprecedented sundering for forty-five years a sundering which is still not wholly healed. (The three years of severence of Madrid in the Spanish Civil War was too short to count as a parallel, and Nicosia since the Turkish conquests of 1974 is not important enough.) This sundering has stunted Berlin, although in a different way, as much as Vienna (itself suffering from a much milder and shorter division in 1945–54) was stunted by the 1918 disintegration of the Austro-Hungarian Empire. In the Viennese case it was like a river losing energy and draining off into agreeable but stagnant pools. In Berlin it was more a question of turbulence over rapids, with for a time the world looking on with bated breath to see what disasters this might produce both *ex urbi et orbi*, and then of the river, freed from the gorges and the boulders, rushing on across the plain of reunification towards a future over which there are many question marks. Whatever else the new Berlin is, it is not placid or stagnant.

There remain a disparate trio of cities, each of them with a special taste for me. In two of them – Brussels and Glasgow – I have actually lived, or rather had a residence, part-time in Brussels, even more so in Glasgow. Brussels was also the first foreign city which I ever saw, in 1929. Nearly half a century later it became my main base for four years. I am glad to have spent those years there, but have a measured view about the city. Glasgow, on the other hand, aroused my passionate enthusiasm. I have tried to explain why. It was not just that I won a cliff-hanging bye-election there, although that no doubt provided a favourable foundation.

Dublin makes my dozen. Again, like Chicago and Barcelona, it is not a city with which I would claim an instinctive and intimate relationship. I first went there in 1961, and have since been about another twenty times. It was always a fascinating place for any amateur of late-nineteenth- and early-twentieth-century British political history, and it has more recently acquired a European-induced surge to prosperity, accompanied by some of the disadvantages of such rushes to wealth.

In addition I ought perhaps to explain why some cities have not been included. There are three which I have in conversations about the shape of this book frequently encountered as false guesses. These are Oxford, London and Washington. Oxford is emphatically not a metropolis – but nor is Bonn, it may be rejoined. But Oxford has never been a capital, not at any rate since a brief and fragile imperium at the time of the Civil War. Most decisively, however, it is to me essentially a university and not a city, and this book is not, except elliptically as in Chicago and Berlin, about universities.

London falls partly because it is too big – although no more so than New York – but more essentially because it has been so comprehensively the background to the whole sixty years of my adult life that I would find it almost impossible to find an outside viewing platform from where to direct shafts of perspective upon it. Where would I start?

Washington does not suffer from that disqualification. I have known it quite well, starting from 1953, although more since the early Kennedy years, but much of my life there has revolved around the massive Lutyens-designed British embassy residence on Massachusetts Avenue – so different from, yet equal with, its rue du Faubourg Saint-Honoré analogue – and I felt that I had done enough on diplomatic life in the Paris essay. I did not want the book to become a sort of Michelin Guide to British embassies. Furthermore I do not think that Washington as a metropolis, with all its spacious beauty, can really hold a candle to the pulsating urban excitements of New York or Chicago.

I owe, as with all my books, considerable debts to those who have assisted in its creation. My wife has of course critically read each of the essays several times, as well as having been with me on at least some of my visits to all the twelve cities, including the special rounding-up ones which we have recently paid to Cardiff, Naples, Barcelona, New York, Chicago, Birmingham, Berlin and Dublin. My secretary, Gimma Macpherson, has had, in order to decipher my handwriting, to make herself familiar with the spelling of such little-known figures as Puig i Cadafalch, Padraig Pearse and Antonio Bassolino.

Then there are a variety of 'experts' on the individual cities, whom I have persuaded to cast their eyes over my amateur judgements.

Paris: Madame Jacques de Beaumarchais; Monsieur Hubert Faure; and Sir Christopher Mallaby.

Cardiff: Lord Anglesey; and Mr David Jones, Librarian of the House of Lords.

Birmingham: Sir Richard Knowles, leader of the Birmingham City Council 1984–93; Professor Peter Marsh of Birmingham University; and Ms Barbara Wren.

Naples: Dott. Renato Ruggiero, native of Naples, graduate of its University and subsequently, *inter alia*, Director-General of the World Trade Organization and Italian Foreign Minister.

New York: Professor Arthur Schlesinger, Jr; Mr Irwin Ross; and Mr Harold Evans.

Bonn: Sir Nicholas Henderson and Sir Christopher Mallaby, former ambassadors.

Chicago: Senator Hillary Rodham Clinton; Ms Eileen Mackevich, President Chicago Humanities Festival; and Sir Colin Lucas, formerly Dean of Science at the University of Chicago and currently Vice-Chancellor of Oxford University.

Brussels: Vicomte Etienne Davignon, member of the European Commission, 1977–84, and subsequently chairman of Societé Général de Belgique; Sir Crispin Tickell, my Brussels *chef de cabinet*; Sir John Kerr, ambassador to the European Commission, 1990–5.

Dublin: Dr Garret FitzGerald, Taoiseach of Ireland, 1981–2 and 1982–7; and Dr Mary Daley, historian.

Glasgow: Dr Donald McFarlane; Lord Maclennan of Rogart.

Barcelona: Alastair Boyd (Lord Kilmarnock), author of *Guide to Catalonia*; Mr David Gilmour, author of *Spanish Cities*; and Professor Lord Thomas of Swynnerton.

Berlin: Dr Hermann Freiherr von Richthofen, German ambassador to London, 1988–93 and currently president of the Deutsch-English Gesellschaft, based in Berlin; and Sir Christopher Mallaby.

ROY JENKINS
East Hendred
June 2002

PARIS

I FIRST SAW PARIS in August 1931, when I was not quite eleven years old. That now seems to me a very long time ago, as indeed it is. Placing one point of a child's geometric compass on today and another on that year, and then swinging it backwards, which I have always found a vivid way of illustrating the distance of an event, takes one to 1860, with the glitter of the Second Empire at its peak and Napoleon III securely ensconced in the Tuileries, St Cloud and Compiègne: with Haussmann in the midst of his great building projects; long before the Belle Epoque, well before the Franco-Prussian War and the horrors of the Commune.

While hardly comparable with the Commune, August 1931 was not a calm month in Britain. The second Labour government was staggering to an ignominious end, although its Prime Minister, Ramsay MacDonald, was to rise again from the ashes, if not exactly in glory, at least, with Conservative support, in a secure tenancy of 10 Downing Street for the next four years. The world economic depression was gaining momentum, and sterling was within a month of severing its tenuous link with gold, which had been restored only six years before. That made France temporarily more expensive until even greater French devaluations made it, for the British, very cheap in the late 1930s. I do not however think that a fine calculation of an exchange rate window played much part in my father's determination to take his small family to Paris in that summer. Neither my mother nor I had ever been there, although we had been to Brussels three years before. And Paris had a great position in my father's life and memory. In 1909–10 he had spent nearly nine months there, after having been a working-class student at Ruskin College, Oxford. Quite how that visit was financed I have never understood, for he did not work except at French, which as a result he spoke better than I have ever done, but devoted himself to learning his way about the city and developing contacts with French socialist leaders.

This meant that francophilia played a continuing nostalgic part in his life. The classics of Russian fiction in his considerable library were, for instance, in French translations, which was unusual in the house of a South Wales miners' agent. And it was no doubt part of the same spirit which made him eager to show us Paris in the summer of 1931. We were accompanied by a local schoolmaster and his wife. We went second class (not first but not third either, for continental boat trains in England as well as across the Channel retained the respectable intermediate class until 1939), via Folkestone and Boulogne. We stayed in a modest hotel in the rue de Turbigo, off the boulevard de Sébastopol. It was almost in the shadow of the sixteenth/seventeenth-century church of Saint Eustache, famous for the quality of its music, although I did not know that until long afterwards.

We spent six days in Paris, visiting most of the obvious sights, as well as engaging in the less obvious pursuit of seeking the hostel near the Bastille, called the Foyer de l'Ouvrier, in which my father had lived twenty years before, and trying (unsuccessfully) to trace its *directeur*, Monsieur Dupuis, who had made a deep impression upon my father. I had heard much about him, although I never knew his Christian name, and always imagined him looking like Jean

Jaurès, bearded, burly and benign, but very unEnglish. Indeed at this stage in my life I thought of nearly everything in Paris as being not at all like our 'own dear home life'. Seventy years ago it was psychologically a long way from Pontypool to Paris, and a very low proportion of our neighbours ever even contemplated making the journey, or a comparable one, at all. It was interesting but strange, and potentially hostile.

I did not go back to Paris until September 1936, when I was fifteen, and then only to pass through it on my way to and from Geneva. I persisted in seeing it as a pre-1914 caricature. I have a blurred memory of breakfasting in a station buffet (whether the Gare Saint-Lazare where we arrived or the Gare de Lyon from where we left I cannot recall) and remember it as being half filled with a lot of men in tall black hats, who looked as though they were Toulouse-Lautrec absinthe drinkers, and half with apache dancers in jerseys, whom one of our party suggested were off to fight in the Spanish Civil War, which had broken out six weeks earlier.

It was not until the two brink-of-war summers, 1938 and 1939, that I came to see Paris through less distorting spectacles. In the first summer, just before going to Oxford, I spent nearly a month there. In the latter I was in France for five weeks, most of them in Paris. In 1938, as in 1931 and 1936, I started very much under my father's aegis. We stayed a few days in the Hôtel Terminus Nord, a somewhat tentative beachhead for British visitors, because it faced the fine 1860s façade of the Gare du Nord, from where most of the English boat trains departed. After those few days, however, I was installed and left in a recommended semi-educational pension off a courtyard behind a *porte-cochère* on the boulevard de Port-Royal in the south-easterly 13th arrondissement. That wide boulevard, with its *pavés*, plane trees and very early Third Republican feel, ran gently uphill from the Avenue des Gobelins to the Carrefour de l'Observatoire, from where there was a perspective up the boulevard Saint-Michel to the southern end of the Luxembourg gardens. It was a district of hospitals, barracks and even a prison (perhaps ironically named Prison de la Santé). I hoped I would not end up in any of them. Beyond the Carrefour, Port-Royal changed its name to the boulevard du Montparnasse and continued to the intersection with the boulevard Raspail, where were the then avant-garde brasseries of Le Dôme, La Rotonde and La Coupole.

In the pension I was supposed to improve my French, which up to a limited extent I did. But, my aptitude for topography being greater than that for languages, what I more strikingly did was to acquire almost a taxi-driver's knowledge of the Paris street plan. This was fortified by my second instalment in 1939, and like many things acquired early in life (telephone numbers of that period are a good parallel example) have remained with me more securely than later knowledge. In 1939 I also acquired a part-time occupation well suited to my interests and talents. I was taken on by the Paris office of the Workers' Travel Association (an Ernest Bevin enterprise, run from his recently built Transport House) to meet parties of British visitors at the Gare du Nord or the Gare Saint-Lazare and conduct them either to small hotels or across Paris to the Gare de Lyon or the Gare d'Orsay. As I loved trains and great termini it was a treat and not a chore. I was not paid, but there was the perquisite of a first-class rail pass all over France. On one occasion I went to Biarritz and the Spanish frontier, on another to Toulon.

In these two summer visits I acquired not only a familiarity with but also a great affection for Paris. My knowledge of it was extensive but also superficial – essentially that of a tourist. I mounted to the top of every *point de vue* in the city from the Arc de Triomphe to one of the towers of Notre-Dame. Apart from an austere lady called Madame Vincent who ran the pension, I hardly knew any French people, although I avoided loneliness mainly through contacts with various transient English. I got to know the Métro system almost inside out, found its characteristic smell evocative rather than offensive, and liked the way in which some lines suddenly swooped to the surface, particularly when crossing the Seine, thereby providing very good urban views. I was also an amateur of Paris buses, which then all had outside rear platforms on which one could smoke exotic (to the English) Gauloises, and be jolted along, healthily apart from the cigarettes, and in touch with Paris street scenes.

As the second half of that 1939 August moved on I became increasingly aware of living on the edge of a precipice of war. Churchill, who spent the same days with his easel in 'the light of this lovely valley at the confluence of the Eure and the Vesgre', said as he completed a canvas, 'This is the last picture we shall paint in peace for a very long time.' Eighty miles away I translated the same sentiment into bathos. Before scuttling home by the night boat from Dieppe I went into a patisserie and bought a large *tarte aux pommes*, which I transported with some difficulty to Victoria Station, across London to Paddington and down to Monmouthshire in a train crowded with evacuees. I think my mother was pleased but surprised to receive this exotic offering. For me it was a very impermanent souvenir of pre-war Paris.

It was nearly eight years before, in the early summer of 1947, I again saw the city. In the meantime I had gobbled up most pieces of nostalgic writing about France which came out in London – from Raymond Mortimer's *Channel Packet* to Alexander Werth's journalistic diaries of the late 1930s. Just as Ernest Bevin once described the object of his foreign policy as being 'to go down to Victoria Station and buy a ticket to where the hell I pleased', so, prominent among my private war aims, was the ability to go to Paris again.

Nevertheless, as is sometimes the case with eagerly awaited pleasures, I did not greatly indulge myself of it much in the decade and a half of the Fourth Republic. I was in Paris perhaps twenty times, not more, in the twelve years between that 1947 first post-war visit and de Gaulle turning the Fourth into the Fifth Republic in 1959.

The Fourth Republic is somewhat unjustly maligned in the history of France. It produced no glorious leaders after de Gaulle retreated to Colombey, and those who made the most impact, with the possible exception of Pierre Mendès-France, were the most respectable relicts of the Third Republic: Léon Blum, Edouard Herriot and Paul Reynaud. With the French Empire at least as untenable as the British, the inevitable retreats and handovers were on the whole managed less well by the Fourth Republic ministers than by Attlee and Macmillan. It was only when the two empires attempted a joint stand at Suez that a real disaster occurred. But, when that is said, the Fourth Republic which inherited the already deeply divided society of the last years of the Third Republic, further embittered by defeat, by the fluctuating fortunes (and supporters) of Vichy and the Resistance, and by vengeful bloodbaths at the end of the war, did manage to pull together the civilized and reasonably stable France of the 1950s. Further, with the Monnet Plan and massive public investment, it laid the foundations of a 1960s and 1970s French economy which, in contrast with the 1930s, was rapidly overhauling that of Britain.

Even so, I did not find that the intoxicating quality of Paris in the 1950s quite matched that which I had experienced in 1938 and 1939. I was in an intermediate phase so far as accommodation was concerned. I never went back to the pension in the boulevard de Port-Royal, except to look at its outside in a nostalgic way. On the other hand I took some time to graduate far upmarket. I never for instance stayed in the British embassy until the mid-1960s. The Hôtel Ritz, beloved by Churchill, remained *terra incognita* to me for somewhat longer. Around 1950, when I was already a young member of Parliament, my wife and I spent several nights of passage, but also one extended stay of a week, in various modest, mainly Left Bank hotels. An exception, however (in its location, not in its modesty), was an establishment implausibly labelled Hôtel des Ministères, which was tucked away somewhere near the Madeleine.

Another exception was a December 1951 visit which was so brief that no question of an hotel arose. A cross-party delegation of about fifteen MPs travelled out by night-ferry *wagons-lits*, spent most of the day at SHAPE, the military headquarters of NATO land forces, then at Rocquecourt on the western edge of Paris, and returned by the same means on the following night. The fact that we were eager to go at all in such circumstances pointed either to a dutiful interest in defence arrangements in that phase of high Cold War tension or to the attractions of any trip out of Britain, or to a combination of the two. I retain three strong impressions of the visit. The first was that Eisenhower as Supreme Commander gave us a polite, conventional and rather dull talk. The second was that his deputy Montgomery, who followed, was determined to upstage him. He strode in with a pointer for use with a blackboard to give us a quick appraisal of force dispositions, and graciously said that we could ask questions provided that we gave our name, spoke clearly and kept them short.

Anthony Crosland reacted to this by leaning back, crossing his long legs and saying in his most languid voice: 'Crosland, not to be confused with [Richard] Crossman, who is sitting in the next row.' Montgomery, who at least could not be accused of deficiency in the art of the put-down, said, 'I wouldn't dream of confusing you. I have heard of Crossman.' The incident, apart from its insight into Montgomery, illustrated the fickleness of reputations, for today, approximately a quarter of a century after both their deaths, Crosland's has survived much more strongly than has Crossman's.

The third impression from that visit is of the glitter of the pre-Christmas shops in the rue du Faubourg Saint-Honoré as Crosland and I walked down it that evening on our way to a restaurant dinner and then to the train. And that sense of glamour was a persistent feature of British 1950s attitudes to France. We instinctively thought that Britain was a more important country, certainly a more dependable member of NATO, head prefect to America's headmaster, with more stable governments, better social provisions (ironical though that would now seem to anyone who has recently experienced both health services), and, we hoped, although with decreasing conviction as the decade wore on, a stronger economy. To the French we were prepared to allow better trains, smarter shops, at least superficially more general sophistication, a language which was still a semi-rival in world terms, and above all incomparably better food, reliably so from *bistrot* to *restaurant de luxe*.

This makes me move on to another quasi-political visit, which was in 1954, the year of the initially hopeful premiership of Mendès-France but also of the crushing French imperial defeat at Dien Bien Phu. The occasion was some sort of conference, but I cannot remember what. I went with Woodrow Wyatt and his about-to-be-married third wife, Lady Moorea Hastings. We stayed in another small hotel, just back from the *quai* south of Notre-Dame, which I think was chosen for romance rather than for *confort cossu*, but we ate rather grandly. I particularly remember a dinner at Lapérouse, half a mile further along the *quai*, where Proust made Swann at the height of his infatuation go and dine alone, because it reminded him of the far-distant (by Paris standards) rue La Pérouse, where Odette de Crécy lived. It was also the restaurant where Churchill in the spring of 1940 had with General Georges, the second man in the French army, what his frequent companion on French expeditions, Louis Spears (another general as well as a participant in the Lapérouse gastronomy), described as 'one of the few pleasant occasions I experienced during the war, three friends enjoying each other's company and remarkable food and drink'.

On that visit we also went, a little unenthusiastically, to a performance in the Second Empire splendours of the Paris Opéra. I suspect that free tickets must have been handed out by the conference organizers. It was only the second time that I had been to that opera house, the Garnier as it is mostly known. The first had been to hear *Rigoletto* in 1938. This time it was Wagner, and none of the three of us at that stage had the perception to see the beauty behind the noise. We left well before the end, maybe making for Lapérouse. The only excuse was that the Paris Opéra was then at one of its low points, with its productions little esteemed among the opera cognoscenti of the world. But that was not much of an excuse, particularly as we were far from belonging to those cognoscenti.

Over the three years of 1955–7 I became a delegate (of the British Parliament) to the Assemblies of the Council of Europe and the Western European Union, the one being a very loose and tentative attempt to bring together a Europe wider than that of the Six, who were already linked in the much more meaningful Coal and Steel Community, and the other an otiose scheme for providing the military arrangements into which seven countries entered under the Brussels Treaty of 1948 with some sort of nominal parliamentary supervision. The first met in Strasbourg, which involved many journeys through Paris. I remember one when, pulling out of the Gare de l'Est, I found myself at a restaurant-car table with Herbert Morrison and Guy Mollet. Morrison's best days were over, and Mollet was within little over a year to be the French Prime Minister of the Suez fiasco. *Wagon-restaurant* food was good in those days, but the luncheon conversation was not memorably scintillating.

The WEU Assembly, which performed for only a few days a year, did so in Paris, in the Palais de Chaillot, latterly the Musée de l'Homme. The Palais de Chaillot was a relic of the International Exhibition of 1937, just as the Eiffel Tower was of that of 1889. I am unaware of any contribution which I made to European statecraft in the Chaillot, but the expenses scale of WEU at least extended somewhat upwards my knowledge of Paris hotels. At first in this phase I stayed in the fashionably placed but not grand Castiglione, opposite and a little down the street from the British embassy. Then I became seduced by the slightly Germanic grandeur (it was indeed the favourite Paris base of Adenauer and of some subsequent Chancellors) of the Hôtel Bristol, further up the rue du Faubourg Saint-Honoré and nearer to the Elysée.

I discovered that there was a large low room under the eaves – and perhaps not for this reason much sought after, number 806 I think, which could be had for a surprisingly modest sum and certainly well within the WEU expense limit. More important, however, was the room's command, through three mansard windows, of a wide sweeping southern Paris panorama from the Tour Eiffel and the Ecole Militaire on the right through the great golden dome of Napoleon's Les Invalides, past the Palais Bourbon to the lesser but still more elegant dome of Mazarin's Institut de France. It was a particularly good view at night, and gave me much pleasure over a dozen or so visits extending well beyond the Council of Europe and WEU years into the early 1960s. Then it came to be replaced for me by the ministerial suite on the second floor of the British embassy, which curiously commanded almost exactly the same view, although with the sweep even less impeded than from the Bristol.

My experience of the Hôtel de Charost has been mixed. Wellington acquired it for the British embassy in 1814 and it has continued to perform that role for nearly 200 years, in spite of one or two unsuccessful attempts, notably that by the government's think-tank in the 1970s, to persuade the Foreign Office that the ambassador could operate more efficiently from a modern flat in Neuilly. It is not the grandest embassy residence in the world. That distinction must belong to the French embassy in Rome, the Palazzo Farnese, although that strikes me as being stronger in grandeur than in amenity. There are also one or two other surprising competitors like the Italian embassy in Lisbon, architecturally splendid, but an island in what has become a semi-slum sea, and, perhaps less surprisingly, the German embassy to France, the Hôtel Beauharnais, across the river from the British and American caravanserai and more in the heart of official Paris. Nevertheless the Palais Chârost has a unique combination of elegance and comfort, and has long been one of Britain's best weapons in the uphill struggle to impress the French.

This does not however mean that my visits to it have been without vicissitudes. These began early. In my second week as a Minister (of Aviation) I had to go to Paris and explain to the French why we had announced, without consultation, that we wanted to cancel the Concorde project. At the time I was in favour of the objective, and even in retrospect I have not changed my mind. I am very doubtful whether Concorde has proved a worthwhile investment for either the British or the French economies, with the French now at least as much disposed to agree as are the British. But

I thought that the method of cancellation had been ill chosen and mishandled. The mission was therefore a difficult ministerial baptism of fire.

The ambassador (Pierson Dixon) who had to look after me was polite but not enthusiastically supportive, for he was even more critical of the method than was I. The luncheon preceding the crunch meeting with French ministers was stiff. Moreover, in my firm conviction, unvarying over what is now nearly four decades, the wine was lightly corked. The ambassador did not appear to notice, which was surprising, for he was a man of sophistication and experience, dating back to his having been Eden's private secretary for much of the Second World War. I was then too unselfconfident to put my conviction against his indifference. So we proceeded to the key meeting, which did not go as badly as I had feared, without much prior fortification.

The vicissitude of the next morning, when on my way to the airport I had to make a series of courtesy calls upon other French ministers whose responsibility overlapped marginally with mine, was potentially greater. Awakening in the 'room with a view' I plunged into the bathroom, to discover, when I emerged ten minutes later, that every single item of clothing had been packed by the *valet de chambre*, taken downstairs and put in the boot of a car which was on the point of departing direct to the airport. The suitcase was returned and catastrophe averted by the narrowest of margins. From that morning I learned two lessons: that excessive service can be more of a menace than a convenience, and that one should always keep as close as possible to one's luggage.

My final meeting turning out to be more relaxed than I had expected. It was with Gaston Palewski, who as Minister of Science had a fine room on the corner of the rue Royale in what had been before the war the Ministre de la Marine (and was where Churchill had argued with Admiral Darlan in the winter of 1939–40). Palewski, Gaullist of the first order who had spent the war in London, was a long-standing friend of Nancy Mitford in an *amitié* which was not quite *amoureuse* enough for her, whom she put into literature under the guise of Fabrice, Duc de Sauveterre. This sounded rather a grand designation but as Palewski ended up married to a lady who was born Talleyrand-Périgord and who could lay claim to the title of Duchesse de Sagan, this was not perhaps excessive. At our meeting that morning he only wanted to hear London gossip.

This was not my only difficult bedroom experience in that splendid British embassy. On another visit, nearly two years later when I had become Home Secretary, and in another room which the wife of Dixon's replacement had decided needed modernization with a bed from the then famous firm of Heals, I passed an unrestful night. The new bed was so streamlined that it maintained perpetual motion around the room for several hours. Eventually at about 5.00 a.m. one castor came off and it subsided into immobility, although with a strong list. That was on balance an improvement, and it must also be said that the husband of that innovating wife performed for me a signal ambassadorial service. He informed me that he had invited two up-and-coming French politicians of such promise that he thought I would be glad to meet them to come in, seriatim, for a drink with me that evening. The one was Valéry Giscard d'Estaing and the other was François Mitterrand. He had not done badly by any standards, and it more than made up for the restless bed.

The great majority of my experiences in that embassy have however been without blemish. They have ranged from going there to make a speech on the occasion of Simone Veil's installation as a DBE to the receipt there of my own Légion d'Honneur, and also include a (postponed) eightieth-birthday weekend organized by four dear English friends but with the ambassadorial couple (Michael and Sylvia Jay) hospitably providing the base from which the expedition to the celebratory restaurant meal took place. It was this same ambassadorial couple who not only frequently welcomed my wife and myself, but who went so far beyond the call of duty as to entertain some of our grandchildren too. I hope they got some recompense from the knowledge that one of them (a girl then aged ten) whom I took on a forty-eight-hour visit (we were staying elsewhere) gave the precise reply when asked what she had most liked about it of 'the Sainte Chapelle and being shown round the embassy by Lady Jay'.

Those various experiences extend over the tenure of ten ambassadors, of whom three, maybe four, were close friends. It was however mildly sad that during nearly the whole of the incumbency of our oldest friend among them, Nicko Henderson, I was president of the European Commission and that there was a convention, sensible in its way, that, except on a purely private visit, the president's rising above national affiliations should be underlined by not staying in the embassy of his own country when on a visit to a member state. This meant that I became acquainted with the highest ranks of Paris hotels. If the occasion was organized by the French government they installed me in a grand suite in the Crillon, looking across the Place de la Concorde and the river to the Assemblée Nationale. But they did so with an appropriate regard for the French taxpayer, and on the occasion of my inaugural visit to President Giscard, when two nights were almost inevitable, they paid for one, leaving the Commission to pay for the other. They probably also got cut rates, for the Crillon was very much the government hotel, just as was the Grand Hotel in Rome. The Crillon also had one feature of which the Grand Hotel was free. It was reputed to be almost as heavily if more elegantly bugged as the National Hotel, Moscow.

The Crillon also contains the bar which in the 1950s and 1960s was the clubhouse of the British press in Paris. In that bar, for several hours each day, there gathered nearly all the reporters of France to Britain. Sam White, the monolingual Australian whom Beaverbrook recruited to write for the *Evening Standard* a Paris column as readable as it was generally perceptive, was said to confine his investigations to that hospitable corner of the Crillon. By the time of my Paris visits from Brussels, White was dead and the press coterie had been as completely dispersed as the *Punch* Round Table in London or the Algonquin Hotel literary circle in New York. And, more recently, the vaguely art-deco bar has been redecorated into an unfortunate imitation of a Turkish harem.

So it was not a desire to avoid too close contact with the British press which made me prefer another hotel when I was in Paris on Commission business, but under my own steam rather than that of the French government. The alleged bugging had something to do with it, but more I think was the desire for independence and a feeling that the opposite hill was greener. We made no great leap into the unknown or into the maelstrom of Paris proletarian life. We merely moved half a kilometre to the east and the rigours of the Hôtel Ritz on the Place Vendôme. I had stayed there once before when Chancellor of the Exchequer and in a small suite on the back or garden side. This could be had for what now seems the modest sum of *circa* £180 a night. On this pattern we subsisted over the occasional visits of three years or so. 'While waiting for the new Jerusalem', to paraphase an old bit of Hilaire Belloc mordancy, 'these little huts sufficed for us.'

Then, on the occasion of my farewell visit to Paris as president, this equilibrium was upset. First the Ritz had been revamped and no doubt the prices increased as a result. Second they had put us in a much larger suite, on the Place

Vendôme side. Third I made the mistake of looking on the back of the bathroom door, where French hotels have to display their prices, and discovered that it had become nearly £400. Fourth I was sensitive on the issue at the time, for one of my vice-presidents, admittedly from the richest and most handsomely contributing country of the Community, had an excessive taste for grand hotels and managed to run up phenomenal bills which had attracted the interest of the Audit Court and of the European Parliament.

I summoned Crispin Tickell, my powerful *chef de cabinet* who has since been ambassador to the United Nations, head of an Oxford college and a world climatology expert, and said, 'We cannot pay this. Go down and tell them that they must either move us to our normal small suite, or reduce this price, or we will leave. They can decide while we are paying our call on the President of the Republic.' Ten minutes later Crispin came back looking rather pleased with himself. I asked him what he had said and he replied, 'Il faut que vous sachiez [very accurate use of the subjunctive] que Monsieur Jenkins n'est pas un sheik arabe ni même un roi nègre.' And what did they say, I continued. 'They reduced the price by a half,' he concluded. Rather to my regret I have never, in the intervening years, revisited the Paris Ritz.

French official life over the six decades or so when I have had varying degrees of contact with it, and inevitably measuring it against that of Britain, has struck me in varying ways. Perhaps the steadiest, if not the most serious, change has been that as time has gone by the French (men) have got much better and the English much worse dressed. When I was first taken by my father to the Chamber of Deputies in the 1930s, nearly all those we encountered seemed to be like my description of the (to me) mythical Monsieur Dupuis at the beginning of this essay, burly, often bearded men in ill-fitting, double-breasted serge with rather scruffy shoes and collars. They looked better orators, but they could not hold a candle to the prim neatness of Neville Chamberlain or Samuel Hoare, let alone the more careless elegance of Anthony Eden. Even Léon Blum, rich and fastidious intellectual though he was, looked more gangling than at ease with his socialist faith in his bourgeois clothes. Pierre Laval I never recollect seeing, so that I cannot say with the conviction I would wish that with his trademark white (long) ties he inspired little trust in me. Churchill's erstwhile friend, Pierre-Etienne Flandin, was another slightly ill-at-ease, stiff-collared man who looked as though he got his suits from Old England in the Place de la Madeleine.

The contrast with the French I dealt with in my European Commission days could hardly have been greater. Giscard's sartorial style, I always felt, was not quite sufficiently negligent for his desired impression. But he could not possibly be described as ill dressed. This was even more true of some of his acolytes. Michel Poniatowski, Minister of the Interior, also looked a little too sporting, although with a touch of a boy scout thrown in, but this was largely because his very grand aunt, the Princesse de Caraman-Chimay, firmly treated him as such. This was not at all true of the others. Raymond Barre, Prime Minister for most of Giscard's *septennat*, was friendlily inelegant, although with total self-confidence. Jean François-Poncet, Foreign Minister, and Claude Cheysson, one of my Commissioners, were neat as two pins. François-Poncet, indeed, a very agreeable man who got tetchy only when he was operating under instructions with which he did not agree, was a good match in urbanity for Peter Carrington, who was his *vis-à-vis* at the end of both their periods of office. Jean François-Poncet's one concession to informality, which his father, ambassador to Berlin up to 1939 and after the war to Bonn, would not have approved, was to wear a smart *pull* under his jacket in cold weather. Even André

François-Poncet, however, could not rival the exquisite refinement of one of his successors in Bonn, Olivier Wormser. Wormser, although I greatly both liked and respected him, always made me feel slightly vulgar when eating or drinking anything in his presence.

Jacques Chaban-Delmas, who had been Prime Minister but was currently president of the Assemblée Nationale, also had a sporting touch about him but it was more that of tennis balls than of gun dogs. François Mitterrand's short stature, although he never had the demeanour of a 'little man', was not an aid to elegance, although his extraordinary physical immobility more than made up for it. He could sit absolutely still while waiting to make an important speech, giving the impression of a very powerful spider sitting confidently at the centre of a very convoluted web. Lionel Jospin, by contrast, reverted more to the shagginess of the left in the Third Republic. Few however of the British figures at ministerial meetings in Brussels were by comparison much of an advertisement for Savile Row superiority – certainly not Denis Healey, Geoffrey Howe or Kenneth Clarke.

There are, however, comparisons between French and British official life more important than the sartorial, amusing a diversion (to the writer at least) although these may offer. The first and most obvious one is that the French government, under at least the first four Presidents of the Fifth Republic, was the most co-ordinated and/or disciplined in the Western world. When, in 1979, I had a mild passage of arms with President Giscard at a Paris press conference on a Tuesday afternoon I detected a distinct unease in the attitude to me at lunch in Strasbourg on the Wednesday of even such a normally friendly man as François-Poncet. When there was a turn at the top they all turned, and with great speed. That would not have been so in the British government. Neither Peter Carrington nor Geoffrey Howe would have even marginally shifted their attitude to me because of the knowledge that I had had a contretemps with Margaret Thatcher.

On the other hand the French and British governments were similar in liking to achieve co-ordinated positions between departments. This may seem an elementary require-ment of government, but it is one without which American administrations have long survived. Messages coming out from State and Defense, or Treasury and Commerce, fre-quently contradict each other. Furthermore it is a tradition in which the Bonn of the Bundesrepublik followed Washing-ton rather than Paris or London. Perhaps it has something to do with federal institutions producing a greater tolerance of difference. Nor is there anything to suggest that the more *étatiste* habits of Britain and France produced a higher level of economic performance or of foreign policy influence than the more relaxed, 'let a thousand flowers grow' attitude of the other two.

During my presidency I found the problems of dealing with the French government as great as dealing with the other eight put together. This was despite President Giscard having been a decisive partisan of my appointment. Yet they were always the most sharply censorious, always looking out for examples of my Anglo-Saxon provincial clodhoppery in relation to the history and conventions of the Europe of the Six. This hypercritical approach reached its epitome in Elysée meetings with President Giscard himself. They typi-cally lasted one and a half hours, and had to be conducted almost entirely in French because, even though his English was better than my French, it was the language in which he believed it appropriate that the President of the French Republic should speak to the president of the European Commission. (To some substantial extent I agreed with him on this, for France was fighting a desperate and losing battle for the international status of its language, which, had English not been fortuitously sustained by the power of the United States, would have produced at least as much defensive neurosis in Britain.) Nevertheless the whole exercise was conducted more like a *concours de dressage* than as a free exchange of international views. It was totally different from an analogous meeting with Helmut Schmidt, despite the great mutual admiration which existed between the German Chancellor and the French President.

This should not be taken as meaning that President Giscard was not a constructive statesman. He had high intelligence and many excellent ideas. But he suffered from the major flaw, which damagingly communicated itself to the French people, that condescension was his stock-in-trade. Sometimes this took faintly ludicrous forms. I remember an interchange which gave great pleasure to those among the French official classes who were not his greatest fans. He wished to pay me a mild compliment, and said, 'Ah, Monsieur Jenkins, votre français s'est beaucoup amélioré récemment.' He continued: 'Il y a quelqu'un d'autre qui me l'a dit la semaine dernière.' Then he paused and said, 'Si j'ai bonne mémoire, c'était le Roi d'Espagne.' I could not resist replying: 'Mais c'est un peu bizarre, Monsieur le Président de la République, parce que le Roi d'Espagne et moi nous avons toujours parlé en anglais.'

It would however be quite wrong not to set alongside the fencing-match quality of relations with the French government and its top officials the simple fact that all my principal, long-lasting and deeply loved non-English-speaking (as a maternal language) friends have been French. There have been about eight of them, and with none of them have differences of view about the organization of Europe, or disputes about the relative status of the Commission and of the governments of the member states (particularly of one), or Anglo-French budgetary arguments ever made the slightest difference to the untroubled face of friendship. Pre-eminent among these have been the Beaumarchais, whom we first met in 1953. Jacques de Beaumarchais was then a forty-year-old counsellor at the French embassy in London, who subsequently became the adjutant of Maurice Couve de Murville, the leader of that school of French Gaullist diplomacy which believed that Britain (which they claimed greatly to admire) could best be saved from her own follies by keeping her out of Europe. Beaumarchais wielded many a sharp sword in this cause until he became ambassador to London in 1972. In the eyes of nearly everybody except for Giscard d'Estaing, with whom he did not get on, he was a brilliant success in the exacting post, and it was a great sadness when he died only two years after his return. He was elegant both in body and in mind, but with no trace of pomposity. There was nothing of Proust's Monsieur de Norpois about him.

Marie-Alice de Beaumarchais, to whom also the success of their London embassy owes a great deal, lives on in discriminatory vigour, the companion to us both on many holidays, mainly now of sightseeing January excursions from Lisbon to Istanbul, and my wholly trusted court of last resort on questions of French diction or writing. (Should she ever need a supporting opinion, their son, Professeur de l'Université Jean-Pierre de Beaumarchais, and author of widely selling encyclopaedias of French literature, can always be called in as an assistant justice.) The Beaumarchais apartment, at the river end of the Avenue Franklin D. Roosevelt, and Marie-Alice herself remain the anchors of our Paris life. I remember it when the street door leading into the *porte-cochère* was *plastiquée* in the Algerian troubles of the late 1950s. There I have taken first a son and then two grandchildren to stay. There I have provoked a long-running argument between nearly a dozen literati as to whether or not the 's' at the end of Palamède de Charlus is silent.

In summer the first-floor apartment is dark in the shadow of the horse-chestnut leaves. But it is illuminated by the Nattier portrait of the original maker of the family name, Pierre-Augustin Caron de Beaumarchis. A statuette of him also there shows him insouciantly holding a silver-topped cane. That cane was once equally insouciantly left by me in a café, but fortunately only for a few hundred yards and a couple of minutes, when a jerk of memory enabled me to go back and safely retrieve it. Otherwise I am not sure that even the powerful sinews of our great friendship would have survived. Caron de Beaumarchais was the creator of the character of Figaro, from which, with a little assistance from Mozart and Rossini, at least a half of Seville's great operatic reputation has stemmed. We (more than Marie-Alice) were therefore somewhat shocked when, on a visit to the large Alfonso XIII hotel in that Andalusian city, we found ourselves in a grand suite while the bearer of the name to which it should be most grateful was given a *chambre de bonne*. Perhaps the management allowed their proximity to the old tobacco factory (now the University) to lead them to the mistaken view that Bizet's Carmen was more important.

One of the difficulties of having known a city over seventy years, and through a series of very different circumstances, is that of trying to reconcile the very different images of Paris which float vaguely through the mind. The Paris of the Fifth Republic, at any rate the more fashionable parts of it, seems to me immensely more glossy, even brittle, perhaps less *gemütlich*, and certainly less fertile of cultural achievement than that of the Third Republic. This has the effect of making me enjoy areas of the city where the spirit of the early twentieth century seems best to have survived. The façades and immediate surrounds of the great railway stations have something of that quality, although once within everything is different, with the access to the *quais* having increased in difficulty almost as much as has the speed of the TGV.

There are other central areas where something the same applies: the old newspaper and Bourse area just to the east of the Opéra, where restaurants as redolent of the 1930s as Au Petit Riche and L'Escargot (although I have not been to either of them for many years) suddenly appear through a taxi window. It is, however, most striking in the infrequently visited eastern arrondissements that there has been the least change. The paradox of Paris is that the poorer parts have much the most interesting natural landscape. Apart from the gentle slope of the Champs-Elysées and the still gentler one of the rue de Rennes or the boulevard Raspail to Montparnasse, the Paris both of the ancient city and of the foreigners' playground is flat. The streak of the Seine is its only interesting natural feature. The more working-class areas by contrast are rich in slopes and *points de vue*. The hills of Ménilmontant live up to their evocative name. This contradicts the pattern in nearly every other major city of the world. New York and Berlin are both uniformly flat, but the better areas of the former look on either one of the two rivers or on Central Park, and of the latter are interspersed by the woods and lakes of Dahlem and Grünewald. London has Hampstead and Highgate, and nearly all Scottish or English provincial cities have their local high points on which, in most cases, the university is situated. This is true of Edinburgh, Glasgow, Aberdeen, Bristol, Birmingham, Liverpool, Leeds, Nottingham and Newcastle.

Paris is in reverse. The most exciting park is the Buttes Chaumont, deep in the heart of the 19th arrondissement, facing its splendid *mairie*, built in 1886 in the style and colour of a very passable imitation of a François Premier château. The Parc itself is a dramatically landscaped collection of lakes and ravines created by Barillet, an acolyte of Haussmann, out of the quarries from which that building baron got his stone. This recreative work of construction followed very soon after the destructions of the Commune, the horrors of which – on both sides – are most vividly commemorated by the Mur des Federés in the great cemetery of Père Lachaise only a mile or so to the south.

No other city has such a famous and visited graveyard. Glasgow has its Necropolis. London (incongruously as the greatest capitalist city of the period) has the last resting place of Karl Marx. Rome has its discreet Protestant cemetery which houses Keats and Shelley. And New York has the grandiose mausoleum of General (and President) Ulysses S. Grant, who was not even a New Yorker. But Paris is unique in the impact of Père Lachaise. I was first taken there by my father on a hot August day in 1931, and I was last taken there by a British ambassador on a sleeting February day in 1996. It is not exactly a cheerful place – such quality would indeed be inappropriate – but its large hillside site, with its variety of often florid monuments, is a remarkable tribute to the sweep and variety of French nineteenth- and early-twentieth-century achievements, and to their concentration in the city of Paris.

CARDIFF

CARDIFF WAS THE CITY of my childhood. We did not live there. Indeed I do not think that I have ever spent more than a total of ten or twelve nights under one of its roofs. We were twenty-two miles away. But it was very much the local metropolis. My father had a lot of meetings there. Often my mother and I accompanied him. We went there for Christmas shopping, generally as late as Christmas Eve, for the festivity was much more compressed in those days, and often for more routine purchases as well. We went for semi-celebratory meals in the Park or Angel Hotels. We went occasionally to contemporary plays – I remember particularly Priestley's *Time and the Conways* at the Prince of Wales Theatre; and, an even more conspicuous excitement, to occasional rugby internationals at Cardiff Arms Park. Then, not wholly seriously I am afraid, for I knew I was subsequently destined for Oxford, I went at the age of sixteen for six months in 1937–8 to the Cardiff University College. I travelled each way by bus on about four days a week and rather enjoyed the journeys. In Cardiff my main recollection is of occasional lectures, some reading for which I preferred the city public library to the college facility and of endless cups of coffee (or Russian tea in glasses, then thought rather smart) in the adjacent Kardomah Café.

Taken together these experiences gave me a wide if

superficial knowledge of 1930s Cardiff. That period for
Cardiff was like a relatively tranquil valley lying between two
more upland and memorable tongues of ground. Already
by the end of the First War it was past the peak of an
economic development which had turned it from a semi-rural
east Glamorganshire habitation (population almost exactly
matching the date in 1800) scattered around a twelfth-century
cathedral at Llandaff and the remains of a Roman fort and
later a border castle two miles away, into a city with a population of a quarter of a million. It had become the greatest
coal-exporting port in the world. Already in 1889 its near
monopoly position had been challenged when David Davies,
the founder of a dynasty of wealth and public generosity, had
built a new railway which outflanked it by running direct
from the Rhondda to the more modern and single-purpose
outlet of Barry, eight miles to the west. But the coal flow was
so great that this diversion did not immediately do much
more than prevent it choking the Cardiff docks. In 1913 a
record tonnage (13½ million) of very high-quality steam coal
went out through Cardiff.

There was then little emphasis upon what has become
Cardiff's more recent role as a capital city. Welsh nationalism
was weak in the great days of the coal trade, and insofar as
it existed it was more an affair of rural nonconformity resisting an Anglican and alien establishment. Lloyd George's
Llanystumdwy was about as far from Cardiff, both geographically and sociologically, as it was possible to be in the small
Principality of Wales. Cardiff, while admirably placed to
convey the product of the South Wales mining valleys to the
world, and also for quick rail travel to London, was far less
satisfactory as a hub of Welsh nationalism. The more Welsh
areas of the north looked paradoxically to Liverpool as a
semi-local metropolis in the way that we did to Cardiff. The
Liverpool Daily Post was the regional newspaper along the

North Wales littoral and Liverpool's medical resources which, nearly a hundred years later, grew up around Gladstone's Rodney Street 1809 birthplace were also North Wales's call of last resort.

It was difficult to get to Cardiff from most of Welsh Wales. If all-Wales committees or conferences were to be summoned the point of greatest mutual convenience was Shrewsbury, ten miles over the English border. This was a little humiliating but it was frequently accepted. As a result the Cardiff of my childhood and adolescence was not a very Welsh city. I remember being told that if you went into a shop in Cardiff and spoke Welsh (not an option for me or other Monmouthshire English monoglots) you would be looked at askance, whereas if you did so in Swansea, forty miles to the west, it would be regarded as perfectly normal. Today Cardiff is somewhat more Welsh and Swansea a little less so.

To add to the paradoxes, Cardiff in the inter-war years was not only the largely English- and non-Welsh-speaking principal city of a nonconformist Wales in which nearly a quarter naturally spoke the local language, but was also still (just) presided over by a Scottish Roman Catholic magnate. Toward the end of the eighteenth century the third Earl and first Marquess of Bute, son of one of George III's early Prime Ministers, acquired a Welsh heiress wife and a vast chunk of property in Cardiff and its hinterland. The Butes, their title for once accurately bearing geographical validity (unlike that of Devonshires, Derbys or Salisburys) were a Scottish family with their principal house in the complicated seascape of the western approaches to the Clyde and Glasgow. They were Stuarts, to which surname they added the second barrel of Crichton *circa* 1800. This did not prevent that marquess and his first heir from paying full commerical attention to their South Wales dowry. Cardiff had hitherto been like Valencia in Spain in turning its back upon the nearby sea, which was used for a little desultory fishing but not for much else. Bute built the first dock in 1839 and joined it to the existing town centre with a mile-and-a-half-long artery. Both the dock (which was only the first of a cluster) and the street bore the name of their creator, and logically the area which it opened up became known as Butetown. Both superficially and in reality therefore the impact of the Butes upon Cardiff was major. (They also imported some of the family's favourite Christian names into Sophia Gardens and Ninian Park.) They put a lot of money into Cardiff (the second wife of the first marquess was a Miss Coutts, which provided a strong supplementary cashflow) and they made a vast amount out of it. The coal poured down from the valleys (where the Butes also owned a lot of properties, although they preferred mining royalties to running collieries) through Cardiff and, paying fairly high port dues, out into the world. By the third quarter of the nineteenth century the Butes were one of the richest families in Britain.

They were stronger in wealth than in longevity. The second marquess succeeded his grandfather and survived for thirty-four years as head of the family but nonetheless died when his own son was only a year old. This third marquess did not come of age until 1868, but then made an impact at once romantic and fantastic before he died in 1900. He was said to be the model for Disraeli's *Lothair*. He was a determined opponent of blood sports and he wrote a book about the dying language of the island of Tenerife, which pointed to a mind at once eclectic and eccentric. More important in public imprint was his conversion to the Church of Rome at a time when the ostentation of 'pageant Catholicism' was rather shocking the old recusant families, and his desire to give expression to it by flamboyant high-gothic-revival architecture. For this purpose he acquired an almost perfect partner in William Burges, architect and decorator. Bute gave him several commissions to build new churches in Scotland and he also strongly imbibed his medicine at home. Burges, in the early 1870s, began work at Mountstuart, the family seat facing the Ayrshire coast and the Firth of Clyde, and set a splendidly extravagant pattern, which others continued for twenty years. But Mountstuart is relatively hidden, not least in rhododendron bushes. Burges's great work for Bute was his 'stupendously decorated additions' (Jan Morris) to Cardiff Castle, on one of the most prominent urban sites in Britain. It dominates central Cardiff, facing the main shopping area. Even 130 years later no one can visit Cardiff without being aware of Burges's work, and very splendidly did he fill his showcase. Not content with this, however, Bute got Burges to work on a medieval ruin at Castell Coch, six miles to the north, a sentinel site where the River Taff debouches into the plain. Here the motif was that of Rhineland fantasy, but the detailed decoration was sufficiently the same that Lord Bute could find his surroundings familiar, even if not exactly homely, whether looking across the northern waters from Mountstuart, or sitting in the heart of his wealth in Cardiff Castle, or looking benevolently from Castell Coch over the innumerable coal trains which made their way from the valleys to the Pierhead. On the Castell Coch site Burges was not able to finish his work. He died in 1881. William Frame, a more local but Burges-trained architect, finished the job.

Bute's benevolent gaze encouraged him in 1898 to sell to the Corporation of Cardiff, of which he had been mayor six years before, for neither an exorbitant nor an eleemosynary sum, fifty-nine acres of Cathays Park, adjacent to the Castle on the west side. This enabled Cardiff, which was still being borne forward on a rising flow of 'black gold', to give itself some of the appurtenances of a capital city. Gradually over the next quarter-century there arose a spaciously planned and grandly designed group of public buildings to which there is, in total, no parallel in any provincial city in England. They have a faintly artificial air about them, as if a papier-mâché model had been created for the centre of government in, say, Winston Churchill's only and somewhat Ruritanian novel *Savrola* (1901). Given the pomposity of Edwardian and early George V building styles, however, they were individually remarkably good. They were finished in Portland stone, which set them clearly apart from the rest of Cardiff, to which that white gloss was wholly alien. But they have on the whole achieved a fine combination of being impressive without being oppressive. They compare very well with most London building of the period – Kingsway, the added front of Buckingham Palace or the 'New Government Offices' as they were originally known, on the south-west corner of Whitehall.

The core Cardiff building was the City Hall, which by the narrowest of margins never had to bear a lesser title. When King Edward VII opened it, in 1905, he made Cardiff a city and elevated its chief magistrate to the dignity of a lord mayor. Adjacent to the left and finished a year earlier were the Law Courts. Behind that was the Glamorgan County Hall (opened in 1912), in many ways the most elegant and subtle of the three and the work of a hitherto unknown twenty-nine-year-old architect. Beyond to the north was a space and then the Technical College, later the University of Wales Insitute for Science and Technology. Opposite that, across Alexandra Gardens as the centre of the site was known, was the University College of South Wales and Monmouth-shire, to give it its full title, which began to move there in 1906 and has sporadically gone on building ever since. It has been the most sprawling of the Cathays Park edifices, but again it is not offensive. It is a little dingier. The college no doubt preferred academic needs to the pristine quality of the Portland stone, which is not a bad order of priorities.

There are four other elements in the Cathays Park ensemble, supplemented by one attachment on the south side, not strictly in the Park but worth mentioning. The largest of the four is the Welsh Office on the north side. It was begun, under a different name, in 1914, and it went on growing, in a quiet bureaucratic way, at least until 1979. It is neither interesting nor horrific. In the middle there is an exceptionally delicate First World War memorial, done by Sir Ninian Comper in the mid-1920s and a considerable relief from the solidity of Lutyens, whether in Whitehall or at Mons. The third and most significant building is that of the National Museum of Wales, for during the fifteen years which had intervened between foundation stone and coping stone (1912–27) its designation rose. It had originally been thought of as a local city museum, but its status and Cardiff's claim to be a capital increased with the delay. This building flanks the City Hall on the right, just as the Law Courts does on the left, and was in good Beaux Arts style. It would have made a fine railroad station for Philadelphia.

The contents of the Museum are well up to the exterior. There is a remarkable collection of French Impressionists, acquired with verve and given with public spirit by 'the Misses Davies', as they are always known. They were the two spinster daughters of the David Davies who challenged the Bute/Cardiff monopoly by building Barry docks. These two ladies bought in the early 1900s with an adventurous discrimination which rivalled Mrs Potter Palmer in Chicago and Reid and Lefebre in Glasgow, and provide an interesting indigenous juxtaposition to the Butes. In 1898 the Butes half gave the land. In 1927 the Davieses gave the pictures. Beyond that, in 1937–8 their nephew, the first Lord Davies of

Llandinam, further tilted the balance by paying for and seeing created the third building on the left-hand side, the Temple of Peace and Health, as it was admirably if a little grandiloquently called. It was designed by the fashionable Welsh architect of the 1930s, Sir Percy Thomas, the local equivalent of Baker for the last phase of empire, or of Foster for the millennium. Thomas produced a hall of lightness and optimism, which was appropriate to its declared objects, but unfortunately also of very bad acoustics, which was inappropriate to its main purpose as a venue for semi-ceremonial lectures. I was present at its opening by Lloyd George in 1938, and found it difficult to catch much more than a half of what emerged in that golden but already declining voice. And when I spoke there myself, nearly forty years later, I had a strong feeling of battling against my words being lost in the elegant ceiling.

The attachment to the south is a group of four statues in what is known as Gorsedd Gardens (because of the sub-Stonehenge relicts left in the various places where Welsh National Eisteddfods have taken place) opposite the imposing front of the Museum. They represent figures appropriate to early-twentieth-century Cardiff. The first is of the second Lord Tredegar who, unusually for a South Wales coal magnate, took part as a cavalry captain in the 1854 Charge of the Light Brigade. However the Morgans of Tredegar were always atypical, except in their wealth; the last of the line (1893–1949) was a homosexual aesthete more at home in an Evelyn Waugh novel than in a coalowners' conference.

The second statue is of John Cory (1828–1910), a straight-down-the-line mining magnate who balanced his rich takings with significant philanthropy. The third is of Lord Ninian Crichton-Stuart, a younger son of the third Marquess of Bute, who was MP for Cardiff until he was killed in France in September 1915. The fourth, and much later, statue is of

Lloyd George, who, although a non-Cardiffian, was the most famous Welshman since Owen Glendower, a more shadowy figure, even with LlG's ambiguities. Futhermore, the peak of Lloyd George's fame coincided with Cardiff's highest prosperity, of which the whole Cathays complex is a fine symbol and legacy.

Before the Butes are allowed to disappear from the scene (which they most abruptly did in 1947, when the newly succeeded fifth marquess sold up his leasehold grip on a vast swathe of Cardiff houses to the unreassuringly named Western Ground Rents Company, ceremoniously lowered the family flag over Cardiff Castle and departed whence they had come) reference must be made to the alternative city centre which they created at the waterfront end of Bute Street. It was on a small scale reminiscent of the New York financial district in relation to midtown Manhattan or, in London, of the City to the West End and Westminster. Mountstuart Square, as it was typically christened, and one or two adjacent streets achieved a rare commercial dignity. With the Coal and Shipping Exchange (1884–8) in the middle, banks, mining and shipping companies competed with each other to produce neo-classical façades of five- or six-storey buildings which sheltered entrance halls of opulent mahogany. Clustered around were the offices of the twenty-eight foreign consuls whose governments then thought it necessary to maintain a representation in the Cardiff that exported so much of the coal which fuelled their ships and industries.

When the South Wales coal trade declined after 1918 the purpose of this grand commercial centre declined with it. Mountstuart Square became a sad relic until in the late 1980s it began to achieve a new and different vitality with the vast Cardiff Bay development scheme. But this was nothing to do with coal or foreign trade. It was much more to do with government and recreation. The Coal Exchange was intended to provide a temporary house for the new devolved Welsh Assembly, but the scheme fell through. The Mid Glamorgan County Hall (the county having been split into three in the 1970s) moved to the area. There were great arguments about how grand a waterfront home should be provided for the Welsh National Opera Company. This had been founded in the late 1940s by Mr W. H. Smith, no relation of the great stationer, but a successful Cardiff garage owner born in London. As a result of this enthusiasm for opera as a hobby (and especially the discipline with which he inspired the excellent, initially amateur chorus) it eventually evolved into (and remains) one of the four leading professional opera companies of Britain.

All this was a very long way into the future as the coal crisis of 1925–6 settled into the mass mining unemployment of the 1930s. The Rhondda and the other valleys, which had been the essential hinterland to the making of the Butes' Cardiff, became in the full meaning of a then current piece of bureaucratic jargon 'distressed areas'. Yet the Cardiff of my childhood and youth never seemed to me a poor city set on an inevitable course of decline. It harboured much less obvious poverty than Glasgow. It never gave the impression of having lost its mainspring as Liverpool did when, except for a battering Second World War revival, it was displaced by Southampton as the main Atlantic terminal.

How did Cardiff manage it? Jan Morris, epitomizing the rural jealousy of 'city slickers', wrote in her 1984 book *The Matter of Wales*, of 'the chocolate-voiced all-but-English businessmen [who] drive about in their Mercedes, or scoff at the Welsh language in lounge bars . . . while their wives practise their Knightsbridge idioms over calorie-light lunches with Perrier'. A little less prejudicially she went on to describe the city's bouncing back from successive depressions 'in a heady effervescence of opportunism, fuelled frequently with nepotism and publicity campaigns. Cardiff is Post-Industrial Wales, living by its wits and its service trades.'

What has undoubtedly paid Cardiff very well has been the growing return from its determination to be the capital of Wales. As we have seen earlier it is by no means ideally placed for this, either geographically or linguistically. Ms Morris would prefer the capital to be at Machynlleth, Owen Glendower's *circa* 1400 headquarters in the heart of Welsh Wales, and preferably accompanied by full independence, with the 2,000 population of that west Montgomeryshire town enhanced by a full diplomatic corps infusion. But the size of Cardiff has nonetheless proved irresistible, although it took until 1955 for the status of capital to be formally conferred. The bold first-quarter-of-the-twentieth-century decision of the city fathers to provide the appurtenances of a capital has proved a brilliant investment, not only for their own repute but for the prosperity of their electorate. And its results began to come on stream just as the coal trade declined. Cardiff had a very prosperous First World War, and beyond the great coal and steel empires a lot of auxiliary fortunes were made. Under the Lloyd George regime these new figures were rewarded (maybe after suitable political payment) with status as well as wealth, and Cardiff was for a time known as 'the city of dreadful knights'.

That boom crashed in 1921, and there was no full recovery for the traditional trade. But, even in the 1930s, the number of public servants and doctors and lawyers increased nearly as fast as the number of dockers decreased, and they were better paid. Moreover such industry as continued moved down from the heads of the valleys to the coastal strip, with the East Moors steel plant moving from Dowlais (alongside Merthyr Tydfil) to the Cardiff mudflats in 1934. Production there lasted only until the 1970s, but it was an important transitional source of employment for forty years. Steel apart,

Cardiff was becoming rather a genteel town. Gabled villas, detached and semi-detached, sprang up on a northern arc. It was a good shopping centre, notable for one of the most intensive complexes of arcades to be found anywhere outside the Galleria of Milan and maybe that of Naples too. Its resources were such that sixty-two years ago it provided the evening tailcoat (necessary for Oxford Union debates) which I still wear for occasional state banquets – an evening coat having the advantage over a morning one that it does not have to be done up in the middle.

Even the impoverished valleys provided Cardiff with a lot of day visitors, intent not only on shopping but on rugby internationals followed by high tea in one of the several establishments which were halfway between a teashop and a proper restaurant. Sometimes a cinema with a newly released famous film or some lesser sporting event had to fill in for the absence of a full-scale treat in Cardiff Arms Park.

Central to the whole transitional enterprise was the Cathays Park group of buildings, becoming, as the Second World War loomed, almost a third of a century old, but still looking pristine and impressive. Swansea had a better bay, Newport had a better railway station, but as Butes and coal exports foundered it was this Cathays Park ensemble which gave Cardiff its clear superiority over the other towns of the South Wales littoral. Without this Cathays Park focus, Cardiff would have resembled an inky splodge which had spread out, lacking much design, in a variety of haphazard directions. It would have lacked the centrepoint of Liverpool's waterfront, Newcastle's Tyne bridges or Norwich's cathedral. With them it looked a city above its size, still no more than a quarter of a million.

It is therefore not perhaps surprising that my most vivid post-war Cardiff memories should be concentrated on those fifty-nine acres. In December 1968, as Chancellor of the

Exchequer, I came to Cardiff for the opening of the new Royal Mint, which had been moved from Tower Hill on the eastern edge of the City of London to Llantrisant, a few miles to the west of the City of Cardiff. The decision, well justified on dispersal-of-employment grounds, had been made by my predecessor James Callaghan, and was not without controversy, particularly among long-term Cockney employees of the old establishment. There was even a mordant joke, following a well-known advertisement of the time for 'the mint with a hole', that Llantrisant had become 'the hole with a mint'.

Nevertheless a very grand ceremonial opening had been planned, and the whole of Britain's financial establishment, all the Treasury ministers and chief permanent officials, the Governor of the Bank of England and his adjutants, as well as the chairmen of all the main comercial banks, entrained for Cardiff at nine o'clock that morning. We were in pullman comfort, but the day was of a Stygian blackness, both literally and psychologically. It was still almost completely dark when we left Paddington thanks largely to one of my reforms in my previous role as Home Secretary, which had been to impose single summer time in the winter – and double summer time in the summer, which of course had the effect of making it darker in the mornings even if lighter in the evenings. However this was only contributory, for nothing more than a dismal half-light developed during the entire day. Moreover, the poor vulnerable sterling of those days was taking a terrible exchange-market battering, and seemed almost on the brink of another devaluation, which hardly contributed to the gaiety of the official party. However, by the time we all got back to London that evening the markets had staged a temporary but most welcome turn-round which suggested that the best contribution we could make was to keep out of the way.

In Cardiff the celebrations began with a very grand luncheon in the City Hall. George Thomas, who was later to be Speaker of the House of Commons before becoming a last but not fecund hereditary peer as the Viscount Tonypandy, was then Secretary of State for Wales, and in charge of the arrangements. He had shared the parliamentary representation of the City of Cardiff with James Callaghan for nearly the previous quarter-century, and no doubt a little comradely rivalry and friction had occasionally developed between these 'two kings in Brentford'. Thomas was very Welsh. Callaghan was not. Furthermore Callaghan was temporarily down in the political stakes, having been relegated from Chancellor to Home Secretary, and I was temporarily up, having had the reverse experience, although it need hardly be said that Callaghan eventually got much further up Disraeli's greasy pole than I did.

Thomas was very sensitive to these temporary fluctuations, and as we milled around the City Hall portico waiting for the royal party to arrive he said to me, 'Oh, Roy, I hope you will like where I have put you at lunch. I have put you between the Queen and the Prince of Wales.' He then paused before, with even more than his usual Welsh intonation, adding, 'It is very different, I can tell you, from where I have put Jim.' The exact words have long remained in my mind as a fascinating tutorial in the Cardiff politics of the day, although perhaps perversely they left me more pro-Callaghan than pro-Thomas.

In 1975 I became President of the University of Wales Institute of Science and Technology, previously mentioned as one of the four buildings on the left aisle of Cathays Park, and held the office for six years. Only the over-arching if somewhat shadowy University of Wales was allowed the full dignity of a chancellor, but the individual colleges at Aberystwyth, Bangor, Swansea and Cardiff, plus the upstart of UWIST and later the Medical School, also in Cardiff, were allowed presidents, who performed much the same light duties as chancellors in the more monolithic English provincial universities. I went to Cardiff for these duties only on average a couple of times a year, for a morning and afternoon degree-giving ceremony in July and perhaps for a December Council meeting, and found the commitment easily sustainable, even during the four years when I was Brussels-based, and on the whole enjoyable. It was also a very useful apprenticeship for Oxford (just as was my 1937–8 six months in Cardiff for my subsequent undergraduate years at Balliol) although there the structure is different again, and the duties of chancellor considerably more onerous.

There were only two disadvantages to the summer ceremonies, which were held in the imposing neo-baroque assembly room of the City Hall. The first was that – and we were heavily robed – they always seemed to coincide with that rare phenomenon, a Cardiff heatwave. The second was that the benedictions of each group of graduates had to be pronounced in three or four lines of Welsh. Hitherto I had always mistakenly believed that I could instinctively pronounce Welsh, even though I could not speak or understand it. I had after all been brought up among the Welsh place and family names as well as the lilting accent of the western half of Monmouthshire. How mistaken I was. Perhaps there is force in the view of a North Wales marchioness, no great shakes at the language herself, who believes I have one of the worst Welsh accents she has ever heard. I found it more difficult than my subsequent experience of getting my tongue round Oxford's Latin allocutions, very inadequate a classicist though I also am. From the moment I was told that, according to the rules of Welsh mutation, the central word for the purpose, that for university, could be either Bryviscol or Pryviscol, according to what it followed, I reckoned that

I was in for something much more subtle and complex than knowing how to pronounce Abersychan or Ystradgynlais.

My embarrassment was somewhat reduced by the Principal of UWIST, who bore the splendid name of Aubrey Trotman-Dickenson, and had answering responses to make, being even worse at Welsh than I was. Compared with his rendering of the language, I felt that I sounded almost like a druid. But he had no pretensions to be Welsh. Furthermore whatever his Cymric deficiencies, he was such an effective principal that, when in 1987 UWIST came to be amalgamated into University College, Cardiff, it was almost a reverse takeover. UWIST was more the whale than Jonah. Together the two colleges have had a highly successful decade and a half under the new designation of University of Wales Cardiff.

I look back on those UWIST ceremonies of twenty-five years ago with pleasure, but also with a feeling that there was something very typical of the ambiguities of Cardiff about them. An Englishman and an expatriate border Welshman unconvincingly addressed an audience of successful students in a language which, even had the speakers done it well, would have been incomprehensible to the majority of their listeners. Furthermore they did it in a fine marbled hall modelled on South German baroque, although with an obeisance also to Garnier's late Second Empire Paris Opéra. And the whole ambience of Cathays Park, successfully built at an unpromising period in a style about as unWelsh as it is possible to imagine, helped to enhance Cardiff's Welsh capital status and to get it through some difficult decades when it might easily have sunk into being little more than a former coal port with decaying monuments, whether the opulent office blocks of Mountstuart Square or the over-decorated clock tower of Cardiff Castle, coming to look almost as archaic as the ruined skyscrapers of San Gimignano.

That has emphatically not happened, and although one may mock with Jan Morris some of the 'opportunism', 'nepotism', eclecticism and even gentility of Cardiff, stronger tribute should be paid to its resilience and to its ability to be at once (and increasingly) the epicentre of Welsh politics and culture, an open gateway to England, and a three-arm bridge between the old industrial South Wales of coal and steel, the rural areas of West, Mid- and North Wales, and the civic post-industrialiam of which it is itself such a striking example.

BIRMINGHAM

BIRMINGHAM IS NOT a city which easily clutches the heart strings. Yet I am deeply grateful to it. It sustained me in Parliament for twenty-seven years, the core of my House of Commons career, and did so with steady and undemanding generosity. By modern standards it imposed light constituency duties. I was never expected to live in the city, and I was left plenty of time both for London politics and for writing books. Birmingham (or more accurately the one-twelfth of the city that was the Stechford constituency) enabled me to be a latter-day example of that now distinctly endangered species – the part-time MP.

When I was a minister all my working time was devoted to the duties, constituency, departmental and Cabinet, which stemmed from that. But during the nineteen out of twenty-seven Stechford years when I was not in office, I was able to do a lot of other things. Had this not been so, I would not have stayed in Parliament to the end of the long opposition backbench stretch from 1951 to 1964. In particular I would have been tempted away by the 1963 offer of the editorship of the *Economist*. My vanity stops short of believing that this would have been a major national loss, although I do know that it would have been for me a major deprivation never to have been Home Secretary, Chancellor of the Exchequer or President of the European Commission. Still more strongly, however, do I believe that the House of Commons, as it has become more full time and professional, has also become less interesting, less rewarding for its members, and therefore relatively less attractive to high talent than the media or the City, less of a national forum for exciting debates, and less of an effective check upon the executive.

That is a digression but a heartfelt one. It increases my gratitude to Birmingham, and it certainly does not mean that I treated the city merely as a convenience. Such constituency duties as I was asked to perform I took seriously and executed diligently. Some extra ones I even sought, being eager in the 1950s to become chairman of the Birmingham group of Labour MPs. I was very fortunate in my constituency supporters, and retain a vivid affection for what is now mostly only their memory. Furthermore the very strong political history of the city from about 1870 onwards, exactly the period on which my amateur historian's attention was becoming concentrated, gave it a special, almost romantic appeal to my imagination.

Birmingham, of course, did not start in 1870. Medievally it was no more than a few square miles of upland (500 feet) north Warwickshire, although with some good thirteenth- and fourteenth-century parish churches – Northfield, King's Norton, Yardley, in what are now the outer suburbs. From the fifteenth to the seventeenth centuries there was a fair ration of mostly half-timbered manor houses, although no more than in any other area of Warwickshire, which have been swallowed, although some of them preserved, in the vast urban growth of the nineteenth and twentieth centuries. There are three notable churches more or less within the city centre. The first is the Birmingham parish church of St Martin's in the Bull Ring. It started in the thirteenth century, decayed in the seventeenth and eighteenth centuries, and was effectively rebuilt in 1873–5 (by Chatwin), except for the tower and spire which had themselves been rebuilt a hundred years earlier. Its adventures did not stop there. It was bombed in 1941 and rebuilt again in the decade after the war by the grandson of its 1870s re-creator. Its spire, although of no more than eighteenth-century antiquity, survived these vicissitudes, and dominates the lower or southern parts of the city centre, as it has done for the 200 years of dramatic Birmingham growth.

St Martin's relationship to the second church of the trio, that of St Philip, elegantly built on the highest point in old Birmingham by Thomas Archer in the early eighteenth century, which became the cathedral in 1905 when the independent diocese began its life under the charismatic Anglo-Catholic Bishop Gore, is reminiscent of a Bristol juxtaposition. There the Perpendicular St Mary Redcliffe, in the view of Queen Elizabeth I, 'the fairest, godliest, and most famous parish church in England', stands lower than the more heterogeneously styled cathedral, but is nonetheless more dominating. They are both however older and of higher architectural quality than their Birmingham opposite numbers. But that is natural, for Bristol is the only major English provincial city which was great before the industrial revolution. It then stood alongside only York and Norwich, but is as much bigger than them today as it is smaller than Birmingham, which was then negligible.

The third Birmingham church is St Paul's in the Jewellery Quarter, 'a pattern-book church for the period' (late eighteenth century) according to Pevsner. It stands, classically solid, just to the north of the city centre, dominating what was for a time but is no longer a desolate area. The other notable buildings which predate Joseph Chamberlain's Birmingham were the Town Hall (designed by Hansom of cab fame, and a good copy of the Temple of Castor and Pollux in the Roman Forum), which was started in 1832 but took more than a decade to complete, St Chad's Roman Catholic cathedral, which Pugin built more quickly in 1839–41, and three railway stations. The first of these, and the most architecturally distinguished, was Curzon Street, built in 1839 but early relegated to be only a goods and suburban terminus, and now no more than an isolated building to which no tracks run. The two mainline stations were Snow Hill (1852) and New Street (1854). The original buildings have both now disappeared. Snow Hill, the Great Western station, went out of railway use *circa* 1970 and is now back in local and some wider use; New Street which became a vast hub of the LMS (London, Midland and Scottish) system, and was supplemented later by a fine railway hotel famous for its chandeliers, was torn down and replaced, in the mid-1960s, by an inconvenient and anonymous unidentical twin to the new Euston Station at the other end of the line in London.

Joseph Chamberlain, born and educated (only to sixteen) in London, came to Birmingham in 1854 at the age of eighteen to join an uncle's screw-making business. This was a typical Birmingham trade of the times. Less than twenty years earlier Alexis de Tocqueville had written of the town as being 'an immense workshop, a huge forge, a vast shop. One only sees busy people and faces brown with smoke. One hears nothing but the sound of hammers and the whistle of steam escaping from boilers.' And, referring back to 1832, George Eliot in the introduction to *Felix Holt the Radical*, wrote of the prospect of Birmingham from adjacent rural Warwickshire: 'The breath of the manufacturing town, which made a cloudy day and a red gloom of night on the horizon, diffused itself over all the surrounding country, filling the air with eager unrest.'

Joseph Chamberlain operated at the upper end of this small workshop trade, and by the age of thirty-nine had made enough money to retire, live in grand bourgeois affluence and promote his various political purposes, at first strongly radical, later imperialistic, until his stroke in 1906 and his death in 1914. His impact upon Birmingham and then national politics was immense. He wrecked two parties, but he was nonetheless (or perhaps in consequence) the most powerful non-Prime Minister in the classical period of British politics. He made the political weather. When he launched his last great campaign (for Imperial Preference) he told the Chief Whip of the opposing party: 'You may burn your pamphlets: we are going to talk about something else.' It was supreme arrogance, but not misplaced.

Even before his early retirement from business Chamberlain had been elected to the Birmingham Town Council, in 1869. Within five years he began a three-year spell as mayor, and made Birmingham the *fons et origo* of 'gas and water' municipal socialism. During his 1873–6 mayoralty, apart from his schemes for public provision of essential services, he oversaw the building of the massive and vaguely Italian-renaissance-style Council House (an administrative centre supplementing the more austere Town Hall, which is essentially an assembly room), and set in train a programme of town-centre slum clearance which led to the creation of the broad new boulevard of Corporation Street. Chamberlain was probably Haussmann-inspired here, although he did not obtain a Parisian quality of buildings to line his creation.

In 1876 Joseph Chamberlain became a Birmingham member of Parliament and remained so (even though totally incapacitated over his last two general elections) for thirty-eight years. In 1876 his direct control over civic affairs ceased but his power remained pervading. When he broke with Gladstone over Home Rule in 1886 and moved sharply across the political spectrum from left to right he took with him the representation of all seven parliamentary seats into which

Birmingham was then divided. His two sons, Austen and Neville, followed him as members for the city (as it became in 1889, with the mayor raised to the dignity of a lord mayor in 1896), and indeed as national statesmen. He was almost single-handedly responsible for the hatching in 1900 of a commercial college into a full-scale new university on a commanding hill-top site a mile or so from the city centre. His impact upon both the politics and the appearance of Birmingham was immense. As late as 1935, twenty-one years after his death, the city was a bastion of the Unionism (by then called Conservatism) into which he had led it. There was not a single Labour member among the twelve which Birmingham returned at the general election of that year. The one blot upon his devotion to the reality of power rather than to the trappings of office was that he allowed a Chamberlain memorial fountain to be erected in Chamberlain Square, in the heart of official Birmingham, when he was still only forty-four years old.

When I came to know Birmingham the purely political power of the Chamberlain tradition was about to be sundered. Austen Chamberlain, who was always a little remote from the city, fighting his last few elections from the already mentioned station hotel rather than from some more indigenous base, had died in 1937. Neville Chamberlain followed in 1940, soon after his ejection from the premiership in favour of Churchill. It was nonetheless a paradoxical outcome that Neville had got to 10 Downing Street at all, for he had been trained as the pack-horse of the family, whereas his elder half-brother Austen had been trained as the racehorse. But he was a racehorse who, alone with William Hague among Conservative leaders of the twentieth century, failed to reach the winning post.

In the 1945 election the Conservatives lost ten out of the thirteen seats into which the city had then been divided, and have never since come back to anything approaching their extraordinary dominance of 1886–1945, although a near equality with the Labour party was temporarily achieved in 1959. It is however the case that today (2002) Birmingham is the only major city outside London in England, Scotland or Wales which has a trace of Conservative representation in the House of Commons. That is not because of the persistence of Chamberlainism but because the boundary commissioners decided in the 1980s parliamentarily to tack on to the city the purely middle-class Warwickshire residential area of Sutton Coldfield, which sits like a poultice on its north-eastern face.

One other part of the Chamberlain legacy (primarily Joseph's but with Neville as auxiliary) remained intact up to and throughout nearly all my Birmingham years. This was the tradition of a strong City Corporation exercising firm civic power from the Council House. It was the biggest single-tier authority in Britain, and most of its senior officials were of an appropriately high quality with adequate but not excessive deference towards the elected councillors. Between them they managed vast housing estates. They administered many schools, both primary and secondary. The hospitals had already gone from their control following the creation of the National Health Service in 1948. But they still ran their reservoirs in Wales, their own gas company and their own intensive bus services within the city. Perhaps not surprisingly in these circumstances the Council, and indeed the councillors – three to a ward with a senior layer of aldermen, who had all graduated through previous service as councillors – were a considerable presence in the minds of the electorate. They were men and women of substance and the yearly elections by which one-third came up for renewal or rejection, the *municipal* elections as they were always known, were events of significance in the life of the city, certainly of its

MPs, and maybe of its citizens too. The majority of the few who attended my advice bureaux and who contributed to my fairly exiguous constituency correspondence were more concerned with municipal than with national issues. The Council election turn-outs were not magnificent, but far from negligible either, about the same as in present-day general elections.

The political control of the Council fluctuated. Labour slightly predominated, but the Conservatives, who were mostly of a social reform rather than a hard-faced tendency, often coming, as did a few of the Labour councillors, from the old Unitarian families into which Joseph Chamberlain had twice married, had a significant share of power. The lord mayoralty (and the splendidly visible Rolls-Royce, registered LM 1, which trundled around the city), as well as some other perquisites which went with it, revolved according to a mixture of seniority and acceptability, and was not a monopoly of the majority party. There was occasional party bitterness on the Council, as there was at the parliamentary level, but there was also a good deal of cross-party camaraderie among aldermen and councillors, who made the councillors' library in the Council House (really more of a light luncheon bar than a serious reading room) into at least as good a cross-party meeting point as the smoking room of the House of Commons. They nearly all thought that they were the heirs to a somewhat authoritarian but nonetheless highly public-spirited tradition. The few speculative builders who thought that getting on the Council was a route to quick profits by fixing planning permissions soon found themselves frozen out.

The national influence of the Birmingham Corporation was far from negligible. It was not quite comparable with the first Mayor Daley's Chicago but it was probably greater than that of any other local authority in Britain. I remember leading a Birmingham delegation to Harold Macmillan during his 1956 year as Chancellor of the Exchequer. Some new Treasury banking regulation threatened the position of the Birmingham Muncipal Bank (a Neville Chamberlain creation) and my pleas and those of the City Treasurer, who had all the authority of a Whitehall permanent secretary, were received with the utmost attention (although Macmillan was never a Chamberlainite) and a favourable compromise quickly reached. It encapsulated the reasons why I found Birmingham a very worthwhile place to represent.

The generally misconceived 1973 local government reorganization considerably weakened the position of the City Council. A lot of its powers were taken away and given to the amorphous West Midlands County Council, an authority which never achieved either effective leadership or any place in the hearts and minds of the citizens. One or two of these so-called metropolitan counties may have achieved some success – most notably Merseyside – but the West Midlands Council embracing Coventry, Wolverhampton and the Black Country as well as Birmingham, emphatically did not. Unloved and unlamented, it was wound up in the mid-1980s, by which time however local government as a whole was subject to the centralizing subjugation of the middle and later Thatcher years. Aided, however, by a strong leader from 1984 to 1993 in the shape of Sir Richard Knowles, the Birmingham Council regained much of its élan and set in train a major reconstruction of the city centre.

Although I had probably made a dozen brief excursions to Birmingham in the quarter-century since I ceased to be one of its MPs, it was only during a 'round-up' visit on a perfect April day in 2002 for the purposes of completing this essay (which is nonetheless unashamedly about the Birmingham of and before my years there) that I realized what a dramatically exuberant change there has been in the city at the end of the twentieth century. The Birmingham of the 1950s, when I first knew it well, was, as I have described, a prosperous but hardly an exciting and certainly not a cosmopolitan city. It was riddled with canals, which had been its crucial communication with the outside world in the late eighteenth and first half of the nineteenth centuries. But they had been almost as hidden from public gaze and appreciation as were its sewers. It had a distinct city centre but was bounded on the western side by a fairly sombre avenue, Broad Street, with a few good brick houses and one or two second-hand bookshops, running up half a mile or so to the intersection Five Ways and the beginning of Edgbaston. The city's restaurant resources were minimal. The three main hotels had dining rooms, as did the handful of lesser ones. These apart, I can remember only one proper restaurant, the Burlington, in a basement between New Street and the station to which it gave its name.

In the 1960s things if anything became worse. The central area – a pinhead in relation to the population of a million – was marginally extended by the building of the southern section of an inner ring road, but it was flanked by some of the most third-rate buildings of that architecturally dismal decade, including a fourth (fairly) big city-centre hotel, of which the most notable characteristic was its total anonymity. In response to this catering desert a few semi-roadhouse, semi-suburban hostelries began to spring up. The foremost was the Plough and Harrow, on the northern edge of Edgbaston, with its very name proclaiming how unmetropolitan it was.

The contrast between this picture and the Birmingham of half a century later is as great as it is possible to imagine. The canals have been transformed from culverts into waterways of pleasure. Well-fitted-up barges, some of them with eating facilities, echoing the *bateaux-mouches* of Paris, offer short cruises. The one restaurant of *circa* 1950 seems to have performed miracles of parturition into a multiplicity of eating places, no doubt of varying gastronomic quality, but with most of them providing outdoor café facilities. Broad Street has been transformed from a sombre thoroughfare into a boulevard of entertainment and culture. To the south of it lies a new Chinatown, certainly artificially created, for thirty years ago there was no trace of it, but nonetheless looking almost as convincing as that which San Francisco spawned nearly a hundred years earlier. A pagoda at a crossroads, upturned dragon-relief eves and multi-coloured fronts proclaim that the cuisines of Szechwan, Nanking, Kuantung and Beijing, as well as other entertainments, are to be found within.

Even more striking than this is the succession of pedestrian carrefours which lead for half a mile or more from Brindley Place in the west, interspersed with two great open-access buildings, the first mainly a shopping complex and the second the combined convention centre and concert hall, through to the again familiar territory of the Town Hall, Chamberlain Square, the Art Gallery and the Council House. The front prospect of the Council House has however been transformed by the remodelling of Victoria Square which faces it and has been embellished with an ornamental fountain officially called *The River* but which following an earlier Dublin demotic joke is mostly known locally as the Floozie in the Jacuzzi. The whole post-1990 development has been a remarkable example of how success can build upon success, of how determined public enterprise can be rewarded, of how if you can get even a sluggish aeroplane far enough down the runway it can soar into the air. Birmingham can now begin to hold a candle to the other great provincial cities, Barcelona, Chicago and Glasgow, which I include in these essays.

My route into Birmingham politics was both haphazard

and crab-like, although perhaps not untypical for an aspiring British politician with no very strong local roots or prejudices. The first time that Birmingham made an impression on me was in the early summer of 1937 when, aged sixteen, I accompanied my father who was addressing a bye-election meeting in the old West constituency following the death of Austen Chamberlain. Richard Crossman was the unsuccessful Labour candidate, but I remember less well the speech of that sparklingly irresponsible intellectual, who thirty years later was to be my immediate neighbour at the Cabinet table, or indeed the speech of my father, than I do the bewildering effects of the one-way street system (then a very innovative concept) which Birmingham had just introduced. We went round and round looking for the Queen's Hotel where we were to meet Crossman. Occasionally we caught a passing glimpse of it like a holy grail, at the end of a street to which entry was firmly forbidden, but then went into another mile circuit.

After this mildly traumatic experience, which however, together with the chandeliers of the Queen's Hotel, impressed me with Birmingham being a very important place, I do not think that I saw it again until I presumptuously attempted to be adopted as a parliamentary candidate in the dark gloom of the last winter of the war. I was defeated first by Woodrow Wyatt for the Aston division and then (this time by only one vote) by a local alderman for the Sparkbrook division. By late April, with an election imminent, I was happy to settle just outside the city for the middle-class suburb of Solihull, a sort of Esher in Warwickshire. Psephologically it was a hopeless prospect, as much so as the previously mentioned Sutton Coldfield which has given Birmingham a touch of the robe of a Tory MP, even in the elections of 1997 and 2001.

However I much enjoyed fighting the losing battle of

Solihull in the summer of 1945, partly because I did not realize how hopeless it was. It provided very good packed schoolroom meetings of 200 or so, and taught me to speak at them. When I lost by about 5,000 votes I was foolishly disappointed, but the contest had nevertheless put me in the Birmingham Labour loop. After a brief twenty-one month sojourn as an MP for Central Southwark in 1948–50 (where the population was heavily shrinking and seven constituencies have eventually gone into one), I went back to Birmingham and became member for the new but fairly safe Labour division of Stechford. This, combined with my much later 1980s foray to the Hillhead division of Glasgow, has given me the unique attribute of being the only person in British politics who has ever sat in Parliament for the three largest cities of the United Kingdom. I regard this as a curiosity and not a distinction. It is rather like, had I moved at an early age in such elevated circles, putting in *Who's Who* 'educated Eton, Winchester and Harrow', an entry more likely to arouse curiosity as to what happened in the interstices than to impress.

My part of Birmingham was not rich in ancient monuments or in twentieth-century institutions of note. In this respect it was in sharp contrast, as I later came to appreciate, with the Hillhead division of Glasgow. The Stechford constituency was almost entirely a product of two waves of Birmingham industrialism. The inner ward – Washwood Heath, which pointed like a triangular wedge towards the heart of the city – was part of Joseph Chamberlain's Birmingham, a place of small, mainly metal-processing workshops and still smaller dark-brick late-Victorian terraces, sometimes with closes containing a cluster of houses and known as 'tunnel-backs' behind the streets. This ward, wholly 'Brum' in Chamberlain's period and in my early years, became fairly heavily Asian towards the end of my Birmingham time.

The other two wards, Stechford and Shard End, were largely creations of inter-war and early post-Second World War council housing schemes. The Stechford division as a whole had a minimal professional quota. The necessary scattering of clergymen and doctors was about it. This again was in the sharpest possible contrast with Hillhead. But Stechford, in the quarter-century after 1945, was not poor, either absolutely or relatively. It was essentially a skilled manual workers' constituency, with very full employment, and with Birmingham wages, maybe marginally behind Coventry's but at least the second highest in the country, had a considerable prosperity. The constituency did not itself contain many factories. Three-quarters of the employed population must have gone outside the boundaries to work, principally to a ring of great factories with resonant Midland and motor-industry names which surrounded it like grandstands around a football pitch: Dunlop Rubber, Fisher and Ludlow, BSA, Lucas Industries, Rover Motors and, a little further away, the Austin works at Longbridge. These were all creations of the second and largely post-1918 age of Birmingham industrialism. Compared with the first wave the units were much bigger, the locations were on the periphery rather than in the city centre, and the labour relations were sometimes but not always much worse. Joseph Chamberlain would not have recognized the factories or the hitherto greenfield sites on which most of them were placed.

The migration had however started almost at the beginning of Chamberlain's period as an MP for Birmingham, and by an important if far from typical Birmingham firm. In 1879 Cadburys moved four miles from the city centre to Bournville, then a thickly wooded part of rural north Worcestershire. It is a feature of Birmingham that, like so many of the provincial cities which sprang to prominence in the nineteenth century, it is on the edge of a county, embracing bits of others, rather than securely in the centre of one. Birmingham, primarily in Warwickshire, spills into both Staffordshire and Worcestershire. Manchester does the same with Lancashire and Cheshire, as does Glasgow with Lanarkshire and Renfrewshire, the Newcastle conurbation with Northumberland and Durham, Sheffield with Yorkshire and Derbyshire, Cardiff with Glamorgan and Monmouthshire, Plymouth with Devon and Cornwall, and Bristol with Gloucestershire and Somerset.

Chocolate was a surprising Birmingham product. It had nothing to do with metal, and although its factory was as far from the sea as it was possible to be in Britain, its processing depended entirely upon an imported raw material. But Cadbury Brothers maintained over several generations a position as one of the most successful family firms in the country. It also created, thanks largely to George Cadbury (1839–1925), what is probably the best of all the garden cities. The more or less contemporary outer-London experiments in this direction – the Hampstead Garden Suburb, Letchworth and Welwyn – were all much more detached from a single product and quickly became (particularly the first) firmly middle class. Bournville's main near rival for integrating healthy living with the sponsoring company's employment opportunities was Port Sunlight in the middle of the Wirral, where William Lever (later the first Viscount Leverhulme; the Cadburys being Quakers eschewed peerages) made great profits and a fine memorial out of soap. It is curious that the consumer goods of chocolate and soap should have been the two outstanding engines of artisan spaciousness: all houses in Bournville had considerable gardens and some of the primeval trees were preserved.

Bourneville had the edge over Port Sunlight in that it was less of a company town. Employment in the chocolate factory was never made a condition of continued residence, but Cadbury's paternalism still shows itself in their being no pubs within the confines of Bournville. On the other hand it has never achieved an art collection of the distinction of the Lady Lever Gallery at Port Sunlight. But George Cadbury employed very decent architects over the turn of the nineteenth and twentieth centuries, notably Alexander Harvey, and Bournville has not only long maintained an 'arts and crafts' attraction, but has been an integrated part of the civic life of Birmingham.

It is not possible to leave pre-1950 Birmingham without a passage on Edgbaston, which is one of the two oldest and most architecturally distinguished inner suburbs to be found in Britain. Its real but solitary rival is Clifton, climbing up the hill from Bristol. Liverpool, Manchester, Leeds, Newcastle have nothing to compare. Nor, more surprisingly, do the Scottish cities, for in Edinburgh the New Town is not a suburb and Morningside has little of the Regency and early-Victorian elegance of Edgbaston; and in Glasgow the West End is also somewhat later as well as lacking the peculiar *rus in urbe* quality of Edgbaston. Starting only a mile from the city centre, and extending perhaps another mile further west, Edgbaston was still for most of my Birmingham time an enclave not only of tree-lined streets and stuccoed façades but also of large gardens.

There has since been some infilling as well as an expansion of the University into many adjacent large houses and leafy suburban streets, although this has been done with less brutality than is often the case with university extensions, and Edgbaston retains a very special quality. It has, however, experienced a dramatic change of political allegiance. In the days when Joseph Chamberlain lived there (before in 1880 he moved to a near-mansion in eighteen acres of grounds which he had built two miles away at Moor Green) and he and the Unitarian families were Radicals, it broadly voted that ticket. But from the time that he became a Unionist in 1886 until 1997 it was the most solid Conservative-supporting seat in the city – which did not then include the suburban appurtenance of Sutton Coldfield. When Neville Chamberlain had a close shave in proletarian Ladywood in 1929, he quickly moved with more sense than valour to his home ground (Austen Chamberlain, despite his more patrician manner, stuck it out in the equally proletarian West division until his death). After Neville Chamberlain Edgbaston was represented first by a pedestrian manufacturer of motor parts (if this is not a contradiction in terms) and then, one after the other, by two strident Tory ladies. In 1997 however it succumbed, to another lady, a bright young New Labourite of German origin, and remained fallen, by a much larger majority, in 2001.

I was spared such political upheaval in Birmingham. My majority fluctuated greatly over the nine elections I fought there, but it never disappeared. It began at nearly 12,000, went down nine years later to 2,900 in 1959, recovered in 1964, soared in 1966, declined in 1970 and finished up at 11,900 in the second 1974 election. It had big-dipper qualities. When it went up you could be pretty sure that it would come down next time, and such declines also had a promise of recovery within them.

The counts which produced these results took place in the civic buildings of central Birmingham. Stechford, being an outer constituency, was always relegated to a subsidiary building, the Art Gallery (with contents of considerable quality) which could be reached only across a covered bridge, or the Town Hall, which was wholly separate across a street, while a few favoured inner divisions, perhaps as a subconscious continuing tribute to the real Birmingham of the Chamberlains, were in the Council House itself. These close locations had the advantage that you could move easily and at will into the Council Chamber, where whispered exchanges told what the counts were revealing in the other Birmingham divisions, and television screens showed the results as they came in from the rest of the country. Birmingham neither imposed great secrecy nor entered any race to achieve the short-term fame of early declarations. It left that to such lesser places as Sunderland, Salford, Cheltenham and Guildford, and proceeded at a stately pace to results about 1.00 a.m. The indication that a declaration was about to take place was the movement along the corridors of a little procession composed of the lord mayor in his tailcoat and chain of office, accompanied by a few acolytes, towards the counting room in which he could soon announce a duly elected member. It was faintly reminiscent of the scene described in Lampedusa's *The Leopard*, where the movement of a priestly progress through the streets of Palermo indicated the imminence of a death.

All the satisfactory outcomes, except perhaps for the first, have paradoxically become a sludgy amalgam in my memory. But the two worst results remain vivid. In 1959 we arrived at the count rather late, having been dining in the Edgbaston environs of the University with Solly Zuckerman, the eminent zoologist who was then rapidly becoming a worldwide expert on nuclear weapons. On entering the counting room (that time, I think, in the basement of the Town Hall) I detected a certain balefulness on the part of my supporters, who had been observing what came out of the boxes for the previous hour, and some of whom thought I had lost. Then the Conservative agent, a detached professional, came up and told me not to look so worried. 'You have won all right,' he said, 'but I don't know what has happened to your majority.' It was a good throwaway remark.

This was as nothing compared with the shock of 1970. In the previous parliament my constituency party had supported with heart-warming loyalty both my social libertarian reforms at the Home Office and my severities at the Treasury. They did not, as is often the way with so-called 'activists', entirely represent the ordinary Stechford elector. These rewarded me, not with defeat, or anything approaching it, but with a neat lopping-off of the whole of my 1966 surge. However, what was of much more significance that night was the national defeat. I had been central to the campaign, for Harold Wilson had chosen to fight it very much upon the basis of the recovery in the balance of payments during my years as Chancellor of the Exchequer, and I had not thought that the last days of it, bedevilled by some rogue trade figures, had gone well. But I was not expecting a change of government. It indeed became a long-lasting downbeat family joke, that as we drove in to the count (accompanied unusually by a full complement of our then semi-grown-up children) we had discussed whether we would in future spend weekends at our own house at East Hendred or at Dorneywood, then the country perquisite of the Foreign Secretary, to which office it had been arranged with Wilson that I should switch.

When we arrived at the Council House I went through to the remote Stechford count, where nothing very sensational seemed to be happening, and my wife went to the Council Chamber to watch the national picture. After a few minutes I joined her. 'We've lost, you know,' she said quietly. A very few more results, with their moderate but decisive swings of 5 or 6 per cent to the Conservatives, convinced me she was right. We then both went through to the Art Gallery, sat on a bench under a tondo, which did not receive my full aesthetic attention, and adjusted our expectations. We decided that the most immediately important thing was to be out of 11 Downing Street, the official residence which we temporarily occupied, by early the next evening. In that we succeeded. I was surprised and disappointed, but far from shattered. I instinctively thought that five and a half years in office was about long enough. I also mistakenly believed that, at forty-nine, I had plenty of time in which to achieve all political ambitions.

Birmingham is however far from being associated primarily in my mind with political setback. On the contrary it was the base which made possible most of the worthwhile things that I did manage. It also provided some of the early baubles of ministerial rank which remain in my mind. On my first visit to Birmingham after the 1964 change of government I was greeted upon the platform at Snow Hill by the station-master in a top hat – and I was not then even in the Cabinet, merely the Minister of Aviation. Shortly afterwards Snow Hill station, top hats as a grand railway uniform, and indeed stationmasters themselves, were all abolished.

Almost the last of my vivid Birmingham memories was a sombre and searing one. On 21 November 1974, early in my last Stechford parliament and when I was Home Secretary for the second time, a wave of IRA violence culminated in a vicious Birmingham attack. Two pubs in the centre of the city, packed with young people, were the scene on a Thursday evening of twenty-four deaths and nearly 200 injuries, many of them severe. It was a different order of casualties from anything we had previously known. The next day I made a statement to the House of Commons presaging immediate legislation to strengthen the law against terrorism. It seemed the least that could be done.

Then I took a train to Birmingham. As I wrote much nearer the time:

I was in the city for four hours. It seemed an eternity and was one of the most difficult, draining and unpleasant visits I have ever paid. It was a dry, still, misty, rather cold day, one of the few of that exceptionally wet and windy autumn, and the atmosphere in the unusually deserted centre of the city hung heavy with some not wholly definable but unforgettable and oppressive ingredients . . . Partly no doubt it was the lingering scent of the explosions, but there was also a stench of death and carnage and fear. Maybe this was all in the imagination, but what was certainly physically present was a pervading atmosphere of stricken, hostile resentment such as I had never previously encountered anywhere in the world.

During the four hours I looked at the blasted pubs, interviewed the investigating police, paid a call of formal sympathy on the lord mayor in the Council House and then a less obvious one on the Roman Catholic archbishop because I was deeply worried about a dangerous schism developing between the large Irish community and the more indigenous population of Birmingham, and thought in an inchoate way that this might make a small contribution to preventing it. I then had the most difficult part of the day, my visits to the two hospitals which had received the mutilated. After that I did an ineffective television interview before departing hurt from the scene. It was four months before I again felt at ease in Birmingham. This however had nothing to do with my severing, two years later, my long connection with the city. By then I had fully recovered my Birmingham equanimity, and the causes of my resigning my seat in order to be president of the European Commission lay all in national and international circumstances and not in any local difficulties.

NAPLES

The first time I saw Naples was in January 1949. Although I was a very junior MP (aged twenty-eight and only a member since the previous April) I somehow managed to get on to a parliamentary delegation of about ten which went that month to Italy. I enjoyed it immensely, but although it fortified my taste for Italy, to which I had already paid three post-war visits, it did not make me an enthusiast for group parliamentary travel. I have never been on another delegation in my subsequent fifty-three-year span of membership of the Houses of Commons or Lords.

The main reason why this visit was not only enjoyable but also memorable was that it stands in my mind as poised on two frontiers, both that between a Europe at war and the Europe of the Community, and that between the travel habits of the 1920s and 1930s and those of the modern world. And there was a subsidiary reason. The delegation was led by Rab Butler, for whose subtle ambiguity of character and somewhat crab-like style I conceived a persistent if amused admiration. The latter aspect was epitomized by his teaching me that, whenever confronted by a guard of honour, an uncertain *huissier*, a hotel manager or a papal chamberlain, the best thing to do was silently but graciously to incline one's head and move firmly forward in the direction in which one was previously going.

Of the two frontiers, the first was obvious. It was less than four years after VE Day. The second was perhaps a little less so. But it was probably one of the last occasions when a full-scale parliamentary delegation travelled across Europe by train. We went to Paris by the Golden Arrow, dined at the British embassy, and proceeded by the Simplon Express from the Gare de Lyon. It was like Harold Nicolson's description of Lord Curzon's progress to the 1922 Lausanne Conference. At Milan we transferred to two saloons of the royal train of the House of Savoy which had been taken over by the Republic, and so proceeded to Rome.

These saloons were also at our disposal for the excursion to Naples which took place on the fourth day. We travelled along the so recently war-ravaged coastal strip in more than pullman comfort. On arrival in Naples we were swept up the hillside to a restaurant on the Vomero which combined a panoramic view over the bay and the islands with what seemed to English eyes and stomachs of the period a gargantuan repast. The first real impact of Naples upon me was in a post-prandial glow through the wide windows of that restaurant in the good southern light of a January mid-afternoon. It looked a great but slightly sinister city, rather as Glasgow, at the other end of Europe, was to strike me over thirty years later. Nevertheless it seemed to have recovered almost miraculously from the chaos, at once pitiable and picaresque, of five years before, unforgettably described by Norman Lewis in *Naples '44*.

The still more potent memory of the day, however, was that, in the late afternoon, I was taken off by another member of the delegation, Ivor Bulmer-Thomas, for the special treat of calling upon Benedetto Croce, then aged eighty-two and the sage of Naples, who trailed clouds of glory both as a philosopher/historian and for his firm anti-fascism. Bulmer-Thomas, although then in the process of switching from

Labour to Tory (nearly forty years later he switched back to the newly founded Social Democratic party) had been a Monmouthshire protégé of my father's, and was, and remained, a close family friend. He was also then seen as an Italian expert among MPs, having been involved in anti-Mussolini broadcast propaganda during the war and in consequence knowing all the political exiles from Italy in England. This was the reason for his entrée to Croce.

We found the sage in the epitome of a Neapolitan setting. It was in the old congested centre of the city, off what is now the Via Benedetto Croce, between the Piazza Gésu Nuovo and the Via Santa Chiara, just north of the convent of that name. We entered through a courtyard which had all the intermingled squalor and grandeur of Neapolitan life. On one side the slums were half hidden by a profusion of washing hanging out to dry. On the other we mounted to a *piano nobile*, in which we found polished floors, painted eighteenth-century furniture, and a fine but unheated private library in which sat Croce wrapped up in an overcoat and scarves. It was a pearl set in mud, and I remember the contrast better than any words which he uttered.

After this bit of intellectual one-upmanship we had to find our way back to the rest of the delegation, who had been engaged in more conventional sightseeing. We were short of time for the luxury train back to Rome, and hurried to the Stazione Centrale, where Bulmer-Thomas, whose Italian was thoroughly adequate if not demotic, enquired for *il treno inglese*. We were directed along a fifteen-coach train down a long platform, at the end of which it was alleged we would find that for which we were looking. All we found was a packed train of Mezzogiorno labourers about to depart towards the brickworks of Bedfordshire. It was discouraging. However, with the resilience of relative youth (even Ivor was only forty-three at the time) we galloped back up the platform and down another where we eventually discovered the inhabitants of our royal saloons impatiently waiting for us. Departure had been delayed for ten minutes. We sank into comfort, but were not popular.

After that it was another sixteen years before I again saw Naples. In 1965 came the first of over twenty visits since paid to a large house adventurously built in 1958 by the American mother of Leslie Bonham Carter, the wife of Mark Bonham Carter, my Balliol friend, publisher and House of Lords colleague, and subsequently inherited by Leslie and her two half-brothers. It is near to the Gulf of Policastro, almost exactly halfway between Naples and the tip of the Calabrian toe of Italy. For many of these visits Naples became a staging post and I achieved a considerable familiarity with its railway stations, airport, hotels, restaurants, galleries, museums and even its opera house, the uniquely elegant San Carlo.

In addition I have made two special four- or five-day January expeditions there – an excellent month for Naples, as for Venice in a very different part of Italy. And, when president of the European Commission, I attended a meeting of Foreign Ministers in the Villa Rosebery at Posillipo a few miles along the coast north of Naples. The villa started life as a *nid d'amour* for the brother of the Bourbon King Ferdinand II of the Two Sicilies, who earned the sobriquet King Bomba and provoked the young Gladstone, in one of his more memorable phrases, to describe the regime as 'the negation of God erected into a system of government'. About forty years later it was acquired by Gladstone's immediate successor as Liberal Prime Minister, who was said to use it for still less reputable purposes – harbour boys rather than San Carlo dancers. As however Lord Rosebery kept it for only a dozen years it is curious that it should continue to bear his name. But it provided a good setting for our 1980 meeting, at which the Italians and the Germans blandly relieved the French of the burdens of making clear to the British that their budgetary problem was not the central issue for Europe. Perhaps they thought that we ought to be satisfied by the tribute of the villa's name.

These various layers of impression have left me with the view that Naples is at once the most hidden, even the most sinister, in a way the least modern, but also the most fascinating of Italian cities. It reminds me, King Bomba having brought Gladstone into the story, of that Victorian statesman's diary entry when he first saw Stonehenge in 1852: 'a noble and awful relic, telling much, and telling too that it conceals more'.

What is it that Naples conceals? On the surface it is one of the most open cities in the world. Much of its life is lived in the courtyards or in the streets. It is, again to compare Glasgow, a place where people, particularly the elderly, take the air, but on their own urban doorsteps (or on the innumerable little balconies, present even in the poorer quarters of Naples) rather than on elaborate garden furniture in sylvan retreats. The number of days in a year on which this can be done however is at least five times as great in Naples as in Glasgow. Norman Lewis put 28 February in 1944 as the beginning of spring: 'Last Sunday the sun was so hot that the first of the water-sellers even came on the scene. These picturesque figures and the equipment they carry are hardly changed from representations of them in the frescoes of Pompeii.' And then on 1 May of the same year he wrote:

Today the arrival of summer was announced by the cry of the seller of venetian blinds – sad to the point of anguish in our narrow street – *s'e 'nfucato 'o sole* (the sun's turned fiery). Immediately as if in response to a signal all Naples had awaited, the tempo of life changed and slowed down. As the melancholy howl was heard, first in the distance, then coming closer, people seemed to move cautiously into the shade, and those who hadn't already let down their blinds did so. Fans came out, girls walked about shading their eyes, and the seller of black-market cigarettes immediately under our window unfolded a Communist newspaper and held it over his head.

Glasgow does not see much February sun or feel it necessary to seek shade in early May.

Naples is at least Graeco-Roman as an area of settlement. The Greeks came in the fifth century BC, and changed its name from Parthenope, or virgin city after a siren – maybe a contradiction in terms – said to have been drowned there (Parthenope persists in the name of the street with the best hotels), to Neapolis, or new city, which is nearer to its modern name in German and Spanish than in any other of the main European languages. A hundred or so years later it sought the protection of Rome, but it was not until a third of a millennium later and close to the most devastating of the eruptions of Vesuvius that the area achieved its full classical status as the fashionable resort of the Roman *nomenklatura*. Marius, Pompey and Julius Caesar had villas. Horace was a devotee and Virgil a part-time inhabitant who chose there to be buried. The elder Pliny commanded the Roman fleet anchored in the bay, and the younger Pliny was there to record the catastrophe. It became an amalgam of Brighton, the Côte d'Azur and the Hamptons on Long Island.

AD 79, with the destruction of Pompeii and Hercula-neum, ended all that. There then began an immensely complicated 1,600 years of Dark Ages, medieval and early modern history for Naples. In a very broad-brush summary it emerged from this in 1734 when Don Carlos (not Verdi's hero but a successor of nearly 200 years later) was recognized by the Treaty of Vienna as King Charles II of the oddly named kingdom of the Two Sicilies, with Naples as its capital and Palermo as an Edinburgh- or Dublin-like subsidiary. This began the return of the Spanish Bourbons to Naples, which lasted a century and a quarter until Garibaldi swept them out in 1860 and handed over the Mezzogiorno to the Piedmontese House of Savoy. This Bourbon period of government was interrupted, first by the republic of 1799 and then for nearly ten years by two Bonaparte kings, briefly by Napoleon's brother Joseph and then for longer by his brother-in-law Joachim Murat. That century and a quarter left a vast architectural impression.

The Bourbon period in Naples was dominated by two sovereigns who between them spanned 91 of the 125 years. The first was Charles II of Naples who later became Charles III of Spain and epitomized the elaborate *chassé croisé* of eighteenth-century monarchy. A son of Philip V of Spain by his powerful Italian wife Elizabeth Farnese, everyone seemed to want him as a ruler. At the age of fifteen he set out from Spain, which he did not see again for twenty-eight years, and was gratefully received in Florence by the ineffective last Medici Grand Duke, who was happy to make him his heir. However he was seduced away in 1732 by the prospect of immediate sovereignty in the duchies of Parma and Piacenza, and then further seduced in the next year, after theatrical but largely casualty-free battles between the Spaniards and the Austrians, by the crown of the Two Sicilies. There he reigned for twenty-five years, and maybe gave Naples and the Mezzogiorno one of their better periods of government. He was not an ostentatious man. Obsessive hunting was almost his only personal indulgence. Nonetheless his legacy was extraordinarily showy, even by Neapolitan standards. *Bella figura* was made reality.

He indisputably embellished Naples. The royal palace on the western edge of the old city had been built over a hundred years before by a Spanish viceroy anxious to make a fine impression for a projected visit of Philip III. It was in the strong tradition of nobles semi-bankrupting themselves by extravagant architectural embellishment preparing for a royal visit. Whether or not Philip III ever came, Naples was left with a dominating palace, adjacent to which Charles II/III quickly had built the San Carlo Theatre, which was and remains the most handsome opera house in the world. (This is despite the fact that it had to be rebuilt in 1816 following one of the fires to which opera houses seem so vulnerable.) He also began the transformation of Capodimonte into a Reggia or full palace. Hitherto this property had been little more than a hunting lodge, a mile and a half up a road from the town palace. As its name proclaims it is on a commanding height with spectacular views of the city and the bay. But he wanted it not so much as another residence but as a home for the outstanding collection of paintings, sculptures and *objets* which he had inherited from his Farnese mother. He also erected there a fine porcelain factory, which may have benefited from some of the secrets of Meissen (but not that of 'hard' porcelain) as a result of his wife's Dresden provenance.

He already had another semi-suburban (and seaside) palace at Portici, which spanned the main road to Calabria near Torre del Greco, four miles to the south of the city. It grandly eschewed the need for privacy from passing travellers in a way mildly reminiscent of Chatsworth. These resources did not prevent Charles, in the seventeenth year of his reign, from embarking on the most extravagant of all his projects. Barely twenty miles away to the north he created on the grandest possible scale the vast palace of Caserta. It almost rivalled Versailles, but the wealth and size of France was vastly different from that of the Two Sicilies. Contemporaneously with Caserta, and as though to balance ostentation with concern (although even here not sacrificing any of the former) he built in Naples the Reale Albergo dei Poveri, a huge but elegant 'workhouse' nearly a quarter of a mile long.

These extravagances had several results. The first was that Naples, then a city of about 300,000 inhabitants (London, at the time, was not much more than half a million), gained a fine reputation as a centre of the arts, and indeed of learning, although with a court expenditure three times the size of that of the only other kingdom in Italy, Piedmont and Sardinia with its capital at Turin. It also meant that when, in 1777 and the reign of Charles's son Ferdinand, the National Archaeological Museum came to be established in a *circa* 1600 building, which after starting life as a cavalry barracks had been the seat of the University for 170 years, Naples had two utterly contrasting collections of semi-world class. The University was moved, but improved rather than diminished, to the courtyard of the church of Gésu Vecchio and then expanded at the end of the nineteenth century downhill to a somewhat heavy neo-classical façade on the Corso Umberto I.

The Archaeological Museum is stuffed with artefacts which survived the lava in which Pompeii and Herculaneum were enveloped. For relics of the ancient world it is not quite the equivalent of the Pergamon in Berlin, and Capodimonte is not quite the equivalent of the Uffizi or the Louvre or the Prado. Nonetheless they are between them enough to make Naples a major museum city, and Capodimonte as compelling an attraction (in the sense that I hardly ever go to Naples without a visit there) as I find the Frick in New York. At the time of the millennium it was substantially rehung and improved. Previously the old masters were on the second floor. Now some of the best of them – Titians, Caravaggios, a Botticelli, a Bellini – are on the side of the first floor, but the other side of this first floor remains devoted to Neapolitan portraits, scenes and bric-à-brac of the eighteenth and nineteenth centuries, all displayed in splendid state rooms. And then at the end is a reclining Canova statue of Laetizia Bonaparte – Madame Mère – and a wildly incongruous (to the rest of the collection) Renoir girl painted in Cagnes-sur-Mer in 1919. I find this wing even more enjoyable than the nearly first-rate collection of old masters. They could be anywhere in the world. This wing could only be in Naples.

In 1759 Charles succeeded his half-brother as king of Spain, where he became Charles III rather than Charles II as he had been in Naples. More Italian than Spanish, and benevolently attached to the Naples he had so embellished though he was, he accepted the pull of the greater Bourbon monarchy like metal filings to a magnet. He sailed out of the bay into the sunset (but his own was long delayed, for he reigned in Madrid for another twenty-nine years) on 6 October, and never saw Naples again. It is reported that there was hardly a dry eye on the quayside, or indeed in the departing ship. But the Neapolitans have always been good at regretting the old while quickly welcoming the new.

Charles III ranks high among the sovereigns of the Spanish decline, but for me his main impact was that he founded the order bearing his name, the grand cross of which carries the right to wear a pale blue and white sash, which exceeds even the Garter in its refulgence, if not in its rarity. In the Prado collection of Goya portraits (and in one or two in Capodimonte) nearly all the Spanish royals are wearing it. Until I subsequently took this in I did not appreciate its full status, although I had been given it in 1980 for opening negotiations which led to Spanish entry into the European Community. I sometimes wear it at Buckingham Palace banquets for visiting heads of state, partly as a tease and partly as a bit of peacockery.

When Charles left Naples he handed over that kingdom

to his third son, who became Ferdinand IV of Naples, although to keep up the confusion about sovereigns' numerals which were a feature of eighteenth-century monarchy, particularly in southern Europe, he also became Ferdinand III of Sicily and Ferdinand I of the Two Sicilies. The first son was a semi-imbecile who was left behind in Naples and not taken to Madrid. The second, who became Charles IV of Spain, was offered what seemed the greater prize of the Spanish succession. Ferdinand however showed an impregnable complacency, which was the hallmark of his long reign, by saying to his brother (in 1759): 'Yes, perhaps you will rule one day. But I am a king already!' Ferdinand was only eight years old at the time, but this showed a precocious shrewdness, for his elder brother had to wait until 1788, and then proved a weak sovereign until in 1808 he was forced to abdicate in favour of a Bonaparte.

Ferdinand was married at the age of seventeen to the Habsburg Archduchess Maria Carolina. She was spectacularly well connected, backwards and forwards. Her mother was the Empress Maria Theresa. Her closest sister was Marie Antoinette. Her brothers were the Emperors Joseph II and Leopold II. Her eldest daughter married the Emperor Francis II and she thus became the grandmother of Napoleon's Empress Marie-Louise. Yet as a bride she was a third choice. Two of her sisters who had been destined to be queen of Naples died of smallpox before they could get there – one of them during the near-to-major Vesuvius eruption of 1765. This added to the impression of everything to do with Naples at that period being over several tops and somewhat too extravagant to be true. Everything, for good or ill, was played out as though it was on the stage of the most melodramatic of grand operas. To add to the extravagance there were even more (non-royal) princes, dukes and marquesses – the last being almost a bourgeois title in Naples – than there were earls in Ireland after Pitt had pushed the Act of Union through the Dublin Parliament.

However Maria Carolina survived, even though she had herself been subject to a bout of smallpox, and arrived pockmarked but more or less safely in Naples in 1768. She remained queen until 1814 (sometimes in half-exile in Palermo and sometimes in full exile, but at least then back at home in Vienna), when she died just nine months too early to see the downfall of Napoleon, whom she personally admired but saw as the heir to the murderers of her sister and the cause of terrible trouble to legitimist Europe.

Although she found her chosen husband (the Habsburgs and the Bourbons made modern Muslim arranged marriages seem almost spontaneous) ill educated and immature, she managed to bear him nineteen children of whom nine died in infancy. In their joint 1782 portrait by Angelica Kauffmann, with six of their surviving children, she appears more than adequately attractive and Ferdinand IV was made to look like one of those elegant elongated squires painted by Reynolds or Wright of Derby. But this owed at least as much to the conventions of court portraiture as to reality. Throughout her long consortship Maria Carolina poured out advice, some of it sensible, much of it hysterical, to her husband. He was also receiving near-instructions from his father in Madrid, and there is a strong impression that, even though he twice temporarily lost his throne, there was a good deal to be said for his complacent phlegmatism.

Ferdinand, whatever his limitations, broadly continued his father's pursuit of monumentalism. His resiting of the University and founding of the Archaeological Museum have already been mentioned. Later he celebrated his return to the throne after the defeat of Bonapartism in 115 by the building of a neo-classical, almost aggressively nonspiritual church, San Francesco di Paola, much inspired by the Pantheon in Rome. This was (and is) in the middle of a fine colonnade, the latter commissioned by the second of his Bonapartist usurpers, Joachim Murat, but which served when completed to embellish Ferdinand's memorial to Murat's downfall.

The great space between the Royal Palace and the colonnade he had named the Piazza del Plebiscito, which sounds far too democratic a name for anything to do with the Bourbons, but which nonetheless stems directly from Ferdinand having won a vote to endorse his 1815 restoration. This large piazza is the hinge between old Naples and the late-nineteenth- and early-twentieth-century fashionable district of Santa Lucia, with its grand hotels on the Via Partenope, and, a little beyond it, the Riviera di Chiaia, the local Fifth Avenue (in residential rather than shopping aspect – although the smart shopping area is adjacent), which sounds like a seaside strand but which is in fact a few hundred yards inland, overlooking the long public park of the Villa Communale, which sounds like a municipal building.

On the other side of the Piazza del Plebiscito from the great colonnade is the San Carlo Theatre, and opposite to that is the entrance to the Galleria Umberto I. Beyond that an unmetropolitan grassy hill runs down beside the Castel Nuovo to the Piazza Municipio and the main seafront. The Galleria is a good example of late-nineteenth-century Italy's main contribution to urban architecture. Its cupola of iron and glass rises to nearly 200 feet and its covered arcades are lined with shops and cafés, although perhaps not so animated as they were in its early days. The whole ensemble is not quite up to its Milan analogue, but is a striking second best.

The other notable physical legacy to Naples of Umberto I (who reigned from 1878 until he was assassinated in 1900) was that of closing each alternate arch of the ground-floor

colonnade of the royal palace, thereby leaving eight niches
which he filled with his dynastically ecumenical choice of
the most notable sovereigns who had reigned over Naples
and Sicily. He began with Roger the Norman, who had
conquered Sicily in the eleventh century, then went on to
Frederick II of the Swabian dynasty and to Charles I of the
Angevin one, both in the thirteenth century, then to Alfonso
I (sometimes called 'the Magnificent') of the Aragon dynasty
in the fifteenth century, to the Emperor Charles V in the
sixteenth century, to Charles II/III in the eighteenth century,
then to Joachim Murat at the beginning of the nineteenth,
and ending with his own father, Victor Emmanuel II, the
monarch who was brought to Naples by the Risorgimento.

The result of all this royal monumentalism is that Naples
is for me very much a city of the seventeenth, eighteenth and
nineteenth centuries, and particularly of the latter two. There
are of course some older remnants, of which the most notable
are the three great medieval fortresses of the Castel dell'Ovo
(twelfth century) which dominates the little harbour at
Santa Lucia, the Castel Nuovo (thirteenth century) which
does the same to the central seafront and defies its name by a
century more than does New College, Oxford, and the Castel
Sant'Elmo (fourteenth century) which, with its adjacent and
contemporaneous Certosa of San Martino, overlooks the
whole city from an 800-foot hill.

The road journey up (there is also a funicular) involves a
winding route interspersed with spectacular views – through
the large bourgeois quarter of the Vomero. In the old city
there are also some good earlier churches, although in the
case of two of the best, Gésu Nuovo and San Domenico, the
former precedes the beginning of the seventeeth century by
only seven years and the latter, while originally *circa* 1300,
has been heavily modified. The same is true of the cathedral,
dedicated to San Gennaro, whose blood has to liquefy at a

PARIS

1. The beginning of Paris for me (and many others coming from London) in the 1930s, and again, by Eurostar, sixty years later: the 1859 front of the Gare du Nord.

2. Panoramic Paris: the great south–north axis of the boulevards St Michel, Sébastopol and Strasbourg leading to the two-and-a-half-mile-distant front of the Gare de l'Est. The picture is taken within a few hundred yards of my 1938/9 pension: the Luxembourg Gardens are on the left. Notre Dame is just visible upper-right; and the whole foreground is spattered with the grand educational establishments of the Latin Quarter.

3. *Above.* The garden front of the British Embassy in winter.

4. *Left.* Aerial view of the Place Vendôme (laid out about 1690), with the much later July Column in the centre and the Ritz Hotel on the left.

CARDIFF

5. The grand layout of Cathays Park, the University middle left; the National Museum of Wales beyond; the City Hall upper right; and the War Memorial (1914–18) in the centre.

6. Cardiff Docks (1937); already in semi-decline as a coal port, the whole area is now entirely devoted to leisure, culture and administration.

7. *Above*. Burges's high-Victorian reconstruction of Cardiff Castle.

8. *Left*. A detailed view of the 1905 baroque revival style of the City Hall.

BIRMINGHAM

9. *Right.* The core of public Birmingham in my day: the Town Hall on the left, the Council House and Art Gallery on the right.

10. *Below.* Central Birmingham in the late twentieth century: the vast spread of New Street Station to the right, St Martin's in the Bull Ring top right, Victoria Square in front of the Council House (with that building's cupola just visible) bottom left; and the Cathedral and its surrounding gardens middle left.

11. New Birmingham: the glitter of the recently opened-up canal banks.

12. *Right*. Circa 1900 view of the Bay of Naples with Vesuvius fuming quietly in the background, seen from the site of Virgil's tomb.

13. *Below*. The more modern view of the same hillside of the Vomero, rising up to the Castel Sant'Elmo and the Certosa di San Martino, with the bourgeois terraces and apartment blocks far more developed.

14. *Above*. The main facade of the former Royal Palace, now the Museum and Art Gallery of Capodimonte.

15. *Left*. Late-nineteenth-century scene in the Duomo at the festival of the liquefaction of the blood of San Gennaro.

satisfactory rate three times a year if Naples is to escape calamity. This Duomo was created in the thirteenth century but largely destroyed by earth tremors in 1688 and subsequently heavily baroquized.

In the late morning of 19 September 1988 (the feast of S. Gennaro and therefore the day for the autumn liquefaction) 1988, after two nights in a *pensione* on the Vomero we were on our way by taxi to the Stazione Centrale for a train to the far south when we were held up by police motorcycles on the Corso Umberto I. After a brief pause a large car containing the Cardinal Archbishop drove out of a side street leading from the cathedral. His Eminence was sitting in the back with a look of relief on his face and regarding his hands as a great surgeon might have done had he just performed a peculiarly testing operation. The liquefaction had gone well that year. Whether it led to a good year for Naples I cannot recall. I think it was a couple of years before a new mayor, Antonio Bassolino, achieved a great improvement in the safety (from crime) and the cleanliness of the streets.

These mentioned exceptions and a few others apart, it is the city of the Bourbons (with a Bonaparte interruption) and of the eighty-five years of the House of Savoy in a unified Italy which dominates. The second half of the twentieth century contributed relatively little to the appearance of Naples, which is a good thing. This is perhaps largely a function of Naples not having been an expanding city during this period of potential desecration. In 1939, with a population of just over a million, it was the largest city in Italy, bigger than either Rome or Milan. Now Rome has nearly three times the population and Milan nearly double. Naples has maintained its million plus, but no more. As a result, apart from a cluster of protuberances around the Piazza Garibaldi and the main station and one unfortunate fifteen-storey insurance-company monstrosity near the Piazza

Municipio, the centre of the city is little changed. In this respect it is comparable with Vienna, which has never grown since 1913. It is possible for a city to retain its essential figure with substantial growth around the periphery, rather like an elegant mother with many children. Paris is the outstanding example, which is a tribute to the authority of the French state. Prague also comes to mind, although there, maybe, the dead hand of forty years of Communism deserves the perverse credit.

Even though central Naples escaped so unscathed from the second half of the twentieth century the city has not been without its impact on the life of Italy during this period. It has contributed more than its fair share of leading ministers, some good, some less so. Naples University has great capacity for producing silver-tongued advocates and politicians, many combining both occupations. In this respect the comparison with Glasgow again comes to mind. The University there produces a machine-gun-like debating style which is far more easily recognizable than that of the Oxford Union, and several of its exponents have achieved notable political success. It is perhaps a feature of relatively poor regions that its brightest children take to word-spinning. In richer regions, whether it be Surrey or Lombardy, there is more incentive to commerce than to oratory.

In Naples (and maybe in Glasgow too) there is thought to be the sustaining factor of a large and potentially grateful criminal class to defend. The Naples Camorra, however, is arguably a more benign branch of the Sicilian Mafia. Even before Mayor Bassolino's clean-up Naples never struck me as a peculiarly dangerous city. I would as soon walk in the gardens of the Villa Communale at night as through Hyde Park in London, and much sooner than across Central Park in New York. There used to be a good deal of handbag snatching at traffic lights on the periphery, and maybe still is, but I think that is relatively minor, perhaps because I do not carry a handbag. And I once came out of Naples Airport and while waiting for a taxi was greeted by a rattle of gunfire. It was curiously undisturbing. It struck me as being like one of those last manifestations of Chicago gangsters in the 1920s, more a ballet than a massacre, mildly directed at a rival gang and not imperilling the detached majority.

Criminality apart, Naples is one of those cities where an indigenous cockiness triumphs over often appalling vicissitudes. Berlin and New York are other examples. But above all it is a city where the dramas of life are played out before a backcloth, not always of austere taste, but of exuberant vitality and display.

NEW YORK

I FIRST SAW NEW YORK in the fierce glow of an August dawn fifty years ago. I had made my only westward crossing of the Atlantic by ship, in the stately old *Queen Mary*. This increased the impact of arrival in the New World. Five days' voyage gives much more the impression of having travelled a long way than does seven hours of flight. I watched the then vast Navy Yard and commercial docks of Brooklyn slip past my porthole before going on deck as we came past the Statue of Liberty into the Hudson River, and were manoeuvred to the Cunard pier at West 50th Street. It seemed one of the strangest prospects I had ever seen, made more so by the large freight cars which penetrated to the quays being labelled in English, even if in such exotic names as Chesapeake and Ohio and Erie-Lackawanna, and by the Western Union telegraph agents, who came thronging on to the ship the moment we were tied up, also appearing to speak a version of that language. The scene now feels to me very remote in time and atmosphere. The America of the early Eisenhower years was a different country from that of today.

What has not changed, however, is that from that day to this New York has remained for me near to the epicentre of the world. People divide sharply into those who like and those who cannot bear the city. Which side of the divide they fall is, I find, an interesting early probing question as a route to discovering the outlook on life of a new acquaintance. I, at any rate, am firmly on the side of the Manhattan aficionados.

I have never lived in New York. Indeed I have hardly ever stayed there continuously for more than a week. But in the past five decades I have paid nearly 200 separate visits. I have had a lot of friends there, so that my knowledge of at least a segment of its life has been much more than that of a tourist or of an out-of-town businessman. I have sometimes stayed in hotels (eight or nine different ones), but more frequently in five or six private houses or apartments, and latterly in a Fifth Avenue club. Geographically however my life in the city has been very circumscribed. I have never spent a night south of 44th Street, north of 86th Street, west of Sixth Avenue or east of Sutton Place. This does not of course mean that I have never been in the Financial District or in Greenwich Village or the Upper West Side or in Harlem, Brooklyn, the Bronx or even Staten Island, but it does mean that my social experience of New York has been somewhat skewed in an uptown and upmarket direction. This began at the beginning. When I disembarked from the *Queen Mary* I took a cab to number 3 East 86th Street, a narrow, elegant house of five storeys, now long since pulled down, where I was to stay, and from which chic old New York address a brother of the family quickly had me made a temporary member of the Knickerbocker Club, twenty-four blocks down Fifth Avenue, which nearly forty years later was to become my main Manhattan refuge.

However my early New York experience was not all patrician. Later that same first morning I took a bus down Fifth Avenue and had some difficulty in grasping how to pay (the fare was then twelve cents, recently put up from ten cents, I think, which was part of the difficulty). The driver/conductor with mounting exasperation and even more incomprehensible (to me) New York vowels had several times to

repeat the mantra: 'You put the dime in the machine and you
give the pennies to me.' Then I found a luncheon counter
for a modest meal, but in the August heat my English
innocence was much more impressed by its being fully air-
conditioned than by the food. There I contemplated the
culture shock of the previous seven hours. But I was already
hooked on New York.

On that first visit I stayed only three days and then went
back for a week's visit in the October of that same year of
1953. After that there was a six-year gap, and it was not
until November 1959 that my real New York immersion
began. Accessibility from London improved when the so-
called 'big jets' (in fact very small jets by present standards –
mostly Boeing 707s) came into service about 1958. I was
there a lot in that late autumn of 1959, interspersed with
some Ivy League lecturing, and again in the early fall of
1960, when the Kennedy/Nixon campaigns dominated the
political news. There were some competing excitements. In
September 1960 Fidel Castro led his United Nations delegation away from the Waldorf-Astoria, where they had started,
apparently because the management would not allow them to
pluck and cook chickens in their rooms (although in my view
there were and are other less culinary or ethnic reasons for
not staying a moment longer than one has to in that classic
example of fame and size exceeding quality), and removed
to the Hotel Theresa on Seventh Avenue at 124th Street in
East Harlem. That same year Nikita Khrushchev enlivened
the UN Assembly by taking off one of his shoes and banging
it on his desk in protest against the speech of Harold
Macmillan.

Still more vivid in my memory of that fall, however, was
a spectacular Columbus Day of Indian summer weather spent
with the Kennedy campaign. There was a lot of cavalcading
around the near part of Long Island, but the most notable

event was a mass meeting outside that same Hotel Theresa in East Harlem. From the balcony behind which Castro's men had presumably had their way with the chickens, John Kennedy himself, Eleanor Roosevelt, Senator Herbert Lehmann and the local black Congressman, Adam Clayton Powell, a bit of a charlatan but a brilliant orator, all spoke. Powell was the best, although they were all good. Also present on the balcony was a heavily pregnant Jacqueline Kennedy. It was the first time I had seen her, although she later became quite a close friend. It was heady stuff for a young (thirty-nine-year-old) visiting MP.

During the short years of the Kennedy presidency my main American activity was to write a long (4,000-word) retrospective piece on the Cuban missile crisis for the *Observer* newspaper. The missile-crisis article, which eventually appeared on the first-anniversary Sunday, involved a lot of Washington interviewing from the President through nearly all the figures who have recently been more or less accurately portrayed in the film *Thirteen Days*, but Washington is outside the scope of this essay. It also involved – quite why, I am not sure – a lot of highly pleasurable New York life. I was there twice in 1963, staying high up in the Plaza Hotel, behind one of the dormer windows of the mansard roof on the Park side, for ten days in a cold January and another six in a golden October.

Later in the 1960s, when I had become a government minister, I was nonetheless able to justify a number of official or semi-official visits to New York. These were no fewer than three during my brief year as Minister of Aviation, for New York was an important destination for BOAC (as the relevant part of British Airways was then called), and we inaugurated both a new (VC10) service and launched a separate British terminal at Kennedy, as well as casting a sceptical eye over the F111 (or TFX as it was then known) military plane which was just going into production at Fort Worth. The two visits as Home Secretary required a little more ingenuity of justification, although America was important for the study of drugs, policing methods and race relations.

As Chancellor of the Exchequer – a total of five visits – there was less of a problem. I had to attend and speak at the annual meetings of the World Bank and the International Monetary Fund which took place in Washington in each of those two years. I had also two bilateral visits to American administrations, those of both Lyndon Johnson and Richard Nixon, as well as intensive discussions with the IMF, to whom, until the British balance of payments turned strongly round in the late summer of 1969, we owed a great deal of money. These Washington preoccupations never prevented my fitting in a New York sojourn. Nor did our indebtedness lead to any suggestion that a senior British minister should not keep to the tradition of staying in a suite high up in the tower of the Carlyle Hotel. I remember that I there had my first real day off since becoming Chancellor nearly five months previously. Also on that visit I flew down to Atlanta in the plane of Governor Nelson Rockefeller (as he then was) for the funeral of Martin Luther King. This was not exactly a day off. Indeed when I got back to the Carlyle after seven hours of Georgia services and processions under an intense if vernal sun, plus five hours of travelling, I was exhausted, both physically and emotionally. But it was not a day to be forgotten.

I do not find it easy to analyse exactly why I found New York so inspiring in those days before the Vietnam War cast its shadow (although that had already begun by the time of the King funeral) and the city's financial troubles of the 1970s temporarily depressed its confidence. I think I found its special appeal in a combination of its electricity and its centrality to world events. Maynard Keynes was very good about the former quality. He wrote in 1934 that there is an ingredient in the New York air which makes one need little more than half as much sleep and be able to write an article twice as quickly as anywhere else. But it is not just that. No doubt there are mountain resorts, from Colorado to Switzerland, whose 'air like wine', in the old cliché, may be just as physically stimulating, but are far from equally mentally so.

The New York climate is not particularly good. Difficult though many people find this to believe, it has over one and a half times the rainfall of London. It can be bitterly cold as well as oppressively hot. It can be windy and humid, and sometimes both at the same time. The clouds can lie very low, well down over the tops of the skyscrapers. But not for long. The old joke, about St Louis I think, that if you don't like the weather wait half an hour and it will change, is almost equally applicable to New York. I once met a cold front between Park and Fifth Avenues. It was a muggy November morning near Grand Central Station but by Rockefeller Plaza it had become cold, clear early winter, and remained so for several days.

More important than the weather, however, is the sense of being at the centre of the world. When was this achieved? It was certainly not remotely so in the old Dutch days. And in the early years of independence both Boston and Philadelphia were seen as finer centres of republican virtue. At the time of the Civil War they were thought to have contributed much more to the Union cause. Charles Dilke, visiting in the summer of 1866, was greatly impressed by America generally but thought New York to be 'corrupt, vulgar and, except for its striking physical beauty, generally undesirable'. New York drawing rooms, even this early, might be thought to be the most exclusive in the world, he continued, but 'that was no sign of grace, for those who were kept out included the most eminent and intellectually distinguished'.

The vast post-Civil War surge in North-Eastern industry made New York the unrivalled financial centre, which uniquely mingled elegance and dynamism. Neither these qualities nor the exclusiveness of its drawing rooms prevented some of its most eminent citizens from seeking the illusion of still higher fashion and status in the Old World. In 1891 William Waldorf Astor, the great-grandson of the John Jacob Astor who had come to New York from Germany in 1783 and established a fur-trapping business, although the hold that he almost accidentally acquired on Manhattan real estate proved far more profitable than even the finest pelts, decided on a reverse emigration and removed his family and his fortune (estimated at 100 million nineteenth-century dollars) to England. Although he had been US minister to Rome for three years in the mid-1880s, he did not feel that his desire for public service was adequately recognized in America, and his wife felt miffed by the superiority in those exclusive New York drawing rooms of another Mrs Astor. He therefore reconciled himself to the austerities of Cliveden, Hever Castle and St James's Square, becoming a viscount and founding a notable dynasty in England. However he left behind in New York a younger brother, another John Jacob Astor, whose fortune, although estimated at only 87 million nineteenth-century dollars, was enough to provide continuing lubrication for a philanthropic American branch after he himself perished in the *Titanic* disaster of 1912.

The Jerome family, whose main achievement was to produce Winston Churchill's mother, and whose status and wealth did not quite match those of the Astors, preferred living in Paris. When Lord Randolph Churchill married Jennie Jerome in 1874 he began a strong tradition of British politicians depending upon Americans either as wives or as mothers. Lord Randolph's nephew, with the advantage of being a duke, acquired a Vanderbilt daughter in a notably unhappy marriage, and there was then the remarkable clutch of William Harcourt, Joseph Chamberlain, George Nathaniel Curzon, Harold Macmillan, Quintin Hogg, Anthony Crosland, Keith Joseph, Tony Benn and David Owen, not to mention the Duke of Windsor, who were in one category or the other. By contrast there were remarkably few examples over this period of American politicians or other figures of note acquiring British wives. Almost the only exception (late in life) was Averell Harriman.

Even at the times of the exodus of Mrs Jerome and her daughters, or nearly twenty years later of William Waldorf Astor, New York, so far from being a newly created frontier town, had already been a great metropolis for a long time. It was a world-class city earlier than several European capitals, let alone more remote conurbations from Mexico City to Shanghai. The European capital to which New York's rise is almost exactly contemporary is Berlin. Berlin in 1700 had a population of 25,000. New York (or New Amsterdam as it was until a few decades before) was then smaller, around 10,000. Just over a hundred years later they had come nearer to equality, although Berlin was still leading with 197,000 in 1816, compared with New York's 127,000 in 1820. It was at the middle of the century however that, like two greyhounds waiting in the slips, they both began to take off. New York in 1850 had first gone over half a million, and Berlin, although there was no Prussian census for that year, was just about the same. By 1900 New York had raced to 3,400,000, with Berlin lagging behind. Berlin's maximum was about 4,500,000 in the 1930s when New York had already gone over 7 million and was engaged with London and with nowhere else for the blue riband of being the largest city in the world. Seventy years ago this was a matter of pride, although it has since become a matter of shame, with spreading agglomerations from São Paulo to Calcutta trying to pretend they are smaller than they are.

The Berlin/New York axis, however, is more than a matter of population statistics. It shows itself in considerable similarities of architecture and atmosphere. Many of New York's public buildings from the official ones around City Hall, the Stock Exchange further downtown and the Public Library further uptown have a distinct Wilhelmine feel to them. The Humboldt University or the Staatsoper (now rebuilt in its original shape) do not feel too different. Even more strongly is it the case that many relatively quiet brownstone districts of New York must have given a strong twitch upon the thread for those who had come, voluntarily or involuntarily, from Wilmersdorf or Charlottenburg.

There is no doubt that, well before the end of the nineteenth century, little old New York, as it sometimes self-consciously referred to itself, implying more of both age and intimacy than it actually possessed, was a major world city, not quite then a Paris or a London, but able to look not only Berlin but also Vienna in the face, and to be considered superior in current metropolitan quality to either Rome or Madrid. Theodore Roosevelt who, in spite of his enjoyment of being a 'rough rider', whether in Wyoming or Cuba, was essentially a fashionable New Yorker of an unusually 'good family' for American politics of the time, found Washington when he went there in 1901, first as vice-president and after six months and an assassination as president, an appallingly hick town compared to the glitter and sophistication to which he was used. And this was before the first skyscrapers had given New York its unique physical profile. The academic quality of Columbia University, the beginnings of the Metropolitan Museum, the music of Carnegie Hall and of the first 'Met' (opera house) all came before the Woolworth

Building rose to fifty-five storeys in 1913, let alone before the midtown peaks of the Empire State, Chrysler and Rockefeller Plaza buildings were erected in the late 1920s and the early 1930s. The twin towers of the World Trade Center, which came nearly fifty years later, did not in my view contribute much to the skyscape. The tragedy of their fate was awful, but rather on humanitarian and political than architectural grounds.

New York, however, depends less upon the individual architectural quality of its skyscrapers than does Chicago. They make a backdrop rather than a central contribution to the life of the city. I would guess that most New Yorkers, unless they are workers in high offices or sky-top bartenders, do not go above the forty- or even the twenty-storey mark more than once a month. Fashionable New York life takes place much nearer to the ground, in smallish houses in cross streets or in apartment blocks on the avenues which do not go above a modest fourteen or sixteen storeys. The best restaurants are nearly all on the ground. No notable club or art gallery is on the heights. The skyline gives the city its breathless urban beauty, but the tops of the buildings are mostly for visitors, although also for the Secretary-General of the United Nations, whom I suppose could be regarded as the grandest (and relatively long-term) visitor to New York.

Whether New York has been the right place for the UN, and what has been the impact of its presence upon the city, are questions with by no means obvious answers. In 1945–6 New York almost chose itself by virtue of the predominant power of the United States, of the Latin American countries to which it was a sort of hemisphere capital and junction on the way to almost anywhere else, then constituting nearly 40 per cent of the membership, and of any possible European rival being itself devastated, or surrounded by devastation. The only exception was Geneva and that, important a subsidiary UN base although it has since become, reeked too much of the failures of the League of Nations era. The first UN General Assembly was held in London in the limited amenities of the Methodist Central Hall, Westminster. That gathering underlined the strains the international circus imposed upon any capital which had been near the front line of the war. So New York, with most of the delegations living in midtown Manhattan and travelling out for meetings at the optimistically named Lake Success on Long Island, ineluctably became the seat. When the 42nd to 48th Street complex on the East River was built between 1947 and 1953, the choice was set in steel and concrete.

The UN's impact upon New York has not been comparable with that of the League upon Geneva in the 1920s and 1930s or of the European Union institutions upon Brussels since the 1950s. This is despite the fact that parts of these two cities remain immune from institutional international life. Calvinistic Geneva is still alive on the west bank of the Rhône, and there are large areas of Brussels which remain solidly Belgian. Nevertheless the quantitative impact of the international quarters have been greater in Geneva and Brussels than in New York. It is partly the sheer size of New York, and partly the fact that New York thinks of itself, with or without the UN, as the most international city in the world. Geographically, moreover, the United Nations' impact upon the city has been fairly narrowly confined. Uptown from the complex in the 40s it extends to the Secretary-General's fine residence on 58th Street, while inland from the East River the delegation offices and the ambassadors' residences of the now 189 members hardly go west of Fifth Avenue.

The two questions which remain are first whether a more easterly location (in terms of continents, not of New York avenues), say Vienna or Stockholm, would have made the

Russians and the Chinese feel more at ease in the organization, and second whether the United States being the host
country has tempered American impatience with the UN's
independence of Washington's lead. There is not much
affirmative evidence to answer either of these questions.
Russia and China have been amenable when they so wished,
and sullenly uncooperative when they thought it in their
interest to be so, and it has made little difference whether
they were in New York or Geneva or Vienna or Helsinki.
Furthermore the US Congress has not been persuaded to pay
up its UN dues by any feeling that a hostly generosity was
appropriate for the richest country in the world. Anti-New
York feeling may indeed have joined with xenophobia
(perverse though that is in a country made by immigrants)
to feed the narrow-mindedness of those who do not want to
pay. What, however, has been beneficially the case is that
New York has been the best city in the world painlessly to
absorb these 200 delegations, many of them very large, and
that their presence and the occasional excitements in both
the Security Council and the Assembly have added lustre
even to the city's unique quality.

The UN has played only a peripheral part in my New
York life. I once gave a lecture under the sponsorship of one
of the subsidiary agencies, but I have never addressed the
Assembly or even one of its humbler committees. I support
it, but, as Churchill said he did the Church of England, from
the outside, as a buttress not a pillar. Yet I have always
thought of it as giving an additional dimension to New York.
Nearly four decades ago I used occasionally to go to lunch
with Adlai Stevenson in what is still the United States
ambassador's official residence at the top of the Waldolf
Tower. And I have known, with varying closeness, all British
ambassadors to the UN back to Gladwyn Jebb in the early
1950s. One of them, Crispin Tickell, encountered in the

Paris essay, had been my *chef de cabinet* in Brussels, and in his years (1987–90) I gladly adopted his official residence at the top of a Beekman Place block as one of my two favourite New York temporary abodes, and composed many book pages looking down on the FDR Drive and over the East River to the somewhat nondescript expanses of Queens.

Most of my New York private residence time was however spent in what could be called Tree-houses. Ronald Tree was the heir to a substantial slice of the Marshall Field Chicago department store fortune. He had spent most of his life in England, where he had been a Conservative member of Parliament from 1931 to 1945. He had there acquired and delicately renovated Ditchley, a fine early-eighteenth-century mansion in North Oxfordshire. In the early years of the war it had been an auxiliary country retreat for Churchill. On nights of high moonlight Chequers was thought to be unduly exposed to German aircraft. In consequence the Prime Minister, arriving always with a full complement of secretaries and guests, spent no fewer than fifteen weekends at Ditchley between November 1940 and March 1942. When the war was over Tree lost his parliamentary seat, was not generously rewarded by Churchill (that is, he was not made a peer) and found the burden of British taxation heavy. He therefore returned to the side of the Atlantic from which his ancestors had come and divided the remainder of his life (although with frequent European forays) between Barbados and a large New York house (now the Mexican embassy to the UN) on 79th Street between Park and Lexington Avenues.

I first stayed in the 79th Street house in 1971, repeated this experience in the early and mid-1970s, and then, after his death when his widow, Marietta Tree, moved to a riverside apartment at Sutton Place South, stayed there still more frequently in the late 1970s and 1980s, until that era ended with her death in 1991, and my joining her daughter Frankie

Fitzgerald, Arthur Schlesinger, Mayor Dinkins and Susan Mary Alsop to give memorial addresses in St Thomas' Episcopal Church on Fifth Avenue. Marietta, who had not been the chatelaine of Ditchley during the war for her marriage to Tree took place only in 1947, had been born Peabody. Her father was the Bishop of Syracuse, NY, and her grandfather was the formidable Endicott Peabody, the founder and long-term headmaster of Groton School, who had half intimidated and half inspired Franklin Roosevelt, but was less successful with some of his sons. Her mother was a dedicated civil rights campaigner who was arrested during the Selma (Alabama) march of 1965. At that time Mrs Peabody's second son, another Endicott Peabody, was Governor of Massachusetts, which led to an inter-gubernatorial conversation reminiscent of the fabled exchange between the Governors of North and South Carolina. The Governor of Alabama telephoned to the State House in Boston and said to his opposite number: 'I've got your mother in gaol. What shall I do?' 'Let her out,' Peabody was said to have replied with a brevity worthy of Calvin Coolidge, one of his Massachusetts predecessors.

Marietta Tree therefore, while not brought up to wealth comparable with that of her husband, was of the most reputable New England stock. She also inherited and further added to a tradition of public service. When I first met her (in 1959) she was Commissioner Tree – a splendid title, reminiscent of Shaw's Major Barbara, and appropriate to her appearance, which was at once winsome and commanding – for she was part of Mayor Robert Wagner's City administration, charged with inter-group relations (or, in British terms, race relations) in New York. In her increasing role as the anchor of my New York life this meant that I saw the city somewhat more from an insider's than an outsider's point of view, as well as having the opportunity to develop an exceptional range of acquaintances there.

Marietta Tree was sometimes thought to have a breathless enthusiasm. I remember an occasion when we went to some grand fund-raising dinner (without I fear any contribution from me) in the Egyptian Hall of the Metropolitan Museum. When we drove away, accompanied by Marietta's close friend Kitty Carlyle, as she was known in her singing days, or Kitty Hart as she became through her marriage to Moss Hart, who spanned most Broadway activities, Marietta commented that the 150 or so who had been gathered together that evening probably represented more wealth than the entire national income of Belgium. Mrs Hart, who practised a more deflating style, said: 'Well, they may have been rich, but they were not the cream of New York that I used to look up to. When I first came here such people were often called after telephone exchanges, Rhinelander, Schuyler, Butterfield, Templeton . . . Now they are called Trump or Tramp or some such name.' In spite of this recollection, however, Mrs Tree was not lacking in humour and discrimination, let alone style and public spirit.

In the 1990s inanimate institutions provided substitute anchors. The first was the Knickerbocker Club, and the second was the Random House publishing firm. As mentioned I had a glancing acquaintanceship with that club on my first visit to New York, but it was nearly four decades later that I began to use it frequently. In that long interval it meant nothing more to me than being the venue of a chilling story about Eleanor Roosevelt, although that would have been in the old clubhouse further downtown and not in the new Fifth Avenue and 62nd Street building, erected in 1917. On a cold day in the early 1890s, when she was about eleven, she was given the great treat of an expedition drive with her adored but alcoholic father, Elliott Roosevelt, Theodore Roosevelt's younger brother. All went well until they were passing the Knickerbocker, when he said that he must go in and see if there were any letters for him. She waited outside for several hours until he was carried out dead drunk and feet first.

The Knickerbocker has become for me a real New York haven. Its location almost at the south-east corner of Central Park is perfect. There is only a half-mile walk up to the Frick, my favourite small gallery in the world, because it is intensely pleasurable without being at all hard work, a sort of Venice to the Florence of the great collections in the barracks of the Prado, the Kunsthistoriche or the Rijksmuseum. And a further half-mile gets one to the greater size and range of the more demanding Metropolitan.

The Knickerbocker is also well placed for my more strenuous early-morning walk. This is to go across town while veering a little down to First Avenue around 50th Street, where there are several newsagents (probably the influence of the UN) in which the London papers of the previous day can be bought, and then to come back for breakfast by a slightly different route. In theory I regard the *New York Times* as the most distinguished newspaper in the world, but I do not find, particularly as the British coverage gets smaller and smaller, that it provides me with a wholly sustaining morning diet. One of my most reliable pleasures is to return, with my exercise duty done, and to sit in a window table of the Knickerbocker dining room, slowly eating an excellent American breakfast (the bacon is so much better) and looking at a mixture of both the London and the New York *Times* and the view over Fifth Avenue and the Park. The pleasure of the view is exceeded only by that from the fourth floor of the club, where the bedrooms have access to a spacious balcony and the angle of view is wider.

At weekends when the Knickerbocker dining room is closed and, except for the occasional wedding receptions, the club is left to silence and its few bedroom inhabitants, the best alternative breakfast destination is the first floor (in English parlance) restaurant of the Park Lane Hotel, next door to the Plaza, which has the most attractive low view up the Park of all the Central Park South buildings. The Knickerbocker wedding parties are now, I hope and believe, less excluding and more multicultural than might have been the case in 1953. I remember, in the 1980s, Mrs Tree pushing across to me an invitation which said 'Marriage ceremony at the West End Synagogue, Reception in the Knickerbocker Club', and saying, with approval at the change, 'That would have been inconceivable even twenty years ago.'

From 1990 to 1999 Random House was run by Harold Evans, an old friend whose 1970s editorship of the London *Sunday Times* had given it a new radical panache. Under his direction Random House put into serious New York circulation two of my books: my autobiography, *A Life at the Center*, came out there in the spring of 1993 and *Gladstone* did so in the winter of 1997. In the 1960s and 1970s a number of my previous books had obtained a New York imprint, although mostly that of the Chilmark Press, very much a fringe publishing house, which a rich literary gentlemen called Louis Cowan ran more as a hobby than for profit. His attitude to me must have been distinctly eleemosynary, for he even published in 1968 a dish of reheats called *Essays and Speeches*, of which I would guess the sales must have had difficulty in reaching four figures. Perhaps with my life of Sir Charles Dilke, rechristened *A Victorian Tragedy*, he might have done better, but none of these ventures could be regarded as making a serious impact on the American publishing scene. Harper and Row's publication of my 200-page biographical essay *Truman* in the summer of 1986 was in a higher league, but even then I was a little disappointed with the impact. Maybe it was because America was then at the height of its passion for long books (*Churchill* should more recently have satisfied them in this respect); maybe it was because they thought it presumptuous of a foreigner to write about a president of such heartland origin, even if one who pursued a highly internationalist policy. Or maybe they just did not think it was very good. In any event, I believe it aroused more interest in Canada.

My 1990s ventures with Random House were therefore of considerable importance to me. I needed a publishing lift if my literary New York life was not to lag well behind its political and social counterparts. Harold Evans substantially achieved this for me. Neither *A Life at the Center* nor *Gladstone* was remotely in the category of the blockbusters with which Random House sometimes made (and occasionally lost) a lot of money. But they were both widely and favourably reviewed and sold respectably. The volumes were handsomely produced, so that I marginally prefer them to the London originals. In the case of my autobiography a separate text was produced, Americanized both in the sense that spellings were changed and that, more interestingly, five to ten thousand words of anglocentric passages were taken out and about the same number, expanding on the American interludes in the English version, were added. This exercise was greatly aided by my old friend Irwin Ross, Harvard graduate of 1940, *New York Post*, *Fortune* and *Reader's Digest* journalist for many subsequent decades, and notable author in his own right. He has also over the years performed one necessary and one desirable function: he has kept me in touch with the West Side, correcting my tendency to be far too East Side orientated, and he has been an invaluable guide to New York restaurants. In the case of *Gladstone*, the subject of which never visited the United States although he once spoke of it with an almost sacerdotal awe, the English text was left to reign supreme, with labour instead of labor and traveller instead of traveler. This has also been so with *Churchill*.

Farrar Straus Giroux launched it in 2001, and became for me the peak of an author's dream of publishing houses.

I have not discerned great differences between the New York and the London publishing scenes. London attaches more importance to the exercise of signings in bookshops, so much so that it became a joke at one stage that unsigned copies, because rarer, were more valuable than signed ones. London literary gatherings tend to be more dependent upon the author describing his own work, whereas in New York they often get others to do it for him. I remember Arthur Schlesinger on my autobiography, and Henry Kissinger on *Gladstone*. I also vividly recall a speech by Schlesinger at Le Cirque restaurant, rightly praising the autobiography of Kay Graham, under whose inadvertent proprietorship, precipitated by the suicide of her husband in 1963, the modern *Washington Post* was made.

American reviews are, in my experience, somewhat less generous than British ones, but that may be mainly because, it being a country four times the size, there is less mutual back-scratching. What is more indisputable is that New York publishers' luncheons are infinitely more austere (in intake rather than in cost) than London ones. The literary world crowds each day into the Four Seasons, observing and greeting each other, but making their guests feel infinitely gross and guilty if they consume more than a Caesar salad and one glass of white wine. It is a far cry from what I imagine were the old indulgences at the Algonquin.

The paradox is that New York, so far from being just a new city in the New World, is today for me almost more infused with memories than is London, but that is partly because London has been too omnipresent in my life for seventy years, whereas the fifty years of New York have been more a matter of sudden, brief immersions with all the vividness of scenes in a pageant. My New York memories are almost all as pleasant as they are vivid. And this impression has not been marred by the dreadful events of 11 September 2001. On two subsequent visits I have been far more impressed by New York's resilience than by its resentment.

BONN

Bonn, capital of West Germany from 1949 to 1990, when the East came in and the title West ceased to apply to the Federal Republic, or to 1999, when the formal move of the seat of government back to Berlin took place, should not strictly be in this book, which is intended to be about metropolises, even if in one instance they are as small as Cardiff. And just as I have resolutely rejected Oxford on the ground that it is a university and a county town, but not a metropolis, so Bonn, with which it is twinned, could almost equally be discounted. Bonn's métier, indeed, had been *not* to be a metropolis. But the countervailing consideration is that Bonn was for more than forty years the capital of one of the most important, successful and best-governed countries in the world. Its inclusion is therefore in part an excuse for paying a tribute to the achievements of a polity which started with Adenauer and ran through Erhard, Kiesinger, Brandt and Schmidt to Kohl.

This should not be taken to mean that there is little interest in Bonn as a city apart from its somewhat arbitrary choice as a capital. It claims to be more than 2,000 years old, and indeed it took the claim sufficiently seriously that in May 1989 a celebration of two millennia of civic history was held in the Beethovenhalle there. This took the form of a concert interrupted by speeches from the incongruous combination

of Chancellor Kohl and myself. And the incongruity extended
to the music being mostly by Haydn and not by Beethoven,
Bonn's most eminent son (born there in 1770) in spite of it
being in his eponymous auditorium.

Inevitably any 2,000th anniversary relating to a northern
city is shrouded in some of the mists of antiquity. But there
are substantial straws of evidence of Bonn having been an
ancient settlement where people have long clustered for
safety, worship, commerce and the beginning or ending of
journeys. Still better authenticated is its refounding as an
island of urban culture beyond the Alps by the Emperor
Julian in AD 359. That anniversary will no doubt call
forth another birthday celebration, although whether the
Beethovenhalle will still be there to house it must be an
open question.

Apart from its recent political role, Bonn has at least two
notable characteristics. The first is that its name is unchang-
ing in all the main languages of the world. Neither prefix,
suffix nor internal modification effects its uncompromising
monosyllabic purity. Its only rival in this respect among
capital cities (and even there two syllables are required) is
Madrid. Bonn also has a university whose fame has been
greater than its venerability. I vividly remember asking my
father over seventy years ago which he thought were the
outstanding universities of the world. His reply was precise.
'Oxford and Cambridge,' he said (although not insular he was
sufficiently British inevitably to start there), 'Harvard and
Yale, Heidelberg and Bonn – and Paris.' He obviously liked
to think in national pairs, but was defeated in the search for
a French companion to the Sorbonne. On historical greats
he might have added the Iberian pair of Salamanca and
Coimbra, or the Italian one of Bologna and Pavia, but did
not do so. One interesting feature of this list was that Bonn
was much the youngest of those upon it. Even going back to

its first 1786 incarnation, let alone its second start in 1818, it was 150 years younger than Harvard, 70 years younger than Yale. In the nineteenth century it leaped into the world league with remarkable force and speed.

Even so, it was more than academic eminence which made Konrad Adenauer alight on Bonn as the new capital when the three Western zones came together in 1949 and the Federal Republic achieved near-sovereignty, Anglo-American respect and the opportunity to build prosperity much sooner than had been expected four years before. Adenauer was a Carolingian and a Rhinelander. He instinctively felt that the best date in European history was Christmas Day 800, when Charlemagne was crowned Frankish emperor. He had no warmth of feeling for Prussia or Saxony and in consequence (although he could not publicly say so) no enthusiasm for German reunification on any basis but as a pro-Western democracy, which then was impossible. He saw reunification as bringing a lot of Protestant and/or socialist voters into the Federal Republic.

Religious divisions then played a greater part in German politics than is the case today and they also played a part in Adenauer's choice of capital. He wanted a Federal Republic firmly anchored into the West, in which objective he was brilliantly successful, and he wanted a Rhineland capital, which he also achieved. Hamburg was too far away to the north as well as being too Protestant. Munich, although satisfactorily Catholic, was too remote in the south. Frankfurt was too associated both with the revolutionary tradition of 1848 and latterly with money. In addition all three were large enough cities to be capable of aspiration to national preponderance, and therefore carried the thought of centralization. Adenauer preferred the capital to be, in a phrase of the time, 'almost in the shadow of the spires of Cologne cathedral'. And, if a shadow can be allowed metaphorically to extend for twenty miles, it was. Bonn was also convenient for Rhondorf, where in the years of his disdainful detachment from, but not active opposition to Nazism, he had cultivated a notable garden around a modest villa. Rhondorf was only a few miles upriver from Bonn, although on the opposite bank. There he continued to live, crossing each day by ferry, during the fourteen years of his Chancellorship.

As a result this small town in Germany (pre-war population approximately 80,000) became the capital of the country which rapidly forged forward to being the third most powerful economy in the world. Rarely has such a tiny harbour sheltered such a great ship. Obviously in the circumstances there was a shortage of fine supporting buildings. There were no readymade wharves, customs houses or central welcoming edifices, to continue the maritime metaphor, no equivalent of the Royal Liver Building in Liverpool or the sailors' church of Notre-Dame de la Garde on the hill at Marseille. It was not that Bonn was without some fine architecture, the Münster, the Remigius Church, the Rathaus, and most conspicuously the Elector's Palace, which had become the University and dominates the southern entrance to the old town. But they were all committed to ecclesiastical, civic or academic use; government and parliament, the Villa Hammerschmidt residence of the Federal President apart, had to establish themselves in utilitarian post-1950 structures. Some at least of the embassies were lucky enough to find fairly grand riverside villas in the suburb of Bad Godesberg which Cologne and Düsseldorf businessmen had built for themselves in the period of Wilhelmine prosperity between 1871 and 1914.

Bonn offered a quietly agreeable life to diplomats so installed, as it did to foreign political journalists, as well as to indigenous ones and federal functionaries. There was the interest of dealing with a major government combined with the convenient life in a medium-sized, well-placed town embedded in beautiful countryside bisected by the majestically flowing Rhine. Bonn may not have offered much of the civic excitement of a capital city, but it enabled great issues to be discussed and occasionally resolved in a peculiarly unfrenetic atmosphere. In the second half of the twentieth century this opened up a vast contrast between the capitals of the two German-speaking democracies. Vienna had (and has) the grandest official buildings in the world. Its nearest rival is Paris, for although Rome is rich in Renaissance palazzi, many of which are now in the service of the state, they are not steeped in the traditions of such a role, for the city has little more than a 100-year history of being a seat of secular government. Yet admirable though are some aspects of the small bourgeois Austrian Republic and greatly happier has been its post-1954 than its post-1919 experience, it is impossible not to feel a sad lack of proportion between the splendour of the surroundings and the narrow compass of the issues which now fall for decision within them. The opinions of the Ballhausplatz do not now arouse much interest compared with those of the State Department, the Kremlin, the Great Hall of the People or even the Quai d'Orsay. No modern equivalents of Metternich and Talleyrand fence across the green-baize tables of the Franzensplatz. A Hofburg without the Habsburgs or some regime of equivalent sweep and influence inevitably gives rise to a sense of bathos.

Bonn was the exact opposite. If the government of Austria had been a pea rattling round in a pod too large and grand for it, the government of West Germany was a striking example of power exercised without the props of pomp or circumstance. Bonn as a seat of government was the most quietly modest in Europe. Its marble staircases were few. Its guards of honour were unflamboyantly dressed. And its motorcycle escorts were a model of quiet good manners. In the days when governments provided me with such amenities I always felt that the behaviour of the respective *motards* shone a penetrating light into official styles of governments. The French were much the most ruthless. I have seen them literally kick small Citroën *deux-chevaux* out of the way while slicing through the rush-hour traffic on the Paris Périphérique. The Italians were more given to a ballet performance than to brutal results. There was a lot of pirouetting with hands off the handlebars. The British lacked both the roughness of the French and the exhibitionism of the Italians. They were merely determined to get you there on time, without either brutality or enjoyment. But in the Germany of the Bonn years the primary motive seemed to be that of showing that Prussian arrogance was dead and the rule of law was supreme. They inconvenienced no other motorists. They even waited at traffic lights. It was admirable, although I sometimes thought that I might have arrived more quickly without the escort.

It would be difficult to argue that as the 1950s turned into the 1960s and the 1960s into the 1970s this lack of appurtenances of power in Bonn adversely affected either the performance of the D-mark or the seriousness with which America took Germany as an ally or France took it as a partner. The penalty, if there was one, showed itself much more in the narrowness of social life within the capital. Bonn inevitably became a town of politicians, government officials, journalists, diplomats and little more. It was not unique in this respect. The tradition of the artificial capital, and therefore, to begin with at any rate, of the one-subject civic society, started in Europe at least as early as Philip II's foundation of Madrid in 1561.

Subsequently such implants have been more a matter of the world beyond the oceans: Washington in 1800, Ottawa in 1867, Canberra in 1917, Brasilia in 1960. These greenfield creations (although in the case of Washington at least the original state of the site might have been more appropriately described as 'brown marsh') were often slow to grow. Ottawa took 120 years to reach a population of three-quarters of a million and Canberra 70 years to reach a quarter of million. Brasilia, however, aided by the high human fertility of Brazil, galloped to a million within twenty years of its foundation. Washington is naturally the most interesting of the group, not only by virtue of being the capital of the leading power of the world, but also because it is the only artificially created capital which has ever grown into a great metropolis. It is manifestly not *the* great metropolis of its country, for New York, with Chicago and Los Angeles in reserve, retains that position, but it is nonetheless now a major city by world standards, approximately the same size as the reunited Berlin, larger than anywhere in Europe except for London, Paris, Moscow and Madrid.

It was however a late flowering. As late as 1901, President Theodore Roosevelt, as was seen in the New York essay, regarded it as almost a place of exile, and even when his distant cousin, Franklin Roosevelt, was inaugurated thirty-two years later, Washington's population was still only 480,000. The more interventionist style of FDR's government and then the Second World War changed that. Washington became the capital of the world in a sense that no other city had been since the fall of the Roman Empire. Washington remained (and remains) an overwhelmingly political town compared with New York or Paris or London. The conversation is still too strongly political for many people's taste. But Washington can no longer by any stretch of the imagination be registered as provincial or parochial. It has become a considerable cultural centre. And even within the one-subject world of politics the most famous journalists vie with the most polished ambassadors to produce the most sophisticated witticisms about the most powerful Cabinet officers. Moreover the political talk is less narrowly internal and insular than it mostly is in London. That has been one benefit of world leadership.

These considerations never applied to Bonn. Economically powerful although West Germany became, with the D-mark gradually achieving a position equally powerful and much more benevolent than that which the Wehrmacht had previously enjoyed, there was no aspiration to world leadership. On the contrary, Germany was trying for at least the three decades between 1950 and 1980 to push power away. This was sharply different from both Britain and France, which over the same period were trying by slightly different methods but with equal consistency to cut figures on the world stage greater than those which their economic strengths could easily sustain. I well remember the contrast in the 1960s between Britain trying to cling on to the Sterling Area long after it was capable of providing a hub for such a system and West Germany trying to resist the D-mark becoming a reserve currency long after such a development had become inevitable. Failure attended both endeavours, but the *nolo episcopari* attitude of the Germans was both more dignified and more compatible with an effective management of their home economy.

Equally, in the affairs of the European Community during this period, the Germans were content to provide strong general support and to pay a high proportion of the bills while leaving it to the French to control the *rouages* (or detailed workings) of the Community in Brussels and to get the best jobs for themselves. Apart from Walter Hallstein, who was a formative if somewhat too *protocolaire* first President of the Commission, they rarely sent anyone of top quality to Brussels, either as a Commissioner or as an ambassador (Ralf Dahrendorf was a brief exception).

Yet, in my firm conviction, the Germany of the Bonn years has a high claim to have been the best governed of all the Western democracies, from which it follows, even if Churchill's deliberately downbeat endorsement is accepted ('democracy is the worst of all systems of government until you consider the others'), that it had a very high claim to be the best in the world. In any circumstances this would have been a remarkable achievement. In view of Germany's recent previous history and of the ruined country which was the starting material it was a near miracle. It showed itself in the *Wirtschaftswunder*, which although it has not lasted indefinitely was one of the greatest bursts to prosperity in human history, and which was very well founded on a brilliant exploitation of middle-grade technology – motor cars and machine tools – while leaving others to waste their money on Concordes and rockets. On that hard foundation Germany built a fine welfare state. It subjected governments, both federal and *Länder*, to a firm rule of law, which lived alongside a liberal penal policy and an unassertive police force. Power was at least as devolved as in the United States, which was necessary if cities as large and diverse as Hamburg and Munich were to be governed from Bonn. The electoral system was skilfully designed to provide an adequate proportionality with local roots, and to make the Bundestag a reasonable mirror of opinion in the nation while avoiding the too frequent elections and changes of government of the Weimar Republic.

The result was a threefold triumph. First, the forty-two years between 1949 and reunification were survived in Germany with only two semi-sharp changes of political direction, whereas in both Britain and America there were five. Second, so far from this meaning a dangerous immobilism, the Social Democrats (or SPD), which in Adenauer's day were regarded as a pariah party, threatening both the internal stability and external orientation of the state, moved into full status as a frequently governing party. Third, while Britain and America each needed nine heads of government, Germany got through with only six Federal Chancellors, five of whom were in their differing ways major world figures.

This was clearly true of the founding father Adenauer: partisan, foxy, a limpet for clinging to power, but nonetheless an elderly statesman (between seventy-three and eighty-seven years of age during his fourteen years of power) of breathtaking achievement. Ludwig Erhard, who after many years of impatient waiting eventually succeeded him, was a German Anthony Eden, although of a very different physical shape. In both cases their relative failures as heads of government should not be allowed to obscure their very considerable prior achievements in the number-two position. Erhard, as animator of the economic miracle (about which Adenauer knew little and mainly regarded as *l'intendance* which he hoped would follow), was as important a figure in the evolution of German post-war history as was, three-quarters of a century before, Joseph Chamberlain in the pattern of British party politics or Dean Acheson in America's post-1945 foreign policy commitments.

After Erhard came Kurt-Georg Kiesinger, an aimable Württemberger. He was the weakest of the six, the only one who did not attain world rank. But he had a difficult government over which to preside, the so-called 'Grand Coalition'. All post-war German governments, with a solitary exception, have been coalitions, and very little harm it has done them. But they have normally comprised one or other of the two large parties, CDU or SPD, with a smaller partner, mostly the Frei Demokratische Partei (FDP), or more recently the Greens. Only in the late 1960s did the two heavyweights attempt to span the ideological gap in a broader coalition. It did not work well, partly because from either side of the political spectrum there were figures more powerful than the Chancellor, who were not naturally compatible with each other, Franz-Josef Strauss from the right and Willy Brandt from the left. And Kiesinger did not have Clement Attlee's qualities of coxing a boat containing heavier oarsmen than himself.

In 1969 there began the thirteen years of SPD dominance. First under Brandt, who had great charisma and width of occasionally misty vision, an effective alliance with the FDP was formed. This gave the junior partners, who were essential to the left-of-centre majority, a standing claim on the foreign ministership and on three other Cabinet posts. With Brandt at the head of the government and Walter Scheel at the Foreign Ministry this worked reasonably smoothly. They both believed in a policy of full commitment to the European Community, but also wanted, Brandt in particular, to use it as a secure foundation on which to seek more relaxed relations with East Germany, Poland and the Soviet Union itself, than had been the CDU habit.

In 1973 a Communist spy scandal among his staff led to Brandt's resignation as Chancellor. In retrospect it was a minor affair, not touching his own honour or loyalty, but one in an area in which he was vulnerable, both because of a certain reputation for looseness of administration and because of his *Ostpolitik*, with its greater openness towards, but not greater identity with, the Communist countries of the East. Brandt was in consequence replaced as head of the government by Helmut Schmidt, previously Defence Minister. But Brandt continued as leader and inspirer of the SPD. His leaving the Chancellorship seemed a tragedy at the time, but it may have been a reshuffling of roles which better fitted their respective talents. Schmidt was harder, clearer edged, less visionary than Brandt. They were not exactly a mutual admiration society, but by the standards of relationships throughout the world when one man is succeeded in high office by another, even (perhaps especially) of the same party, they got along averagely well.

I first met Schmidt in Bologna, Italy, in April 1961. A moderately high-level international conference had been convened by an Italian economic periodical. It was also the first occasion at which I got to know Dean Acheson. In addition, it unfortunately coincided with the Bay of Pigs, that early misadventure of the Kennedy administration. This put most Americans on the defensive, which was far from the natural posture of Acheson. Schmidt, then a new member of the Bundestag from Hamburg, and I were both at that time relatively junior participants. Soon after arrival at the Hotel Baglioni I went into the bar where a stocky – and as I at first thought cocky – young middle-aged man was already sitting on a stool. He addressed me in a self-confident semi-American English, expressing some iconoclastic sentiments about the hotel, the prospects for the conference and indeed the world at large. Within five minutes, although I saw him at that stage as carrying a few unnecessary chips on his shoulder, I thought that I was dealing with someone of exceptional quality.

That latter impression has persisted over four decades and many dozens of encounters. During the years of my presidency of the European Commission I found Schmidt the most constructive statesman of the Western world. He was the best head of government to have on one's side, and meetings with him (often even longer than those with Valéry Giscard d'Estaing, and paying little regard to the hours of meals, in which Schmidt was not very interested: a few snacks in the third hour, if one was lucky) were nearly always a pleasure because of the speed of his comprehension, the friendly informality of his manners, and his willingness to argue without rancour. This did not mean that he was free from prejudices or asperities. To an unjust extent, and despite his deep pro-Americanism, Schmidt could not abide Jimmy Carter.

Nearer at home he began with a profound under-appreciation of his political opponent and formidable successor in the Chancellorship, Helmut Kohl. When I made my official inaugural visit to Bonn in 1977, which was naturally much under the aegis of Schmidt as reigning head of government, Kohl had recently become leader of the opposition CDU party. On the second day I paid an hour's morning call on Kohl, which was an habitual exercise for a president of the Commission with a leader of the opposition. At the government luncheon which followed, Schmidt was interested to know what I had thought of Kohl. I replied that I had found him a considerable figure – and I did not just mean in physical bulk. Schmidt affected considerable shock. 'But you can't, you can't,' he said. 'He's nothing. He's just a jumped-up Rheinland-Pfalz local politician.'

The exchange would not have been significant, except for indicating how difficult even the shrewdest politicians find it to appreciate their rivals, had it not been for its sequel, nearly twenty years later. Schmidt, in full retirement, was in the mid-1990s visiting me in London. In the course of a complaint about the sad state of European politics – a refrain which came easily to him – and pointing out the desert of leadership in every country of the Union, he suddenly paused, and, using my Christian name in a way that my wife sometimes does when she has something important but unwelcome to impart, said, 'Except, and Roy, you above all know how much it hurts me to say this' – an impressive shaft of memory – 'except for Helmut Kohl.' I thought both Schmidt and Kohl came well out of this jostling of Teutonic titans, for such they both were, with Kohl, whose sins seem to me minor in relation to his achievements, rounding off the

remarkable run of Federal Chancellors who operated in Bonn
and led a Germany shorn of its eastern third, but also of at
least two-thirds of the problems which have since beset the
reunified country.

How much were the achievements of the Bonn years a
product of the ambience of that small city erected for half a
lifetime into a major capital? Will it be not merely the
surroundings but the style of the German government which
will gradually change with the readjustment to the remnants
of Wilhelmine grandeur and the excitements of early-twenty-
first-century architecture in Berlin? There will be some
advantages from the move. The climate of Berlin with its
wide skies and often exhilarating Pomeranian air is much
better than the perpetual mugginess of Bonn. The mugginess
is born out by the statistics, although happily not by my two
most testing experiences in the Rhineland. The first was the
Bonn monetary conference of November 1968. It was an
appallingly badly conducted conference, thanks largely to the
pedagogic verbal diarrhoea of a now internationally forgotten
German Economics Minister, appropriately known as Professor Schiller. But the sparkling autumn weather made almost
tolerable the dreadful hours which Karl Schiller's verbosity
imposed upon us. I went to bed on the first night at 2.00 a.m.
and on the second at 4.30, but this did not prevent my being
up at 6.30 on the last morning and scribbling away in the
dawn on the mini-budget statement which, thanks partly to
the deficiencies of the conference, I had to make in the
House of Commons at 4.00 that afternoon.

That Bonn experience did however give me a certain
distaste for the ministerial suite on the first floor in the
British ambassador's Rhineside residence, a grand 1904 villa,
built by a prosperous business family from the Ruhr. I was
happy to surrender it on a subsequent visit to Edward Heath,
a year out of Downing Street and a month deprived of even

the Conservative leadership, who would, I judged, appreciate even such a small assuagement. The sacrifice was made less by there being, in my view, a much better room on the second floor, with windows in all directions. The only disadvantage of any bedroom in that house was the intense throbbing noise, at intervals throughout the night, of tugs endeavouring to pull a line of barges upstream against the strong current. It at least conveyed an impression of the power of German commerce proceeding relentlessly by day and by night.

The second memorable occasion when Bonn weather far exceeded its reputation was for the Western Economic Summit of July 1978. This was only the fourth in the series which had begun under French auspices at Rambouillet in 1975. As a result some of the characteristics of the Rambouillet 'fireside chat' were still present. The vast circuses of today were still in the future, although delegations were already made up of three ministers from each government and a moderate retinue of officials and advisers. This relative modesty was well suited to the Bonn ambience. As I recollect it we moved about easily and informally, with no screaming of police sirens, mainly on the small plateau above the Rhine between the buildings of the Federal Parliament and the Chancellery. And we did so in exceptional weather conditions. As I wrote in my diary for the first day: 'A beautiful morning; cool (maximum temperature that day was 63°F – 17°C), settled sun and low humidity, a remarkable and lucky combination for the Rhine Valley in mid-July.' This together with my being at Bonn as president of the European Commission as an almost casually accepted participant, in sharp contrast with London the year before when Giscard was resistant and Callaghan complaisant towards his opposition, made me remember that summit, in spite of a semi-crash landing in a helicopter, with considerable pleasure.

My last visit to Bonn as a capital (and maybe my last ever) was in the summer of 1998 when I conducted my commission on electoral reform there on a highly productive visit of enquiry. We did not recommend the wholesale importation of the German system into Britain. We modified it in several important respects, but it nonetheless had far more influence upon us than any other system of proportional representation. During that visit what impressed me even more than the German system, despite its many virtues, was the spirit of rational enquiry on the part of our interlocutors which informed nearly all our discussions. There was nothing chiliastic about it. Nothing was perfect, but some systems were much better than others, and calm discussion offered the best chance of arriving at a sensible solution. It was the reverse in this respect of the spirit which had influenced the Nazi regime and indeed that of the Hohenzollern Empire. It seemed to me the epitome of the Bonn spirit. Bonn as a capital may have been dull, it may have been monocultural, but it was calm, co-operative and sensible. And it certainly achieved results. In the modern (or any other) world there is a great deal to be said for these modest 'bourgeois' attributes.

NEW YORK

16. *Right*. The Statue of Liberty and Lower Manhattan as I first saw them in the early 1950s.

17. *Below*. The Upper East Side of New York by night a generation ago. The Plaza Hotel is at (A), the Knickerbocker Club at (B), the Frick Collection at (C) and the Metropolitan Museum of Art at (D).

18. View of Central Park (laid out in 1858) in autumn, New York's best season.

BONN

FOUR CHANCELLORS

19. *Right*. Konrad Adenauer and Willy Brandt: the 'old fox' looks persuasive though his successor-but-two seems sceptical.

20. *Below, left*. Helmut Schmidt: in the late 1970s 'the most constructive statesman of the Western world'.

21. *Below, right*. Helmut Kohl in the days when he towered over Bonn and Europe.

The British Embassy
22. *Above*. The entrance from the land side.
23. *Below*. The view over the Rhine from the river side.

CHICAGO

THE 'LITTLE HUTS'
OF TWO TYCOONS

24. *Right.* George M.
Pullman's mini-British
Museum on Prairie
Avenue.

25. *Below, right.*
Potter Palmer's
Rhenish castle of the
1880s which began
the development of
Chicago's Gold Coast.

26. *Below.* The
convolutions of the
Carson, Pirie, Scott
department store
(Louis Sullivan, 1899)
with a glimpse of the
earlier and more austere
first 'Chicago style' to
the left of the picture.

27. *Above.* Chicago's early 1920s architecture, exemplified by the twin sentinels of the Wrigley Building (left foreground) and the Tribune Tower (right foreground) at the southern end of 'the Magnificent Mile' of North Michigan Avenue.

28. *Left.* The Water Tower (1848), a rare survival from pre-Fire Chicago, with the John Hancock Center (1990) and its antennae behind, and another example of late-twentieth-century high building also visible to the left.

29. *Below.* Nineteen Chicago 'literati' sit or stand around an exhausted luncheon table at Schlogl's in 1925.

BRUSSELS

30. *Above*. The Grand' Place: some of it is old, some of it is 'repro', but the blending is well done.

31. *Right*. The European Commission in session in the 1970s.

32. *Above.* The drawing room of 10 rue de Praetère, our temporary residence.

33. *Below.* The art nouveau interior of Comme Chez Soi.

CHICAGO

On my first and 'grand circle' visit to the United States in 1953 I, like Toqueville 122 years before, missed Chicago. He had more excuse than I did, for its population in 1831 was no more than 250, whereas I missed a place of 3½ million inhabitants. But I had a strong and sad family reason for having to go back home for the four days which should have been my Chicago allocation and therefore for interrupting my planned schedule in Detroit and resuming it only in Minneapolis. It was a major gap, for to do a tour of the Mid-West, or indeed of America at all, without Chicago was like visiting Athens and missing the Parthenon.

I did not therefore see Chicago until October 1960, the autumn of the Kennedy/Nixon campaigns. The circumstances were perhaps peculiarly propitious, and I was completely bowled over by it. I have since been back on, I think, another dozen occasions, and have never failed to be enthralled by its unique mixture of vigour and sophistication. They come together in giving it the best modern architecture in the world. Technically the first skyscrapers (about 250 feet high) were in New York in the 1870s. But in the next decade Chicago surged ahead, not only in the number and concentration of high buildings but also in the inventiveness of their design and the technical strength of their construction. Nor was this only a sudden spurt. The highest excitement and refinement in the history of the skyscraper have been achieved in the Chicago of the last quarter of the twentieth century. I remain a considerable New York fan but Chicago is for me simply the greatest non-capital city in the world (New York, in any event, in all but the strictly political sense has most capital-city attributes). America's twin capitals apart, Chicago is a metropolis far superior to any other North American rival. It has a depth and an all-round quality which leave Los Angeles or San Francisco, Philadelphia or Dallas well behind. Indeed if a rival 'provincial' candidate from the North American continent is to be put up, I would choose Toronto, although as 'a qualified candidate willing to lose' in the words of the 'Politics and Poker' song from the old musical. Chicago's only European rival in this category is Barcelona.

Chicago has had a remarkably short history for such a city of world class. It was first touched by Christendom in 1673 when Marquette, a Jesuit priest born in the eastern France town of Laon, and Joliet, a Canadian-born Frenchman, were sent by Tulon, a viceroy of Louis XIV, to head a seven-man canoe exploration with the main object of discovering whether the Mississippi flowed out into the Atlantic in or near Virginia, or west into the 'Californian Sea', or south to the gulf of Mexico.

One hundred and sixty years after that, when Chicago was incorporated as a town in 1833 it had a population of barely 300, and when it graduated to be a city in 1837 (a rapid promotion) it was still only 4,000. Other surrounding places were substantially bigger until the end of the 1840s. This was mainly because the Chicago site although macro-magnificent, a meeting point potentially commanding two-thirds of the North American continent, was micro-squalid. The climate was, as it has not unnaturally remained, inclement. Chicago acquired the sobriquet of 'the windy city' only in 1892, when New York, competing unsuccessfully against it to be the host city of the World's Columbian Exposition, designed to commemorate the 400th anniversary of Christopher Columbus' expedition to the west, was eager to plant some denigratory blows on Chicago. Nearly a generation before, however, Chicago had experienced the most appalling consequences of the wind in the Great Fire of 1871.

The wind was still memorably there on my third visit to Chicago in January 1970, when on an only three- or four-block walk to the Art Institute I experienced its peculiar cutting quality. The temperature was not particularly low for the region and the season, perhaps 5° or 6°F (−16 or −17°C), but on that short walk I nonetheless experienced a sensation that I have never felt before or since. I was more or less adequately covered from the knees up. Nevertheless I had the strong impression that the weave in my trousers was disintegrating, and was surprised but relieved to discover on gaining the shelter of the august Institute that this was entirely false.

Nor was Chicago's winter cold, less than that of Minneapolis or Montreal, its major disadvantage. The wind gave a certain harshness to all seasons, with the result, for example, that the lake, although a fine sheet of water, never has much softness or subtlety about it. Compared with an Italian lake or a Mediterranean seascape, its surface looks metallic. More than the weather, however, there was the disadvantage of the mud which even its moderate rainfall (about thirty-three inches) was sufficient to produce. The old core of the city (there was no penumbra then) was set in a semi-drained marsh, which made early walkers liable to sink to the tops of their boots and early wagons or carriages liable to do so to the tops of their axles. It was not an environment superficially conducive either to commercial development or to the amenities of social intercourse.

The first limited but essential phase of Chicago's transition from mudhole to metropolis was achieved between the early 1830s and 1848. William Butler Ogden had much to do with this surge. Ogden was a New Yorker (State rather than City) born in 1805, who came to Chicago in the mid-1830s and stayed there until his death in 1877, during which forty years he witnessed and substantially contributed to one of the most rapid and dramatic urban transformations in the history of the world. Within a couple of years of arrival he had been elected mayor, and after his term he remained a powerful alderman for many years.

Ogden was a necessary spearhead of New York capital into Chicago. Such an influx was crucial to the city's rapid development. The irony was that Chicago, which within fifty years became the great marketing city of America, had in the 1830s nothing to sell. Imports in 1837 were valued at $370,000 and exports at $11,600. Ships which arrived fully laden went back across the lake in ballast. A high proportion of those who created early Chicago came from rural backgrounds in New England or upper New York State. If one stands in a Vermont hamlet, now of only a few houses and surrounded by rocky, no longer cultivated land, but with a full graveyard, and asks where did all their descendants go, the answer quite frequently is that they went to rescue Chicago from the mud. After 1850 they were joined by a mass influx of immigrants who were born neither in America nor in Britain, who for one if not two generations constituted a mostly docile but occasionally threatening store of proletarian labour. This early link of men and money to and from the East meant that Chicago, although then thought of as very much 'the West', grew up and remains, although with its own special characteristics, essentially an extension of East Coast America rather than a city of the new West which grew up in the late nineteenth and early twentieth centuries.

In 1848 Cyrus H. McCormick arrived in the city from Virginia, where he had developed a mechanical reaper. McCormick was doubly significant. He founded a dynasty which had the interesting characteristics of being Anglo-Saxon, patrician-minded and anti-British, and which has left great physical imprints on the city, from the Tribune Tower (1922) to the McCormick Place convention and exhibition centre (1993–7). And his mid-nineteenth-century McCormick Reaper Works, set up alongside the river, soon employing 120 men and sending harvesters out to the corn-fields, was the first example of Chicago actually making something substantial as opposed to trading in land values and other people's commodities. In spite of these figuratively and literally ground-breaking innovations of 1848, the population of Chicago in 1850 was still only 30,000.

Thereafter it bounded forward. The post-Famine Irish came in great numbers, and were followed by Germans, Poles, Lithuanians and Italians. In one single day in 1857, some 3,400 immigrants arrived by train from New York. In the two decades of the 1850s and 1860s Chicago's population multiplied tenfold to 300,000 and its role as the hub city of the continent was firmly established. Despite its relatively late start as a rail centre it had by the beginning of the Civil War become the pre-eminent meeting point of different lines and different systems. St Louis, an older city, was the rival, but it was soon firmly overtaken. The populations of the two cities in 1870 were approximately equal, but it was an unstable equality, as, to use a simile appropriate to the basis of their rivalry, when two trains momentarily run alongside each other at the same speed before the one with greater power inevitably draws away. So it was with Chicago, which by 1889 reached a population of a million. By 1914 it was at 2½ million. And by 1950 (the maximum) it was over 3½ million. St Louis never rose above 850,000.

The Great Fire of 8–9 October 1871 marked another decisive breakpoint in the short history of Chicago. The Fire was a massive catastrophe, an unprecedented urban disaster, greater even in area destroyed (a corridor approximately four miles long and one mile wide) than that which had struck London in 1666 or that which followed from Napoleon's deliberate setting alight of Moscow in 1812. The catastrophe did not halt the breakneck growth of Chicago. If anything it accelerated the surge, as when a river, checked momentarily, flows faster when it comes out of the constriction. It was often a rough flow. Max Weber wrote of Chicago 'resembling a human being with his skin removed, and in which all the physiological process can be seen going on'. Before that cataract, however, there had been several signs that Chicago was on the way to becoming a metropolis. It was in 1860 that its role as the great centre of national political conventions began. The Republicans met in their specially constructed 'wigwam' and there nominated Abraham Lincoln; so it was no commonplace convention. The Democrats also met there in 1864 and unsuccessfully nominated General George B. McClellan. And in 1868 the Republicans came back to the city but not to the wigwam and nominated General Ulysses S. Grant in Crosby's Opera House. So by the end of the 1860s Chicago was firmly on the political map for presidential conventions.

Contemporary with and perhaps partly because of this rise to political eminence, Chicago had by the 1860s begun to assume some signs of advancing amenity and even of luxury and/or eminence. Extraordinary acts of elevation took place in the late 1850s. To assist the process of pulling the city out of the mud entire blocks and in one case the largest existing hotel were raised by four feet. This was one of the earliest enterprises of George M. Pullman in the city, although it was minor compared with his subsequent equipping of America, and indeed by influence Europe too, with comfortable sleeping, dining and club railroad cars. The hotel which went up by four feet as part of the process of making central Chicago a drier and a healthier place was the Tremont House, then the principal establishment and one with an impressive six-storey façade. But it was soon to be overtaken by the first Palmer House.

Potter Palmer had arrived in Chicago from New York in 1852 and had developed a successful dry-goods store on Lake Street. His ambitions in various directions were however higher. First he did not think that Lake Street, a mixed trading area, was a location which could be made to rival the rue de la Paix, Bond Street or even Fifth Avenue. So he determined to shift the smart retail centre of Chicago about a quarter of a mile to the east on State Street, and almost single-handedly accomplished it. There, having widened and paved the new location, he built a six-storeyed, marbled-faced emporium, popularly called Palmer's Palace, which he leased to a couple of up-and-coming dry-goods merchants named respectively Marshall Field and Levi Z. Leiter. Leiter became the first of two American fathers-in-law of George Nathaniel Curzon, ultimately the first and only Marquess Curzon, although many other things on the way, which showed that Leiter had made a great deal of money out of his dry-goods and associated activities. Marshall Field also made enough to sustain several generations of urbane living. Potter Palmer rose well above even the highest peaks of the dry-goods trade. At first his ascent was merely to become an 'innkeeper', but the inn, the 1870-completed Palmer House, was by far the grandest that Chicago then had, with eight storeys, 225 rooms and a staff of several hundred crisply uniformed blacks, and all in his new boulevard of State Street. He even brought together with shopping the prospect of matrimony. He first met his bride, Bertha Honoré, the daughter of well-established Kentuckians settled in Chicago, when she was shopping (with her mother) in his Lake Street store. They were married in 1870, when he was forty-four and she twenty-one.

Potter Palmer gradually over the next twenty-five years made himself the greatest landlord and wealthiest man in Chicago, and enabled his wife to be the queen of society. The name of Mrs Potter Palmer resounded in New York as well as in Chicago, and even to some extent in London and Paris. Fortunately she was a woman of discrimination and even some approach to liberal views, particularly on women's rights. While he performed an even more extraordinary feat of reorientation with the fashionable living districts of the city than he had done with the fashionable shopping streets, she among other things bought pictures. Before Palmer's real-estate revolution the smartest places to live in Chicago were Prairie Avenue and Michigan Terrace, a nearby stretch of South Michigan Avenue, both in what is now called the South Loop. Pullman, for instance, had a well-designed mansion, almost in the shape of a mini-British Museum, on Prairie Avenue. Palmer in the 1880s simply moved this centre of fashion three miles to the north. He bought an area of dune and marsh, got the city to drain it and make what is now Lake Shore Drive, built a fantastical imitation Rhenish castle there for himself, persuaded some of his friends to cluster around, and thereby created the 'Gold Coast' which from that day to this has remained the home territory of the Chicago *ton*.

Mrs Potter Palmer meanwhile was assembling a prodigious collection of French pictures, some of the safe Barbizon school, but many more of the then far from safe Impressionists. She acquired no fewer than thirty Monets, as well as Renoirs, a Degas and Pissaros and Sisleys. Eventually they came to the Art Institute as an invaluable addition to its collection, but only after her death in 1918. While she was alive she could not bear to part with them. It is a remarkable fact that, twenty years before Roger Fry's exhibition of Impressionists and Post-Impressionists was laughed at in London, some of their best works were being knowledgeably bought in Glasgow and Chicago. But, thanks largely to Mrs Potter Palmer, Chicago got more of them.

The Potter Palmers spanned the Great Fire. Most of the other tycoons belonged essentially to one side of it or the other. Even Pullman, although he had his first car ready for Abraham Lincoln's funeral, was essentially a post-Fire phenomenon. It was not until the 1880s that he built his company town, bearing his own name and situated on the Calumet River about thirteen miles south of the Loop. It was a harsher version, both architecturally and in company-imposed discipline, of Cadbury's Bournville in Birmingham. And it was 1894 before his model town was stained by the killing of thirty-four people in the notorious Pullman strike which was one of the two most reverberating examples of labour unrest in late-nineteenth-century Chicago – or indeed in America as a whole. (The other was the Haymarket 'insurrection' of 1886.) Between them they provided the somewhat slender justification for Chicago earning a line to itself in the little-known second verse of the Red Flag, the socialist hymn set to the tune of Maryland:

> Look round the Frenchman loves its blaze;
> The sturdy German chants its praise;
> In Moscow's vaults its hymns are sung;
> Chicago swells the surging throng.

There is a neat but false theory that the 1871 Fire had the direct and happy result of turning Chicago from a shanty town into an architect's paradise and one of the two sky-scraper capitals of the world. The first fallacy here is that there were a lot of pre-1871 buildings which were far from shanties: the Chamber of Commerce building, Crosby's Opera House, Marshall Field's first State Street store, the Courthouse, the New Tremont Hotel and the first Palmer House, to name only a few examples. Second, the 1870s rebuilding was not at all architecturally exciting. It was done in too much of a rush and in a way reminiscent of British 1950s city-centre rebuilding after bomb damage – the Bristol and Plymouth shopping areas and much of Coventry (apart from the cathedral) are examples – to have much style or quality. When Chicago did become architecturally innovative and interesting was in the 1880s, and often involved, in a typical Chicago way, the pulling down of much of what had been put up a decade earlier.

When so-called 'skyscrapers' began in New York in the 1870s they were a very modest affair. Ten storeys was enough to qualify for the somewhat hyperbolic label. This meant that they came little nearer to scraping the sky than did the highest of the Edinburgh seventeenth-century tenements, or the sombre smoke-blackened fourteen-storey form of Queen Anne's Mansions which was created on the south side of St James's Park in London between 1873 and 1889 (and was pulled down in the early 1970s to make way for the new Home Office building on the same site), and quite considerably less so than did the thirteenth-century towers of San Gimignano in Tuscany. An essential difference however between London on the one hand and both New York and Chicago on the other was that, following the over-the-top Queen Anne's Mansions, the London County Council in 1890 imposed an eighty-feet (roughly eight-storey) limit which persisted until the beginning of the 1960s, when the presumptuous Hilton Hotel at the lower end of Park Lane sprang to thirty storeys.

An important difference was that the American cities, with their 'can do' and 'money talks' ethos, avoided, except for one short period in Chicago, such public authority restriction as was acceptable in London and still more in Paris. But more than that was needed to create vertical metropolises. There had to be conducive or at least containable physical conditions. In this respect it was surprising that New York and Chicago should have been the twin pioneers, for their physical circumstances were sharply contrasting. New York, or more precisely Manhattan, the relevant borough, suffered as a narrow and not very long island from the most obvious constriction of land space balanced by its geology providing the hardest of surface rock and therefore the most secure foundations.

Chicago was a spread-out city on a flat plain with no natural restrictions to its growth to the west, but with foundation problems 'probably not equalled for perverseness anywhere in the world', as an architectural journal article noted in 1888. Solid bedrock was about a hundred feet below the surface but the water level was only fifteen feet down, an unfortunate combination. The Loop, a term which curiously became synonymous with Chicago's downtown area about fifteen years before the completion of the elevated railway system from which its name is derived, imposed a certain voluntary constriction, and that a very tight one, for the looped enclave is only half a mile square, in other words only a quarter of the historic size of the City of London. The total Chicago city area, on the other hand, was by the beginning of the twentieth century half as big again as that of the 1880–1963 twenty-eight-borough London County Council, and in the days before Los Angeles showed that suburban sprawl can encompass even a peak significantly higher than Ben Nevis, was exceeded as a metropolitan area by Berlin with its lakes and woods, and by little else in the world.

Independently of these considerations of topography, the age of the skyscraper also required three technical advances.

First it was wholly dependent on the development of the hydraulic elevator. No one was going to regard it as a privilege to walk up ten or twenty or thirty floors, later eighty or a hundred. The 'cliff-dwellers' had to be propelled there fast, and this was crucially facilitated by elevator patents taken out in Chicago in 1878. Second the technical problems of making tall buildings stand securely had to be overcome. Only too many four- or five-storey edifices had tumbled down of their own volition in Chicago before the Fire. No one in that highly commercially minded city – and the skyscraper fashion was very much commerce-driven – was going to provide the money for ten- to twenty-floor buildings, which might easily contain two or three thousand daytime clerkly inhabitants, if the whole structure was liable to crumble. To avoid this required both secure foundations – easy in New York, difficult in Chicago – and an above-ground structure which could be depended upon not to collapse. The first problem was solved mainly by an architectural partnership of David Burnham and John Root which developed in the late 1870s and early 1880s the idea of a floating foundation, a concrete and steel raft which spread the load over a large area of subsoil. Then, fifteen years or so afterwards, caisson-created foundations reaching right down to the far-submerged hard rock were developed.

These successive solutions corrected for Chicago's handicap *vis-à-vis* New York. The above-ground revolution of technique, on the other hand, put the Mid-Western city ahead in this respect of its larger rival on the Eastern seaboard. To this Burnham and Root also contributed, although it was the somewhat older architect bearing the impressive designation of Major William Le Baron Jenney who had the decisive idea. Jenney, after Civil War service close to both Grant and Sherman, went for a Paris sojourn where he was much influenced by his friend and fellow countryman James McNeill Whistler and by Viollet-le-Duc, the restorer of gothic cathedrals. These, together with the two American generals, were a remarkable quartet of 'god-fathers', although Jenney's most innovatory idea is said to have come from more homespun sources. He saw his wife place a heavy book on top of a delicately wire-framed bird-cage. Might not a cage of steel therefore serve as a frame for even the most massive of buildings?

As the idea more or less coincided with Chicago (including its environs stretching down across the state line into Gary, Indiana) becoming the second (after Pittsburgh) most important steel centre in the United States, it could be regarded as one whose time and place had come. It led on directly to the development of the 'Chicago style' which was essentially based on a light, strong steel frame, leaving the outer walls as decorative curtains with no structural functions. The key attributions of the style were said to be 'simplicity, stability, breadth, dignity'. This plain functionalism paved the way to the Bauhaus style in Germany in the first quarter of the twentieth century, and was very different from the derivative and ornamental tops to many of New York's tall buildings. Frank Lloyd Wright, who as a young man came in 1887 to work in the office of another famous Chicago architectural partnership, that of Dankmar Adler and Louis Sullivan, and who ended up a more renowned although more horizontal architect than any of those thus far mentioned, wrote many years later of the modernist movement that 'it all started in the long grass of the Prairies'.

The fourth problem which had to be solved before the Chicago skyscraper boom could take off was that of fire-proofing. Chicago's experience, an extreme form of that of nineteenth-century America as a whole, made it inevitable that developers would not put money into vast buildings which the insurance companies would not underwrite so long as they thought that there was a real risk that the buildings might incinerate themselves and their two or three thousand inhabitants. A combination of steel frames and terracotta insulation went a long way towards achieving this. By the mid-1880s the Loop was claiming to be more secure against the spread of fire than any other business district in the world. Chicago was a great place for all-embracing terrestrial boasts, and it might have been expected that, as with the *Titanic*'s claims to unsinkability, this was inviting the retaliation of fate. Fate, however, was for once unvengeful, and there has for a hundred and more years been no major Chicago high-rise fire disaster, although a ground-level theatre blaze in 1903 killed about 600 people.

The four problems solved, Chicago had a tremendous architectural decade. The buildings were not in fact very high. The Montauk Block (Burnham and Root, 1881–2) with which the wave began was only ten storeys, and the Masonic Temple (the same architects, 1891) only twenty-two, although it was then the tallest in the world. But they were clean-cut, massive, indigenous and self-confident. Between them, both in height and in time, was the laterally vast Auditorium Building (Sullivan and Adler, 1887–9), which combined an hotel and a theatre with 4,000 seats, nearly half as many again (a carefully noted point) as the New York Metropolitan Opera House. Its opening in 1889 (three years before the Art Institute, a gallery which soon became and remains more distinguished for its contents than for its architecture) was said to mark Chicago's cultural coming of age. Any moderation in the height of these achievements was balanced by the hyperbole of the comparisons which they aroused in the minds of contemporary Chicagoans and even more in some others later. Professor Donald L. Miller's brilliantly informative 1996 *City of the Century*, a socio-topographical history of pre-1900 Chicago, cites several of them and adds a few of his own. 'What Chartres was to the Gothic cathedral,' Thomas E. Talmadge wrote in the 1930s, 'the Montauk Block was to the high commercial building.' Miller himself preferred to compare it with quattrocento Florence and sustains this with some well-directed arguments. 'John Root's Chicago, like Brunelleschi's Florence,' he writes, 'was built in an age of élan by merchants and visionaries fired by the resolve to make their city the marvel of its age.' And again: 'we need to remember what fifteenth-century Florence was realy like. A great art capital, it was also a lusty, aggressive city, hated and feared by urban rivals it put down in its furious drive for commercial supremacy in Tuscany. Its economic might, like Chicago's, came through its near total domination of its *contado*, or hinterland.' And then, in a nice touch, 'St Louis was Chicago's Siena.'

Another breakpoint came in 1893. This should have been a year not only of triumph with the successful opening of the World Columbian Exposition, but also the beginning of a second lap of architectural innovation. In fact, however, for a variety of reasons, it marked a loss of building momentum. This was partly because a financial panic of that year meant that money was less freely available. This check was acute but short term. The other factors, while not permanent, were longer lasting. The buildings for the World's Fair, mainly by Burnham, were in their temporary exhibition-style way a splendid success. But, as was appropriate for the occasion, they belonged very much to the derivative-pastiche style. They were mostly white, not a natural Chicago colour, and embraced many domes, minarets and Venetian-like bridges and waterways. They turned the city's back on the austere but original 'form following function' Chicago style which had made the city's reputation in the 1880s. This did not mean that no innovative buildings were created in the remainder of the nineteeth century. Louis Sullivan's Carson,

Pirie, Scott department store of 1899 was perhaps the best of all his buildings. It still exists, is not particularly high, but has an original decorative quality, which, so far from being derivative, could be regarded as the forerunner to the early-twentieth-century creations of Gaudí, Domènech and Puig in Barcelona.

The third factor was that, in 1893 and in a very un-Chicago-like way, the City Council put a 130-feet limit on the height of buildings. This ordinance had a few loopholes but it was sufficiently strictly observed that the Masonic Temple remained Chicago's highest building for over two decades. The windy city offered no immediate competition to New York's sixty-storey Woolworth Tower of 1913. It was only in the boom years of the 1920s that the middle wave of Chicago skyscrapers restored the city to the world tall-building league.

There were however plenty of other ways in which Chicago could assert itself. Two years before the 1893 Exposition the University of Chicago had been refounded, and lavishly endowed on a greenfield site eight miles south of the Loop and adjacent to the Exposition buildings. Its sponsors were the quartet of Marshall Field, who gave the land; John D. Rockefeller, who paid for the buildings and went on doing so until the vast chapel which bears his name was completed in 1927; the central funds of the Baptist Church; and Martin A. Ryerson, a patrician Chicago aesthete, who, having shown his paces in both the building and the contents of the Art Institute, was a good catalyst for the raising of local funds to complement Rockefeller's Eastern dollars. Together they provided a powerful quadrilateral of support. The University of Chicago's record over more than a hundred years has been one of uncompromising success. Within ten years it had become a major research university. It has since been (at least the temporary) home to sixty-five Nobel prizewinners, a greater number than has been achieved by any other American university.

The University began with a liberal ethos, admitting women and members of ethnic minorities long before the best-known Eastern universities did so. In spite or perhaps because of these credentials, it has been determined to eschew modern forms of political correctness. This showed itself in several ways when I participated in the centennial celebrations in October 1991. They had several memorable aspects. There was the eve-of-ceremony dinner in a great tent on the edge of the campus, when the rain beat down with a ferocity (and a noise) reminiscent of the weather and the resultant mud which Joliet and Marquette had experienced 300 years before. A counter-bombardment was however achieved by at least one of the fraternally visiting academic speakers. Professor Jaroslav Pelikan of Yale riveted my attention by proclaiming the axion that 'the reason academic disputes are so bitter is that the stakes are so small'. (I subsequently learned that the epigram was not as original as I thought it at the time; but of which really good joke is this not true?)

The following morning, under a washed-out sky and a few temporarily exhausted clouds, we assembled for an academic procession to the core commemoration ceremony in the Rockefeller Chapel. The University of Chicago in its broad wisdom had decided that the greetings of older-sister institutions should be conveyed by the envoys of Harvard and Oxford. President Bok (who had in fact just stepped down from the presidency of that famous seat of richly endowed learning on the Charles River) and I (in my capacity as Chancellor of Oxford) subsequently addressed the assembled 3,000 guests in what I trust were suitably but not excessively sonorous tones. We then marched out side by side, and as we reached the end of that impressive nave I turned to Derek

Bok and asked him whether he had not been struck, as I was, by one feature which was curious in modern American academia. In all the large congregation there were barely ten black faces. 'It would surely have been quite different at Harvard or Yale,' I ventured, to which he assented. It was not the University of Chicago being racist, which it certainly is not, but just its calm refusal to illustrate unnecessary denial in its exhibition case. There was nonetheless a certain piquancy in its insouciance, situated as it is on the southern edge of perhaps the largest black ghetto in the whole of the United States.

The large luncheon following the ceremony was addressed by the Provost (the second-in-command in the hierarchy of an American university). This one, Gerhard Casper, departed soon afterwards to become president of Stanford, a typical move in a highly administratively successful academic career. I wondered what on earth new he could find to say after the welter of commemorative oratory to which we had in some cases contributed and in all to have listened. In fact he held us once again riveted by giving a 'full and frank' account of Chicago's history and rationale for limiting honorary degrees to genuine *academic* excellence. He was at once frivolous and fascinating. The centre of interest for me in view particularly of Oxford's trauma with Margaret Thatcher's non-degree in 1985 (before my time as Chancellor, fortunately) was his uncovering of Queen Elizabeth II's similar but better-hidden experience at Chicago prior to her 1959 visit.

The conferment upon her of such an honour had been proposed by an anglophile professor of law and carried through the nominating body, as with Lady Thatcher at Oxford, but had then, again analogously, been rejected by the wider body whose endorsement was required. But at Chicago the rejection had been much more subtly done.

It had been made a matter not of politics but of academic qualification. When the proposition had been put, an elderly but respected professor with a quavering voice had risen and announced that, before he could agree, he must be informed of the publications of the proposed honorand. Her jurisprudential sponsor tried to bluster his way through. In the case of a sovereign, he replied, he or she could be regarded as communicating through the accumulated writings and pronouncements of her judges and other constitutional advisers. Everything from Blackstone or Dicey to the judgments of Hewart or Goddard could be seen as in a sense hers. It did not work. She was turned down.

I do not suppose the Queen ever knew this, or would have felt unduly deprived had she done so. But Chicago's austere academic standards had been upheld, and a recondite semi-precedent to the Lady Thatcher contretemps been provided. Altogether I felt that my twenty-four-hour visit to the University of Chicago had provided almost as unforgettable a window on to an aspect of American life as in an utterly different direction had my attendance at the funeral of Martin Luther King in Atlanta twenty-three years earlier.

The 1893 Columbian Exposition, or the World's Fair as it was more commonly known, was in itself a great success. During its six-month season it was reported to have attracted 27 million visitors. But the two following decades were in some ways a period of slack water for Chicago. There were no particularly exciting architectural developments. The old generation of creative if tyrannical tycoons died off. The first McCormick had gone well before. Pullman followed in 1897. Potter Palmer in 1902, the two great meat-packers Armour and Swift in 1901 and 1903, and Marshall Field in 1906. They were not adequately succeeded. On the other hand, the foundation of Hull House by Jane Addams in 1912 was a symbol of early social concern in Chicago. And it was not only a symbol. Hull House was an early training ground for two of Franklin Roosevelt's most progressive Cabinet officers – Frances Perkins and Harold Ickes – just as Toynbee Hall in the East End of London was for Clement Attlee.

Nevertheless the turn of the nineteenth century was a period when Chicago consolidated its position as a metropolis of *circa* 2 million people, the second largest American city. It managed at the same time to stand high among world conurbations for the size of its German, Polish, Italian, Greek and Scandinavian populations, which exceeded those of all but the largest home cities. The Germans, a fairly steady quarter of Chicago's population throughout the great expansion from 1840 to 1910, were the most concentrated minority (although the Irish were ahead of them in grip on local political power), living a life of geographical and linguistic separateness until the effect of the two world wars undermined their ethnicity. On the other hand there were relatively few blacks – only 15,000 in the 1890s – until two wars (and particularly the second) sucked many more of them up what had been the old 'underground' for escaping slaves in the 1850s and the great South Side ghetto was created.

A thicker layer of indigenous culture was also built up. Even before the Fire some of the great singing and acting stars, such as Adelina Patti and Edmund Kean, had been lured by a mixture of fees and curiosity to give Chicago performances. But they did so rather in the way that, a generation later, their successors went to the temporary glory of the opera house at Manáus, which briefly flourished in the Amazonian jungle on the rubber boom. By the end of the century, however, Chicago had something much more solid. The Symphony Orchestra, first under Theodore Thomas and then under Frederick Stock, was founded in 1890 and got its own Michigan Avenue auditorium a few years later. It did not play much American let alone Illinois music, and indeed there was little to play until the 'Chicago beat' (not played by the Symphony Orchestra) grew out of New Orleans jazz thirty years later. But Thomas and Stock were the beginning of a strong orchestral tradition which has run through to Solti and Barenboim.

A strong writing fraternity on the borders of literature and journalism also grew up. Theodore Dreiser, Jack London and Upton Sinclair were Chicago novelists at the start of a line which has led to Saul Bellow. Harriet Monroe was the centre of a group of poets in which category Carl Sandburg was still more eminent. These were all at least secondarily engaged in journalism, and there were others who, equally famously at the time, stuck rigidly to that more ephemeral side of the writing trade. Ray Stannard Baker, George Ade and Finley Peter Dunne, the last creating his famous Chicago/Irish homespun street philosopher Mr Dooley, were well-known reporter/columnists, although more in the subsequent style of Art Buchwald than of Walter Lippmann or Joseph Alsop. Apart from Ade they seemed to think that a three-barrel name gave them additional impact, and their local fame was such as to justify this. Ade with his bye-line 'Stories of the Streets and of the Town' epitomized a new demotic approach which revolutionized journalism at least as much as did Harmsworth's *Daily Mail* in London. Three-quarters of a century later they inspired nostalgic Chicago films like *Front Page* and *The Sting*, for which Scott Joplin's syncopated ragtime music, developed about 1900, provided an entirely appropriate background. Two pictures well capture the spirit of their milieu and time: the first is of a yuppy of his day sitting on a bar stool in a by no means squalid horseshoe-buffet with a grey derby perched on the back of his jaunty head and chatting up a comely but respectable-looking barmaid; and the second (from a little later) is of twenty or so literati sitting or standing around an exhausted

luncheon table, all of them quite glossy but perhaps a little
more naively eager than would have been their equivalents at
the Algonquin in New York or around the *Punch* table in
London.

Chicago's world-famous gangsterdom of the 1920s is
frequently attributed to the eighteenth amendment to the
American constitution which imposed alcoholic prohibition
from 1919 until repealed at the beginning of the Roosevelt
administration in 1933. However there was quite a lot of
organized crime well before that act of intolerant and misplaced 'do-goodism'. 'Big Jim' Colosimo (anyone over six feet
was liable to attract the accolade of 'big', which in his case
matched well with his surname) was sufficiently established
that in 1910 he imported one John Torrio from New York
as his personal protection officer and hitman. Colosimo was
in some ways a man of discrimination. He ran a restaurant
on Wabash Avenue which produced some of the best food in
Chicago and became the equivalent of London's Ivy (less
noisy maybe, except for an occasional burst of gunfire) with a
high-grade theatrical and operatic clientele. But he did not
exercise discrimination in his choice of a bodyguard. A few
years later Torrio had Colosimo shot dead, or 'rubbed out',
in the expressive phrase of the period, in his own gourmet
restaurant, while he was supervising the delivery of two
truckloads of bootleg whisky (Colosimo did not do things by
halves).

Torrio did not fire the shot himself. No self-respecting
gang leader, or one aspiring to leadership, ever pulled his
own trigger. He hired or terrorized someone else to do it for
him. But Torrio was the direct beneficiary. He succeeded to
Colosimo's command, and in turn imported a young New
York gangster called Al Capone as his adjutant. Thereafter
the action assumed something of the well-rehearsed formality
of a crazy ballet, all played out on a stage covered with great

banks of expensive flowers. One rival of Torrio's kept a flower shop and did very well out of orders of vastly expensive wreaths for the funerals of his fellow gangsters. He himself was finally gunned down – in 1924 and in his own floral parlour.

The biggest single bloodbath was the so-called St Valentine's Day massacre of 1929. Four Capone men, giving a comic twist to the ballet by being disguised as policemen, slaughtered with machine guns seven members of a rival gang. But although this was the peak of the killings it was also the beginning of the move to a quieter period. The massacre was the effective end of any challenge to Capone's suzerainty of the Chicago underworld. And then, in 1931, he was at last arrested, needless to say not in Chicago, but in Philadelphia where a combination of the spirit of William Penn and of the 'signers' (of the Declaration of Independence) seemed to give a greater courage to law enforcers, and was there indicted, convicted, and imprisoned for ten years on a federal charge of income tax evasion – a final irony.

Chicago has recently shed its crime-ridden aspect. It nonetheless retained for some decades at least the shadow of its 1920s reputation as the criminal capital of the world. In the autumn of 1966, early in my first period as Home Secretary, I paid a visit to the Chicago police. This was occasioned not by their indifferent record of the 1920s when they treated discretion as the better part of valour and left the gangs to shoot it out among themselves, but by the fact that their chief of police, Professor Orlando Wilson, a fairly new import from the University of California at Berkeley Department of Criminology, was thought to have made the Chicago police uniquely well equipped with advanced technology. This view proved well founded, and the permanent under-secretary of the Home Office and I learned a good deal on the visit. From it there flowed several important equipment advances for the British police. Nevertheless some images from the old reputation remained in my mind, and when the professor said that he would take us out on a night expedition to see his force in operation in the most difficult part of the city, I accepted with alacrity but not entirely without apprehension. As we ate an early dinner I felt more tension than had we been preparing for a similar expedition in, say, Bath or Bournemouth. The apprehension was entirely misplaced. So far from our being regaled with hails of bullets and screaming tyres, nothing happened at all. Not even the most minor criminal incident could be uncovered. After a couple of hours two police cars ran into each other at a crossroads. It was reminiscent of a scene from that old Alec Guinness film *The Lavender Hill Mob*. Perhaps the Chicago police thought it was the least they could do for us.

On that visit I also had an encounter with Mayor Richard J. Daley – he has since been succeeded by his son, another Richard Daley. Daley was then at the height of his power. Orlando Wilson took the view that we ought to call upon Daley in the City Hall. The mayor however seemed preoccupied during the meeting and distinctly vague about the role of a British Home Secretary. We then half enjoyed hearing him say on television that evening, 'as I told that London police official who called on me this morning . . .' I, rather proud of having been recently promoted to the office of Peel and Palmerston, Asquith and Churchill, was not too pleased to be regarded as a sort of precinct captain.

Daley had first been elected in 1955 and was in his sixth four-year term when he died suddenly in 1976. Ed Kelly had previously enjoyed an almost equally long mayoralty, and during these two periods of office (with a short interregnum) Chicago gradually become one of the safer cities in the United States. 'The City that Works,' which was Daley's slogan, had enough truth in it not to be a bad joke. It sustained the 1960s and 1970s inner-city decay and the flight to the suburbs better than did nearly every other American conurbation of the North and the East. In contrast with Detroit, Cleveland, Pittsburgh, Buffalo, St Louis, Kansas City, it retained a large prosperous, middle-class element living close to the city centre. Population passed its peak (of 3,620,962) in 1950 and is now nearly a million less than that figure within the city limits. The Stock Yards, vast slaughter-houses created to meet the voracious needs of Armour and Swift, after a period of decline finally closed in 1971, as symbolic a blow to Chicago's traditional role as it is possible to imagine. But, equally symbolically for Chicago's position as the crossroads and merchandising mart of the nation, the McCormick Place convention centre, the largest in the world, was opened on the lake front in the same year.

The decline of American railroads also meant that Union Station, almost as much the epitome of Chicago's late-nineteenth- and early-twentieth-century nodal vitality as the Stock Yards, is no longer a background to the romance of the arrival and departure of great long-distance trains like the Twentieth Century Limited to New York. It remains a hub of suburban traffic, but there is not much romance in commuting. This loss has however been fully replaced in economic and statistical terms, if not wholly in terms of literary evocativeness, by the growth of O'Hare Airport into the busiest in the world. (I doubt if a new Scott Fitzgerald, writing three-quarters of a century on, would make some of the most vivid memories of Dick Diver's youth his return from school in the East for the Christmas holidays in Minnesota through, not the smoke and the frost of changing trains at Union Station, but the bustle and foetid air of transferring from the United to the North-Western desks at O'Hare.) About the dominance and busyness of O'Hare – what a memorial for a fairly obscure alderman, comparable, *mutatis* a good deal *mutandis*, with the immortality achieved by John Harvard and Elihu Yale – there can be no doubt. In my own experience it is the only airport in the world in which I have ever sat for three hours in a plane on the ground waiting for take-off. And equally, it is the only one above which, while circling to land in intermittent cloud, I noticed that there were at least another dozen planes in the close-packed pattern, and hoped that the Chicago air traffic controllers were as good as, on the record, they appear to be. Both these experiences were in the 1970s. More recently I have found O'Hare, massively impersonal although it may be, smoothly efficient.

Chicago in the Second World War, in sharp contrast with its disengaged attitude in the First War, was wholly committed once the Japanese had struck, and was famous for the warmth of welcome (almost everything free) which it gave to US servicemen. More decisive, if less popularly heart-warming, was the work which Enrico Ferni and a team of scientists did in the University of Chicago leading up in 1942 to the biggest nuclear breakthrough since that achieved at Cambridge (England) by Rutherford nearly a decade earlier. It was a crucial step towards the successful explosions at Alamogordo three years later.

The biggest impact of the Second World War upon Chicago was a vast increase in the black population. The 15,000 of the 1890s had become just over 100,000 by 1920. By the end of the Second World War it was 800,000 and subsequently went to over a million which, accompanied by a somewhat falling overall population, makes Chicago today an almost 40 per cent black city. On the whole it has accepted this infusion and integrated well. Nineteen-sixty-eight was the difficult year. Following the assassination of Martin Luther King in April there was widespread rioting in the ghetto areas of the South and West Sides. But it was no worse than in many American cities and much less bad than in the poor areas of Washington east of the Capitol. Then, in August, at the height of the Vietnam War and following the June assassination of Robert Kennedy, there was very rough police handling of demonstrations provoked by the Democratic Convention which nominated the (reluctantly) pro-war Hubert Humphrey. It made a bad enough television image to keep the Democrats away from another Chicago convention until 1996. However, the batons of Mayor Daley's police were exercised just as much against affluent white liberals, with even the towering form of Professor John Kenneth Galbraith narrowly escaping, as against deprived minorities, and it could at least be said that, contrary to the full-blooded Chicago tradition, there were no fatalities.

To set against this blot, Daley's twenty-one-year reign saw the revival of innovative architecture in Chicago. There had not been much building excitement in the first half of the twentieth century, nothing comparable with the last quarter of the nineteenth. The exception was a short 1920s burst. The Drake Hotel dated from 1920, but it was of more significance for the solid authority of affluent comfort with which it looked out over Lincoln Park and the Oak Street Beach than for any novelty of design. It was reminiscent of one of the major Swiss hotels of the period. A little later the Tribune Tower and the Wrigley Building (topped by its copy of Seville Cathedral's Giralda tower) arose as twin sentinels at the Chicago River end of the Magnificent Mile, a sobriquet which came to be applied to North Michigan Avenue in 1947. But that was about it.

Then in 1949 Mies van der Rohe, who (as a refugee from Germany) had been for a few years teaching architecture at the Illinois Insitute of Technology, designed a building with the modest description of 860–880 North Lake Shore Drive, but which, when it was completed two years later, exhibited a new stripped-down steel-and-glass style depending on a precise calculation of proportion, which was the first swallow of the summer of what became known as the Second Chicago School. Other notable buildings followed in the 1950s and 1960s, some by van der Rohe (notably his two-years-posthumous IBM Building of 1971) and some by those who followed in his slipstream. One was the Inland Steel Building of 1959. Another was appropriately called the Richard J. Daley Center and dated from 1965. The culmination of this phase was the 1969 John Hancock Center, which arose like an icy pinnacle of tinted glass and aluminium pointing to the sky. Its hundred storeys and 1,100 feet of height dominates the Gold Coast end of North Michigan Avenue and looks down on the Drake Hotel in front and the two surviving pre-Fire monuments of the Water Tower and the Pumping Station behind. It is now only the third tallest building in Chicago (and until recently the sixth in America), having been superseded by the 1973 Amoco Building (not a success) and the Sears Tower, completed in 1974, which at 1,454 feet, or 1,707 if its antenna be included, was the tallest building in the world for twenty years, and has remained unsurpassed in America, although overtaken by a Kuala Lumpur 'tiger economy' exuberance in 1996. The Sears Tower (in the Loop), like the Hancock Center, is in black aluminium and dark-tinted glass, although it is distinguished from it by important differences of construction.

Towards the end of the 1970s post-modernism began to take over from the so-called international style which had dominated in Chicago from the first days of van der Rohe. Once again it was a German-born architect, Helmut Jahn, who was the leader of the school. His first Chicago building was the 1980 Xerox Center, now redesignated as 55 West Monroe Street, but his 1985 curved James R. Thompson Center, housing mostly State of Illinois public offices and named after the Governor of the time, is more successful. Height for height's sake, except for that of the atrium, which rises to the full seventeen storeys of the building, is eschewed. Some of Jahn's followers went back to a more upright shape with art-deco influences, as with Adrian Smith's NBC Tower of 1990; and there were even plans for Cesar Pelli, the architect of the Malaysian building which out-topped the Sears Tower, to re-out-top himself with a 125-storey building in the Loop. Perhaps fortunately these plans were overtaken by the property recession of 1990 and have not since been revived.

Meanwhile the regime at City Hall, a modestly dowdy building around which many of these glittering architectural exhibits arose, went through a series of metamorphoses, although with the mayoralty, whether in strong or relatively weak hands, continuing to be a major factor in the life of the city. Sometimes the power in federal politics of Chicago's chief citizen may be exaggerated. Whatever Mayor Daley did or did not do to the Cook County ballots in the 1960 presidential election was not crucial to John F. Kennedy's victory, contrary to popular legend. Kennedy would have won even without his narrow carrying of Illinois. But the significance of Chicago mayors in the life of their own city is indisputable, and they have frequently measured up to the city's unique combination of brashness and sophistication, with the sophistication fairly steadily gaining ground. Even more strongly than through its mayors, however, it is through its buildings that Chicago has spoken to the world. They provide a unique pageant of American architecture of the past 130 years (Boston and Philadelphia are obviously better on earlier periods), and do so in an idiom more international than parochial.

A final brief visit to Chicago (final in the context of this book at any rate) in March 2002 confirmed rather than

contradicted nearly all the impressions and (often presumptuous) opinions with which this essay is littered. The climate
is still unenticing, with a remarkable capacity for the temperature, particularly in the spring, to leap up and down from day
to day. The Drake Hotel is still a fortress of solid comfort.
The skyscape is still magnificent, although I did not find that
much of outstanding interest had been very recently added.
The emphasis has rather shifted from innovation to conser-
vation, some of it concentrated on the previously decayed
'robber baron' mansions in the South Loop. The metropolitan glitter is still gleaming, although spatially narrow. Only
a few hundred yards from the Magnificent Mile one can be
in streets of vacant lots and nondescript two-storey houses
which could belong to any medium-sized town. Provincialism
rather than poverty laps up against the metropolitan splendour in a way that could not be found in New York, Paris, or
even Barcelona or Naples.

The last visit however confirmed one of my more recently
acquired views of Chicago. It is one of the best cities in the
world in which to give a literary talk. I have done three such
occasions there: a dinner organized by the Council of Foreign
Relations for my autobiography in 1993; a morning lecture
during the annual November Humanities Festival for *Gladstone* in 1997; and a 2002 luncheon for *Churchill*. All these
occasions provided audiences of peculiar perception, thereby
offering a striking example of the victory in Chicago of the
aforesaid sophistication over brashness. And if you are lucky
enough, as I was on the two latter occasions, to be under the
aegis of the Chicago Humanities Council, a cultural organization of exceptional quality, not only an appreciative audience
but also painless arrivals and departures are almost guaran-
teed. This more than makes up for the fact that Chicago
seems to me for the moment to be sensibly going through a
period of consolidation rather than of marauding advance.

BRUSSELS

BRUSSELS IS THE foreign city in which I have spent much the most time. I lived there, although with a lot of excursions away, for the four years from 1977 to 1981 when I was president of the European Commission. Also, by an odd coincidence, it was the first non-British city which I ever saw. Aged eight, I was taken there by my parents for three days in 1929. The recollection that visit now arouses makes the Brussels of the late 1920s much more like the sombre, flesh-potted but slightly sinister provincial capital of Charlotte Brontë's *Villette* or Thackeray's *Vanity Fair* than the plate-glass international centre of today, or even of twenty-five years ago.

Yet, in spite of this more than seventy-year-old early memory, which should be so productive of roseate nostalgia, particularly as it is fortified by the much more recent imprint of what I regard as on balance a well worthwhile segment of my life, which is itself now far enough away to gain a little rose-hue of its own, Brussels does not clutch at my heart strings. Perhaps, like Birmingham, that is not in its nature. It is comfortable rather than romantic. It has been described as the last *vraie ville bourgeoise* of Europe, and if by that is meant that the plumber comes quickly, that the restaurants are outstanding for food, wine and napery, and that the traffic jams have been made minimal by ruthless architectural destruction, the label is wholly justified.

Historically Brussels has been more of a grandstand than an arena. With the exception of a nasty outburst of street fighting in August 1831, it has left revolutions to Paris, and from the émigrés of 1791 to Victor Hugo it provided a safe viewing ground. At least partly for this reason the city and its inhabitants have long been patronized by the French, even though Brabant and Wallonie are instinctive auxiliaries of France. Thackeray was quite right in portraying the Brussels servants to the British officers and camp followers of 1815 as both believing in and hoping for a Bonaparte victory, and the souvenir sellers of Waterloo persist in behaving to this day as though that victory had taken place. Further, somewhat as many of the grand English at the end of the nineteenth century and beyond made a habit of marrying American wives in order to replenish their fortunes, so many rich – and sometimes grand – Belgians for a time made a habit of marrying French wives, but maybe more for social cachet than for wealth, where they could more than stand on their own feet; and the habit seems in any event mostly to have died out.

In all these circumstances it is a little hard that the French should be so resolutely superior. 'Les braves Belges' and 'nos amis Belges' are equally downgrading, as is the widely known even if perhaps apocryphal reaction of a Quai d'Orsay diplomat to a Brussels posting: 'En fin de compte, ce n'est qu'à deux heures et demie de Paris par le train.' An added complication for the francophone Belgians is that in addition to being patronized by the French they have recently found their economic and social superiority within their own country seriously undermined. From the early years of the 1830-created Belgian kingdom it was the coal, iron and steel and associated metal-working industries concentrated along the swathe from Liège through Namur to Charleroi and Mons which provided the bulk of the prosperity of the country. The flax and linen trades of Flanders, although they had provided some fine late-medieval Cloth Halls and Stadhuisen, could not hold a candle to the late-nineteenth- and early-twentieth-century Walloon wealth.

This, coupled to Brussels, with its capital-city prestige, although originally a Flemish town and still surrounded on all sides by Dutch-speaking communes, having become over-whelmingly in the eighteenth and nineteenth centuries a francophone city, meant that French was not only the language of the areas from where the wealth flowed, but also the superior-class language throughout the country. Flemish, or Dutch as its speakers have increasingly come to prefer to call it, was left to be a language only of those in subordinate positions. I came across a remarkable and paradoxical example of this early in my European Commission presidency. In October 1977 Queen Juliana of the Netherlands came to pay an official visit to the Commission. With good international manners and with the linguistic fluency which is one of the most reliable aspects of royalty, she spoke not a word of Dutch throughout the day, sometimes English, sometimes French, except when she suddenly turned to my *huissier* with some simple request. 'Warm water astublieft', I think she said. He looked bewildered, for he was an anglophone Italian. But what was interesting was the instinctive assumption of her generation that the language of the nation of which she was sovereign was, in Belgium, a tongue in which one spoke only to attendants.

In the third quarter of the twentieth century however this hierarchy was upset by the decline of the old industries of Wallonie and balanced by the northern, coastal and Flemish half of the country becoming the magnet for new petrochem-ical and oil-refining developments and hence well the more prosperous part. Thus, with the servant becoming richer than the master, was a new element of linguistic tension intro-

duced. Although by no means an exact parallel, a comparison
with Quebec Province, and above all the city of Montreal,
comes to mind. In Canada, however, the division has been
exacerbated by the remarkable inability of either side to speak
convincingly the other's language, and as a result to get
no pleasure out of trying to do so. This does not apply in
Belgium. I never encountered a Flamand, from that leading
European figure Leo Tindemans, who continued to go home
every night to the Flemish heartland of Antwerp even when
he was Prime Minister, to our skilled but sometimes forbid-
ding cook, Marie-Jeanne Belsack, who could not speak wholly
convincing French when they wanted to do so. Frequently,
however, they (not these two, but others more remote) did
not so choose. I recall once dialling the Brussels equivalent
of Directory Enquiries to ask for the number of a restaurant
south of Namur, in other words as deep in francophonie as it
is possible to imagine. 'Pourquoi vous adressez-vous à moi en
français?' the operator aggressively replied. 'Parce que je suis
Anglais,' I replied with a bland illogicality, although giving
the statement both a little more reason as well as courtesy by
adding, 'et malheureusement je ne sais pas parler le néerlan-
dais.' This appeared to satisfy him for he then continued the
conversation in (of course) wholly fluent French.

The Quebec semi-equivalent of this struck me nearly
twenty years later when, arriving at the splendidly placed and
grandly built Château Frontenac Hotel in that city, we were
greeted (in French) by a large, elderly and top-hatted chief
doorman who handed us on to his almost equally imposing
senior adjutant who took us and our luggage up to the heights
of the hotel. After a perfunctory sentence or so, again in
French, I ventured to say (in English), 'You are not French
Canadian, are you?' 'No, Soir,' he replied, 'Oi'm from Oireland, and there has never been anyone on the door of this

hotel who wasn't from Oireland. But we are not allowed to address any guest in English unless he first does so to us.'

Language can sometimes be as divisive as it is illuminating, which is a pity. It may be that, as a non-Welsh speaking Welshman, who is also far from being a gifted linguist, I am peculiarly alive to this thought. The cause of Scottish nationhood is assisted rather than impeded by the weakness of Gaelic. (So for that matter was that of Ireland nearly a century ago.) Broadly Gaelic is spoken only in a few Hebridean islands and in a Partick enclave of my former Glasgow constituency of Hillhead. This means that it is no challenge to the 98 per cent who do not speak it, and is in this respect quite unlike the 23 or 25 per cent Welsh speakers who certainly agitate the big but not overwhelming majority of non-Welsh speakers with the thought that their chances of major public service positions in the principality diminish with devolution, and would do so even more with independence.

To return to Belgium and Brussels, however, English has in many ways been the beneficiary of the linguistic split. In the Katholieke Universiteit van Leuven, for example, an academic institution of considerable distinction, where the tension led in 1971 to the setting up of a separate French university on a greenfield site christened Louvain-la Neuve, the old establishment, freed by its choice, as they saw it, from the invasion of domestic purity by the insidiousness of French, but realizing that Flemish was not exactly a universal language for a university, took to doing a good deal of its teaching in English.

Futhermore, as goes almost without saying, much of the growth of Brussels as an international city has been inimical to its Flemishness. In one sense this international quality was endemic in its history as a capital of Spaniards and Austrians but in another sense it began its modern international phase only when it became the headquarters of the new European Economic Community in 1958. The Commission started in modest premises, though its first president Walter Hallstein believed in high protocol, and the initial address, rue de la Joyeuse Entrée, was inspiriting. In the late 1960s it expanded into the curious star-like building of the Berlaymont, which, although in a hollow, nonetheless dominated with its thirteen floors the hitherto somewhat nondescript area of Brussels in which it was situated.

Unfortunately it turned out that twelve of the thirteen floors were contaminated with asbestos (I had the luck, or perhaps one might say the predictable privilege, to have been on the only one which was not), and a hasty evacuation to another, almost adjacent and less symbolically dominant building called the Breydel took place in 1990. Meanwhile the Berlaymont has been purged of its poison, and may at some stage revert to European use, although probably not to resume its areopagitical function. Alongside the Berlaymont lay the seat of the Council of Ministers, which had the grander title of the Charlemagne building, although its architecture, and indeed its ambience, was inferior even to that of the Berlaymont. This building has now also been replaced, and rightly so on aesthetic grounds at least. In addition the European Parliament, sensibly in principle but not necessarily in the scale of the result, has revolted against the attempt of the French to confine it to Strasbourg, by establishing a vast presence in Brussels. There is no doubt about the physical impact which Europe has made upon this area of the city of Brussels.

Linguistically the influence has been francophone. Despite the successive enlargements, the European Union, so far at least as its internal working was concerned, became and then long remained the only modern francophone international institution in the world. This has been true of the *services* or permanent staff of the Commission, although less so at Commissioner level, and of Coreper – the Committee of Permanent Representatives or ambassadors of the member states. (It is even less true of the Parliament, for the same reasons writ large that applied to the Commissioners. Politicians' French is inferior to that of either diplomats or lifelong Eurocrats.) This island of international francophonie the French are naturally fanatical about preserving. So would the British be if we had seen our language slip over the past two generations from being the lingua franca of diplomacy and of international rail travel, instead of seeing English swept, largely on the coat-tails of the Americans, to a position of unprecedented world strength.

This has been strongly exemplified by NATO, the other major international organization which Brussels has sheltered since 1966, when General de Gaulle expelled it from France. In Brussels it has at once been relatively unobtrusive – housed in some modest huts on the way to the airport – yet a substantial presence. Apart from anything else it has meant that most Western powers have no fewer than three ambassadors in the city, one accredited to the European Community or Union, one to NATO, and one to the Kingdom of Belgium. This produced a welter of embassies, but more an infusion of English than a further strengthening of French. The acronym of OTAN, a neatly complete inversion of NATO, achieved a Brussels currency, but apart from that the language of Racine or Simenon (the latter a major Belgian contributor to French twentieth-century literature) did not much obtrude upon an organization of which the Secretaries-General have recently been successively Dutch, English, German, Begium, Spanish and Scottish, or upon its military headquarters (at Mons) where General Alexander Haig (the future US Secretary of State), presiding during my Brussels period, at least equalled John Prescott in his fractured use of English and certainly had no linguistic energy to spare for any other language. But if French from its strongpoint of the Marché Commun, as its building was then still known, and English from its rival fortress of NATO, were forever fighting over the Brussels breast, neither of these institutions remotely sustained the use of Flemish in the capital. The balance is however reasserted by the stubbornness with which the surrounding communes, even those on the way to Wallonie, maintain their Flemish linguistic purity.

Road signs seem to be a favourite terrain for such battles. Between Chepstow and Newport in Monmouthshire, for example, where the Welsh language is neither spoken nor understood, roundabouts (or *ffordd-cylch's*) have to be negotiated with great care because of the profuse duality of all signs and the need to remember that Casnewydd, Abertawe and Aberhonddu are not hidden cities arising out of the sea, but just Newport, Swansea and Brecon lurking under Cymric disguise. In Belgium the practice is less ecumenical. Suddenly Mons or Liège disappear completely and are replaced by Bergen (a surprising if logical one that) and Luik, until eight or ten kilometres further on, another linguistic commune boundary having been crossed, they reappear in their prior form.

Of the three great glories of Brussels two of them, to my mind at least, reinforce the French rather than the Flemish quality of the city. These two are the Forêt de Soignes and the *ressources gastronomiques*. The first is made up of vast beechwoods, almost as large as the city itself and genially embracing it on its southern and south-eastern sides. It makes May, if the weather is at all tolerable, the most memorable of the Brussels months, with a concentrated and unmatched verdancy. Around and within the Forêt are a number of Flemish communes, now rich and somewhat internationalized

suburbs, and it has of course a Flemish name, Zonien Woud
– but it seems hardly ever to be used. It is essentially the
Forêt, approached from the upper part of the city centre by
the Avenue Louise, the fashionable boulevard comparable
with the Avenue Foch in Paris or Unter den Linden in
Berlin. The Avenue Louise, which was created in 1864 to
commemorate the consort of Leopold I, Queen Victoria's
uncle, leads to the Bois de la Cambre, which is more lake,
gravel, tarmac and occasional grass banks than woodland, and
then on into the Forêt itself. The latter is a Brussels asset
which surpasses Hyde Park, the Bois de Boulogne or Central
Park in New York.

Brussels restaurants are the second glory, and are formid-
ably good, at least comparable, particularly if allowance is
made for the substantially different size of the two cities, with
the range and quality of those of Paris. The style, even in
the case of the international establishments *de grande luxe*,
is subtly different from that of Paris. The food is perhaps
slightly heavier, the décor certainly so, the service friendlier
and the atmosphere more self-confidently bourgeois. This
applies even to the Belle Epoque Villa Lorraine, which by its
sylvan but not rustic location on the hinge between the Bois
and the Forêt recalls both Pré Catelan in the Bois de Bologne
and Ledoyen in the Jardins de Champs Elysées, both very
Proustian sites. The other eminences are L'Ecailler du Palais
Royal, to my mind the best of all fish restaurants, and Comme
Chez Soi, the highest peak of the lot, now secure in its three
stars, but set in the far from glossy Place Rouppe, through
which the Avenue de Stalingrad runs on its way to the Gare
du Midi, in London terms a sort of Clerkenwell location.

Brussels and indeed Belgian restaurants, however, must
not be seen too exclusively in terms of these metropolitan
heights. The suburbs of Brussels from Jesus-Eik to Gerhoren
and Essine to Groot-Biggarden, thus illustrating by their

names that gastronomy, more than universities, religion or politics, bridges rather than widens the ethnic gap, are littered with Michelin two-stars, as well as with other less decorated establishments of quality. And the old neighbouring Flemish towns, Mechelen and Leuven, Gent and Brugge, Tienen and Aalot, and of course Antwerpen, are rich in resturants as well as in gothic gables. Flemish menus are far from being just an affair of *moules* and *frites*.

For some reason, I suppose partly the old burgher tradition, the good restaurants of Flanders are mostly in the town centres whereas those of Wallonie are mostly in villages or the countryside. This, fortified by our habit, when we spent weekends in Belgium and had guests staying, of taking them out for lunch in the Ardennes if the weather was good, and to a Flemish town if it was bad, created in my memory the illusion that Brussels lay on a climatic divide: to the south were the constantly sunny uplands, to the north were the sodden market places surrounded by cabbage-fields with the compensation of late medieval architecture.

Nevertheless the restaurant eminence of Brussels and its surrounding area must be counted a French rather than a Flemish plus. It would be very odd if the traditional language of gastronomy, which exercises a certain sway at least from Istanbul to San Francisco, assuredly taking in the Low Countries on the way (the main difference between Dutch Dutch and Flemish Dutch is that the latter obsessively extrudes French words whereas the former is liberally welcoming of them), did not dominate Belgian menus. I have never heard of the patron of a good Flemish restaurant resisting a Michelin star or refusing to talk French. And of course the wine lists of the fine establishments, which are of great depth and quality, at least up to those of their Parisian equivalents, are overwhelmingly French, and overwhelmingly red. They are not, contrary to what I had been led to expect

DUBLIN

34. *Right*. The Four Courts (Gandon, completed in 1802): 'the dome I believed I had seen from Snowdon'.

35. *Below*. Fitzwilliam Square: good south Dublin Georgian.

36. *Above*. The Upper Yard of Dublin Castle, the centre of British rule to 1922 and the scene of Margaret Thatcher's 'incarceration' in 1979.

37. *Left*. An insouciant statue of James Joyce, erected in O'Connell Street in 1990.

38. *Below*. The Long Room in Trinity College Library (Thomas Burgh c. 1720, remodelled by Woodward and Deane in 1860).

GLASGOW

39. 'The cranes of Govan proclaim that this is Glasgow . . .'

40. *Above*. George Square, with the Walter Scott Monument in the centre and the City Chambers (William Young, 1883–8) beyond.

41. *Right*. Kirklee Terrace (Charles Wilson, built 1845–64), where we had our small Glasgow apartment.

42. *Left.* St Vincent Street Church (Alexander 'Greek' Thomson, 1859).

43. *Below, left.* Glasgow at its most delicate: the Suspension Bridge (1851) over the Clyde with the Roman Catholic Cathedral of St Andrew (1814–17) to the right.

44. *Below.* The library of Charles Rennie Mackintosh's Glasgow School of Art (1907–9).

BARCELONA

45. *Right*. 'The soaring gothic church of Santa Maria del Mar'.

46. *Middle*. The Plaça de Catalunya with the Passeig de Gràcia, 'Barcelona's very passable imitation of the Champs-Elysées', centre right, and the regularity of the late-nineteenth-century Eixample around it.

47. *Below, left*. Gaudí's 'somewhat hysterical basilica of the Sagrada Familia'.

48. *Below, right*. The 'amazing natural feature of the thirty-mile-distant massif' around the monastery of Monserrat, from which springs the inspiration for much of Gaudí's architecture.

49. *Left*. Casa Amatller
(Puig i Cadafalch, 1895–1900,
and Casa Battlo (Gaudí,
1904–06), Passeig de Gràcia.

50. *Middle, left*. Casa Lleó
Morera (Domènech i Montaner,
1902–6), also in the Passeig
de Gràcia.

51. *Below, left*. The main
stairway of Gaudí's
Parc Güell.

52. *Below, right*. The serpentine
seating on the roof above,
with a view over a somewhat
smoggy city.

The Wilhelmine Capital

53. *Right.* Französischer Dom (built in 1701–5 for Huguenots expelled from France), one of the two small cathedrals which flank the Konzerthaus.

54. *Below, left.* Schinkel's Schauspielhaus (1818–21), now the Konzerthaus, with the Schiller monument in front.

55. *Below, right.* The second cathedral, the Deutsche Dom (1708), which, with the other two buildings, makes the Gendarmenmarkt one of the best (if not best-known) squares of Europe.

56. *Bottom.* The old National Gallery (Stüler, 1866–70), one of the five collections on Museum Island, seen from the River Spree.

57. *Left*. Weimar Berlin
illustrated by the dated traffic in
the Potsdamerplatz, circa 1930.

58. *Below, left*. The Kurfürstendamm
in the summer of 1955: the stump
of the Kaiser Wilhelm [I] Memorial
Church (1895) forms a background
to the 'temporary exhibition'
quality of the main street of
West Berlin.

59. *Below*. The hard face of the
divided city after the Wall was built:
Brandenburger Tor seen from
the West, circa 1975.

BERLIN REVIVED

60. *Right*. The Reichstag
(built 1884–94) as restored and
embellished by Norman Foster
in 1995–99.

before arriving in Brussels, biased by geography in favour of burgundy. The claret lists are at least as strong, with perhaps a more subtle trade-route discrimination, compared with a rare English list of equal quality, in favour of the right-bank and overland-moving St Emilions and Pomerols as opposed to the left-bank Médocs and Graves which were more easily shipped to Britain, Scandinavia or America.

By contrast with the Forêt and the restaruants, however, the third of the Brussels glories, the Grand' Place or Groote Markt, stems much more from the Flemish than from the French tradition. Some of it is old. The Hôtel de Ville for instance is mid-fifteenth century. And some of it is modern, but the 'repro' buildings have been built or rebuilt with a close regard for the unity of the ensemble, and as a result it is a paradigm of the guild-based and essentially urban prosperity which is reflected in similar mostly smaller and less well-known but sometimes architecturally superior market places throughout Flanders.

Although Brussels is incontestably an international city – probably indeed the most so in Europe – and to some a symbol of internationalism at its most hopeful, to others of supranational bureaucracy at its most interfering – it is only very partially so. Not only the functionaries of the European Union and of NATO, together with their attendant embassies and press corps, but also the commercial penumbra which these organizations have attracted to the city, the international law and accountancy firms as well as the various trade and lobbying associations, are confined almost rigidly to the southern and eastern parts of the conurbation, the boroughs of Ixelles and Uccle and the suburbs of Woluwé St Pierre, Audhergen, Tervuren and La Hulpe. This leaves a large area to the north and the west where foreigners are as rare as vegetarians in Comme Chez Soi. Some of these segments of Brussels were traditional working-class areas, but by no means all of them. In a direct line of view from the Berlaymont lie Koekelberg and the heavy but dominating dome of the Basilique, the late-nineteenth-century church reminiscent of St Philippe-du-Roule on the boulevard Malesherbes in Paris, where the surrounding area between there and the Parc Monceau also has much the same air of unostentatious middle-bourgeois respectability. In London, Bayswater and the slopes running up from the Finchley Road to the heights of Hampstead might have been comparable a generation ago, although the odd thing now is that London, the capital of insular Britain, no longer has any semi-central area as purely indigenous as either Brussels around the Basilique or the Paris of the 17th arrondissement.

Brussels of course has, or had, a proletariat, although it has recently become remarkably tucked away. Even the nominally working-class adjacent borough of Anderlecht, famous for its football team, where I used to visit Henri Simonet, former vice-president of the Commission, then Belgian Foreign Minister and altogether a very undoctrinaire Socialist, at his villa in the not notably poor-sounding Avenue de Crocus, never exhibited in my day much sign of deprivation or of left-wing militancy. Yet in the late nineteenth and early twentieth centuries Brussels played an important if on the whole non-combative role in the development of European socialism. In 1847–8 Marx and Engels there drafted and launched the Communist Manifesto. In 1864 a Brussels section of the First International was set up. In 1889 the Second (or Social Democratic) Socialist International was founded there. And in 1894 universal suffrage (except for women) was established earlier than in any other European country. In 1929 also, when as earlier mentioned I first saw Brussels, it was, somewhat typically both for the city and for my pre-1939 travelling destinations, a Socialist International bureau meeting which occasioned the presence of my father and hence of my mother and myself.

I also experienced a last spark of Brussels proletarianism in the late 1950s when I went to a European Movement conference there accompanied by John Hynd, a railwayman Labour MP from Sheffield. Hynd, partly on account of his experience as Chancellor of the Duchy of Lancaster in the Attlee government, under which improbable title he had been ministerially responsible for administering the British zone in Germany, and partly by natural inclination, had become a fervent European and thus a frequent participant in the revolving series of international conferences which were at that stage the necessary lifestyle of the European idea. He was consequently habituated to international hotels, *trains de luxe* and aeroplanes. After a typical conference banquet he took me for a walk around the Palais de Justice and on to the terrace beside it which looks down a couple of hundred feet on to the lower city. 'Down there, Roy,' he said with a mixture of self-mockery, guilt and nostalgia, 'are our people: not in the grand restaurant from which we have just come.' I am not sure the socio-topography was right even then, and still less so when I came to live in Brussels twenty years later, for I think there were nearly as many chocolatiers, smart boutiques and good restuarants below us as there were behind us. But I nonetheless responded to the direction of his thought and have remembered it over a span of fifty years. It was however more a faint *cri de coeur* than an accurate piece of sociological analysis. Brussels is indeed *une vraie ville bourgeoise*, with political energy essentially diverted from the class into the linguistic struggle, which can be equally damaging.

This does not prevent Brussels also being a *ville d'art*. At least from Roger Van de Weyden in the first half of the

fifteenth century to René Magritte in the first half of
the twentieth, Brussels has produced or provided a working
background for a range of painters of remarkable quality,
interest and originality, and sometimes of all three at once.
Even a quick dip yields Memling, Van Eyck, Antonio Moro,
both Breughels, Van Dyck, Rubens, De Vadder, Van der
Storck (the last two vivid representers of the Brabant landscape, particularly that of the Forêt do Soignes), François-
Joseph Navez, Alfred Stevens and Fernand Khnopff.

All are well represented in the Musée Royal des Beaux-
Arts, the contents of which entitle it to be one of the great
galleries of Europe. There is however something in either
the hanging or the lack of authority in the position and
entrance to the building which prevents it making the
impression of the Rijksmuseum, the Prado or the Kunsthis-
torische, let alone the Louvre. The paintings in the churches
are on the whole disappointing, including those in the
cathedral (or more strictly the collegiate church of St
Gudule), although that has good glass and a tremendous
baroque pulpit. There is certainly nothing to compare with
the great Van Eyck triptych in the cathedral at Ghent or with
the Memling in the old hospital at Bruges. The Hôtel de
Ville and a few other public buildings contain magnificent
examples of the tapestries for which the city was famous from
the late fifteenth to the end of the eighteenth centuries. And
at Tervuren there is an unparalleled collection of central
African art. There is also a strong theatrical tradition in the
city. *Le Soir* currently lists no fewer than twenty-seven thea-
tres, mostly small, offering fairly serious pieces. This is more
than is available in London, New York or Paris. Brussels is
also a city spattered with bookshops, both new and second-
hand.

Leopold II, whose boisterous and by no means impeccable
reign lasted from 1865 to 1909, left an impact upon modern

Brussels as great as Napoleon III, with his town-planning adjutant Georges Haussmann, had done upon Paris a generation before. And it was on the whole a beneficial impact. The Palais de Justice, much admired and said to be the largest building in the world when it was completed in 1883, has since, despite its monstrous dominance of an eminent site, gone aesthetically if not literally down hill. It was alleged by an unfriendly critic to have 'imposed the Assyrian style on the Gothic, the Gothic on the Tibetan, the Tibetan on that of Louis Seize, and Louis Seize on that of Papua'. But nearly all the other public and semi-public buildings which sprang up during the second Leopold's reign, including the vast Cinquantenaire, erected for an exhibition to mark the fiftieth anniversary of the independent Belgian kingdom, were decent and dignified examples of the architecture of the period. They make a major contribution to giving present-day Brussels the air of a twentieth-century medium-sized capital city. The process was considerably aided by three long-term and powerful burgomasters, de Brouckère, Anspach and Adolphe Max, although one came before and one after Leopold II.

At the less official and pompous end of what in England would be called late-Victorian and Edwardian architecture there came the (mostly) private developments which made Brussels second perhaps only to Barcelona as a home to art nouveau and later to art deco. Victor Horta was the leading Belgian exponent of this style, the Brussels equivalent of Barcelona's Gaudí or Glasgow's Charles Rennie Mackintosh. Apart from a number of surviving houses, Horta, in his turn-of-the-century period and style, built a department store appropriately called Innovation and a so-called Maison du Peuple, neither of which survived the depredations of the 1960s. His Palais des Beaux-Arts however remains a monument of his creative architecture.

The real man-made disaster for the appearance and

coherence of Brussels began well before that architecturally destructive decade of the 1960s. As early as 1911 works were begun for the joining up, through the middle of the city, of the railway system which spread out from the Gare du Midi with that from the Gare du Nord. They are oddly named stations, for on a through journey from Ostend to Munich or Vienna the train enters Brussels by the Gare du Midi and leaves it by the Gare du Nord, which is on the face of it perverse, for these south Germanic cities, although also well to the east, are indisputably to the south of Ostend. Between them these two stations are the twin hubs of the traditionally important Belgian railway system. One of the earliest trains on the continent of Europe ran from Brussels to Malines in 1835. And the Compagnie Internationale des Wagons-Lits et des Grands Express Européens, founded by Georges Nackelmackers, had its headquarters in the Belgian capital from 1876.

Such a junction of the two systems and the creation between them of a new and conveniently placed (except that no one ever seemed to go from it) Gare Centrale – designed incidentally by Horta in his later and less innovative period – was in itself desirable. But it ought to have been done either deeper or by a more circuitous route. As it was, the price gradually paid was appalling. It was gradual because the works, interrupted by two world wars and by the slump between them, were completed only after forty-one years in 1952. A large swathe of the city had been a building site, sometimes active, sometimes abandoned. An unhealed breach between the commercial centre around the Grand' Place and the official 'Austrian quarter', flanked by the smart *haute ville*, was opened up. The populous district of Saint-Roch was effectively destroyed and the cathedral nearly fell down. But 'progress' at a price, even if not with impressive speed, was eventually achieved. The lasting result has been a rather dead no-man's land at a crucial hinge of the city. Such areas of deadness are however a feature of many cities without the need for half a century of central railway works to produce them. There is one in New York around 20th–30th Streets, one in London around Holborn, and another in Paris where the rue La Fayette approaches, but has not reached, the Gare du Nord or the Gare de l'Est.

Overall, however, Brussels is a reasonably close-knit city and quite good for walking in, although I cannot say that I ever did much there except in the Bois or the Forêt. It can also be a city of sharp contrasts. Very occasionally (when feeling in particular need of exercise beyond my routine early-morning jogging of those days) I walked between our small art-nouveau house off the Bois end of the Avenue Louise and my office in the previously described Berlaymont. There were broadly two routes, each of which took about three-quarters of an hour. The one plunged down hill past the Etangs d'Ixelles, the little lakes naturally attracting desirable surrounding residential property, and then went through the jumbled streets and little carrefours of Etterbeck (all of which seemed crammed with well-stocked but unglossy small foodshops) before gently rising up again to reach the Rond-Point Schuman and the star-shaped centre of Europe.

Alternatively a more flanking route could be taken, which involved crossing the Avenue Franklin Roosevelt, the lavish apartment blocks of which were the epitome of modern international Brussels, and then along the utterly different Avenue Général Jacques before advancing on the Berlaymont from the reverse or Cinquantenaire side. It was further but flatter. Its fascination lay in the General's stretch. General Baron Jules Marie Alphonse Jacques, although already fifty-six in 1914, was a hero of the First War. His avenue looked as it might have done when he made his first stand against the Germans. It was wide *pavé* intersected by tramlines and lined mostly with dark-stoned, sombre rather than handsome nineteenth-century public buildings, including a large barracks, which gave it an appropriate military atmosphere, interspersed with a few shops, which seem to me through the haze of recollection to have mostly been horsemeat butchers. In spite of the valour of the General, who survived to lead the Belgian Corps in the offensive of September 1918, its military atmosphere was one more of defeat than of victory. King Albert, long-cloaked and steel-helmeted, leading a resigned but noble retreat in the rain, would have fitted well into it. It was to me a symbol of the old Belgium in the Europe of 1914, away from which it was easy to see why Paul-Henri Spaak and other less famous but equally Europeanly committed of his countrymen were so anxious to point the way.

The style of the Avenue Général Jacques was distinctly unusual in the Brussels which I frequented, which is the reason that it sticks so vividly in my memory. Mostly my life was lived in the large but uninspiring boxes which were the modest homes of the Community institutions (a British minister has far grander office accommodation); in a couple of nineteenth-century suburban châteaux, Val Duchesse and Ste-Anne, in which we gave luncheons or dinners for visiting ministers or delegations; or in the sylvan and secluded villas ('vineries and pineries' as Lord Randolph Churchill would disparagingly have called them) which were the residences of most embassies to the Community or to NATO. This was mingled with occasional forays into the earlier and grander buildings in which the Belgian state operated, sometimes to see the Foreign or Prime Minister, and less frequently to call on the King at the Palais de Bruxelles or at Laeken, three or four miles away. In my day he was Baudouin, a shyly engaging young man – he was in fact in his late forties but looked younger, although also as if he had the world on his shoulders and hoped that the European idea would help to lift some of the weight.

The missions of the main countries to the Kingdom of Belgium, as distinct from those to the two international institutions, were also mostly in this monumental 'Austrian quarter'. It was pre-eminently the case with the British embassy which with its fine mansion in the rue Ducale, halfway between the Royal Palace and the parliament, overlooked the Parc de Bruxelles and had the Prime Minister's *hôtel particulier* just around the corner. In traditional splendour this is probably second among British embassies only to the Paris residence. The paradox was that the occupant of this semi-palace was only, in the Foreign Office terms then used, a grade-three ambassador, whereas the other two, both in 'vinery and pinery' villas, were of grade-one rank. Moreover British home-based ministers had far more dealings with the ambassador to the Community than with the one to the Kingdom, and indeed spent far more nights (before Council of Ministers meetings) staying with the former in 'the benighted suburbs'.

These factors gathered momentum as the 1980s merged into the 1990s. Consequently, when an ingenious Foreign Office minister of state in 1991 saw the opportunity for a quick shuffle he had all the cards in his hands. His ministerial superiors had a strong interest in supporting him, and when the next bilateral ambassador arrived in Brussels he found that he had been relegated to the remoter quarters of the rue Henri Pirenne (not a bad name for anyone with historical interest) and that the ambassador to the Community was firmly installed in the rue Ducale. Whether the Belgian government was mildly upset I do not know, although this seems unlikely, particularly as the last two bilateral ambassadors had been distinctly sparing in their dispersal of public hospitality, as indeed had been their predecessor in my days as president of the Commission. I think I was in the house only twice in my four years, but that at least was an improvement on the experience of Jean-Luc Dehaene, the long-standingly powerful Belgian politician and at the time Prime Minister, who when he visited the house under the new dispensation in 1992, had never been there before.

The overall efficiency of the British operation in Brussels was undoubtedly improved by the change. Habitually, however, Brussels diplomatic life is more staid than this. Indeed it rather matches the pattern of Brussels life generally, comfortable and smooth functioning rather than exciting. I found it agreeable enough for a limited period, particularly as I believed (and still do) that there was a strong and worthwhile purpose behind the surface boredoms and frustrations of European Community routines.

I began rather negatively by saying that Brussels is not a city which clutches the heart strings. But it did once do precisely that to me. When my four years were up I returned to England without too much regret and did not again visit Brussels for two and three-quarter years. This was not because of any revulsion. It was because I believed, perhaps a little pompously, that when departing from a scene over which one has endeavoured to preside it is better to allow at least some substantial time before getting in the hair of a successor. The interval became longer than I intended because I got involved in founding a new political party. But when I did go back, for a long weekend in October 1983, it was one of the most nostalgic four days of revisiting old haunts and looking at once familiar scenes that I have ever spent. So the 'twitch upon the thread' power of that Brabantine city is not to be dismissed.

DUBLIN

UNTIL 1961 MY ONLY SIGHT of Dublin had been a gleam of light on the domes of its famous Four Courts from the summit of Snowdon, nearly a hundred miles away, which I climbed with my parents in 1936. So, at least, I firmly believed until I came to check records for this essay. Then I discovered that my father's diary (11 August 1936), deflatingly but more realistically in relation to the North Wales climate, recorded, 'Did not see a thing. It was cloud covered.' Such are the frailties of human memory. I think I must have been told by someone else that they had been struck by the sight, and had believed for sixty years that I had experienced it myself. What is indisputable, however, is that in October 1961 I crossed the Irish Sea for twenty-four hours to take part in a Trinity College debate on the merits of Irish (and British) entry in the European Common Market, as it was then known. I was immensely struck, both by Trinity (which in a flattering speech there I was to describe a few years later as making Oxford and Cambridge look almost 'redbrick') and by Dublin as a whole.

This was despite the fact that the city was then, forty years ago, moving towards the end of a flaccid period in its history, both architecturally and politically. Dublin's period of architectural glory started in 1680–4 with the building to William Robinson's design of the Kilmainham Royal

Hospital, and is widely thought to have been torpedoed by Pitt's abolition of the Irish Parliament in 1800, although the sinking ship produced much good early-nineteenth-century building. And the nineteenth century could not possibly be described as a dull period in Dublin and Irish history. To a remarkable extent Britain's Hibernian island, by its tribulations and its turbulence, dominated British politics at a time when Britain was the leading world power.

In the early twentieth century Ireland was even more turbulent and its London repurcussions at least as strong. In 1912–14 the Irish question came nearer to threatening civil war than anything since the seventeenth century. The tensions within the British political system were diminished only by the outbreak of European war. Within Ireland itself they were not so easily (if expensively) resolved. The 1916 Easter rebellion produced not only Yeats's 'terrible beauty', but also the destruction of much of O'Connell (then Sackville) Street, the main thoroughfare of Dublin north of the Liffey, and, still more significantly, of the Irish Parliamentary party, forged by Parnell in the 1880s but later rather too constitutionally led by John Redmond. Sinn Fein ('ourselves alone' in Erse) triumphed at the 1918 election and there ensued two civil wars in and around Dublin.

The first was that of Sinn Fein against the British, which a combination of the exhaustion of the 'rebels', the British liberal conscience and the excesses of the Black and Tans (a sort of Freikorps specially recruited by the British government) forced to a settlement at the end of 1921. The second was an internal war between those who supported the Treaty (of settlement) and those who did not. In the course of this the Four Courts were shelled and Michael Collins, the ablest fighter, first against the British and then against those Irish who wanted to repudiate the Treaty which he (and others) had signed, was ambushed and killed. The paradox was that the intransigents, who had lost in the internecine skirmishes won, after an interval, through the ballot box, and the Irish Free State then settled down under De Valera to decades of narrow, inward-looking but peaceful and theocratic poverty. Almost the only achievement was to keep out of the Second World War, if that was an achievement. It was somewhat reminiscent of Spain after its Civil War, without Franco's vicious reprisals or the proscription of opponents of the government.

The Dublin that I first knew was the capital of a country only beginning to emerge from this dead hand. De Valera's cumulative total of twenty-two years of premiership had ended only eighteen months previously when he had become president of the Republic and begun another fourteen years in this ornamental but non-executive role. The income per head was barely 60 per cent of that of Great Britian, below that of the province of Ulster, which then remained the more prosperous part of the Emerald Isle, as it had been when Asquith in the last year of his premiership was struck by the 'wonderful creation' of Belfast as compared with the 'out of repair' look of Dublin. Membership of the European Community was just a glint of hope beyond the horizon and took another dozen years to be realized. In a book published in 1963, James Morris wrote:

Dublin still has corners of style ... but to the English stranger it comes as a shock to realise that within the perimeter of our common islands there stands the poorest and most stagnant of all the capitals of western Europe. For at a moment when the western world rings with wealth and progress Dublin seems stuck in a forlorn but stubborn rut. Ireland has become the lost soul of Europe, without resources, without leaders, without (one is tempted to say) purpose. The gusto of capitalism, the surge of Communism are both absent from Dublin, which is left waving a little green flag and looking towards Lourdes.

It should be said that eleven years later, in another book, Jan Morris (as she had become) wrote much more affectionately as well as optimistically about Dublin, and I doubt if the improvement can be attributed entirely to her change of sex.

On the other hand the Dublin of 1961 was still a city retaining, maybe a little shabbily, much of its eighteenth-century urbanity. The worst damage to the redbrick squares and terraces (although the destruction can be exaggerated, for much remains) was still to come, and the city retained a size which was reasonable for a head in proportion to the body of the country. It had about 650,000 inhabitants (out of just under 3 million in the Republic as a whole) as against 500,000 in 1918 and 150,000 in 1800. It had grown by between four and five times in the century and a half during which London had grown by eight times.

After 1961 I did not visit Dublin again for nearly ten years, although in the very cold winter of 1963 I overflew it, and had what I decided was an experience previously shared by only a couple of thousand people in the history of the world, that of seeing at a single glance the whole of Southern Ireland snowbound from coast to coast. This was a function of three factors: first that such conditions rarely apply in the soft gulfstream Hibernian climate, and had certainly not previously done so since 1947; second that until what were then called the 'big jets' came into service around 1958 no civilian plane flew high enough to give such a wide perspective; and third, only about ten planes had previously flown that route since the great snowfall of two days before.

In 1970, when I was Chancellor of the Exchequer, immediately after the conclusion of the debate on my third and last budget, we went for a week's April holiday to a good small hotel at the splendidly named Ballylickey in West Cork. This involved two glancing visits to Dublin, which in combination were not without an element of farce. Charles Haughey, who was later in the course of an adventurous career to be three times Taoiseach (or Prime Minister), was then my opposite number in Jack Lynch's Fianna Fáil government. Haughey very courteously said that he would come and greet me at the airport, even though it was the day before his own budget, as well as giving an official lunch on our way back through Dublin a week later. However, when we landed, it was one of his secretaries who came with a message that Haughey had that morning fallen off his horse and concussed himself. We took this with a calm regret. But the next afternoon when we paused in Cork City on our way to Ballylickey, we found screaming evening-newspaper head-lines making it clear that Haughey's trouble was more than concussion and that the Taoiseach (Prime Minister) was delivering the budget in his stead. (A short time later he was dismissed from his post and placed under arrest for gun-running.) Then there was a further message saying that it would now be the Taoiseach and not Haughey who would preside over my next week's luncheon. I reflected that, by comparison, my relations with Harold Wilson, although sub-ject to occasional tensions, seemed satisfactorily steady.

This upheaval did not detract from the pleasure with which I visited for the first time the sites – Dublin Castle, Phoenix Park, Kilmainham Gaol, the General Post Office and the Curragh – around which in the times of two of my biographical subjects Gladstone and Asquith, the hope of an Anglo-Irish 'union of hearts' had died. For anyone captivated by British late-nineteenth- and early-twentieth-century his-tory Dublin is a fascinating city. Also, on that 1970 visit I first encountered my favourite Dublin hotel, the Shelbourne.

There are now others which are more modern and glossier, but I in any event prefer old hotels, and nothing can rival the Shelbourne's commanding position on St Stephen's Green. It looks across at Iveagh House, the seat of the Foreign Ministry and the narrow passageway which leads to the large nave-only church, the main city-centre relic of John Henry Newman's 1852 Catholic University. And at its back the Shelbourne has many of Dublin's most notable institutions: Trinity College, the Mansion House and above all the complex of public buildings surrounding Leinster House, the seat of the Dáil Éireann. These were mostly added around 1865 and include the National Gallery, the National Museum, the National Library, the Natural History Museum and the National Archives. And this makes the Shelbourne the nearest equivalent, allowing a little for the different scale of the various cities, of the Plaza in New York, the Palace Hotel in Madrid, the Adlon in Berlin. This more than makes up for the fact that, like nearly every other major hotel in the world today, it seems to go through a bewildering change of chain ownership between each of my successive visits, and to acquire a series of weakening second barrels to its single resonant name.

My next group of Dublin excursions (nine of them) stemmed directly from my presidency of the European Commission. I thought that a British president ought to pay particular attention to Irish susceptiblities, and I also found the visits both rewarding and informative. There were no dominating Irish politicians of the period, no O'Connell, Parnell or De Valera, but I found nearly all the Taoiseachs and Foreign Ministers aimiable and reliable supporters of the European idea, as they should have been, considering how well Ireland was doing from its European connection. This both freed them from a love/hate relationship with London and gave them a launch pad which, provided they treated it

as a platform of opportunity and not a dole, as they assuredly
have done, enabled them to achieve a surge to prosperity
almost comparable, adjusted for scale, with West Germany's
Wirtschaftswunder of the 1950s and 1960s.

The Irish politician who stood out on grounds both of
companionableness and of intellectual quality was Garret
FitzGerald, although there were several others with whom I
enjoyed dealing. Happily, perhaps, for the office I then
occupied, I felt little partisanship between the two parties of
Fianna Fáil and Fine Gael, and indeed had to exercise a jerk
of memory to recall their differences of origin: De Valera's
Fianna Fáil, the more nationalist party, backed by industrialists benefiting from protection and by many of their workers
as well as by small farmers, and drawing their support from
the countryside and Dublin; Fine Gael, more the heirs of
Arthur Griffith and the Cosgraves, and traditionally drawing
their support from the larger farmers, from shopkeepers and
publicans of the small towns and from the more free-trade
industrialists, in general the heirs of many who had supported
John Redmond.

These visits gave me only a very superficial understanding
of Irish politics, but they did at least give me some familiarity
with the geography of Dublin. By far the most memorable
although not the most productive of them was for the
European Council which met in Dublin Castle at the end of
November 1979. It was the first occasion that the heads of
the other eight governments of the European Community
had encountered Mrs Thatcher in full flood. She made a
profound although doubtfully persuasive impression upon
them. At the heads of government 'working' dinner, on the
question of Britian's justified demand for a budget rebate, she
kept us sitting over the table from 9.00 p.m. to 1.15 in the
morning and gave a fuller meaning to the adjective 'working'.
For the greater part of it she talked without pause, although

not without repetition. Helmut Schmidt pretended (but only pretended) to go to sleep, while Valéry Giscard d'Estaing, who was potentially her most determined antagonist, was able to lean back in contented detachment, watching her embroil with one after another of her potential allies.

Yet I have never been able to decide whether the strenuousness of her performance was in the medium term counter-productive or not. Superficially it was both boring and alienating. But maybe it also made the others realize that they would never have any peace until she got a more or less satisfactory settlement. Six months later this was achieved, although at a price which largely stultified the efforts of her incoming Foreign Secretary, Peter Carrington, to achieve a warmer relationship with the Community countries than that of the Callaghan government.

Of more relevance both to the history and to the topography of Dublin is one scene from those thirty hours which remains imprinted upon my mind. All the other heads of government were in hotels or embassies, and I was in my usual Shelbourne. But Mrs Thatcher, for security reasons decided upon by the Irish government, was installed, almost incarcerated, in Dublin Castle, which was the old seat of British viceregal rule. Lords Lieutenant had lived there until 1782 when they moved to the spacious elegance of an eighteenth-century country house n Phoenix Park, two miles to the west. But British justice and British punishment had continued to be dispensed from the Castle until 1922. And when, on the morning after Mrs Thatcher's dinner extravaganza, I decided to go and tell her that the only hope was to seek a postponement of a decision until the spring, she received me in a sitting room decorated by a plaque saying that it was where 'James Connolly, signatory to the proclamation of the Irish Republic, lay a wounded prisoner prior to his execution [shot, strapped to a chair, for he could not

stand] by the British military forces at Kilmainham Jail . . .
12 May 1916'. This background, bizarre, ironic or lowering
according to taste, did not seem in the least to oppress
her, although I thought it had a dispiriting effect upon her
attendant and distinguished advisory knights, Sir Robert
Armstrong and Sir Michael Palliser.

Another Dublin visit of that autumn also retains a posi-
tive, perhaps frivolous but enjoyable position in my memory.
A month or so before the European Council I went, as was
the habit for a president of the Commission, to discuss the
agenda for the Council with the Irish Prime Minister, who
was then its rotating president. After the meeting I took the
opportunity to have Garret FitzGerald, temporarily in opposition, to dine in a private room at the top of the Shelbourne.
There we had a wide-ranging and largely non-political conversation. Such conversations are a speciality of Irish life. At
a Chamber of Commerce luncheon in County Wicklow
nearly twenty years later there was a poetry reading, which I
cannot imagine happening at such an event in England.
Equally I once saw a large banner at Dublin Airport proclaiming that 'Ireland welcomes Harold Pinter'. It would be
impossible to imagine a similar welcome at Heathrow or even
Charles de Gaulle airports.

At the FitzGerald dinner the waiter had peculiar difficulty
in opening the wine – a most uncharacteristic Irish weakness
which led me to think up a joke based on the fairly well-
known aphorism that 'the trouble with France is that it is an
anti-semitic republic presided over by a Jewish royal family –
the Rothschilds'. I suggested, tongue in cheek, that the Irish
analogue was 'the trouble with Ireland is that it is a teetotal
republic presided over by a brewing royal family – the
Guinnesses'. There was plenty of supporting evidence around
for the second half of the proposition. Across St Stephen's
Green was Iveagh House, the earldom of Iveagh being the

senior Guinness title, although acquired only under Lloyd George. A side-glance to the west took one to the mile-distant great St James' Gate Guinness brewery, founded in 1759, at one time the largest brewery in the world and still a dominant Dublin presence. Then a little south of that was the over-restored (1860) St Patrick's Cathedral paid for by Guinness money. And in the hinterland there was a splatter-ing of country houses – some now hotels – which at one time or another had been either built for or owned by Guinnesses.

The 1980s were for me an empty Dublin decade. But the 1990s were the reverse. A variety of reasons led me to pay at least eight Dublin visits, nearly all of them in the springtime, although the spring is at least as unreliable a season there as it is almost everywhere else in the temperate world. The publication of my biography of Gladstone was one of the reasons. Gladstone in practice was not a great Hibernian. He paid only two visits, one of thirty days in 1877, mainly to great houses within the Pale, the part of Ireland, broadly the counties of Dublin, Kildare, Meath and Louth, which had remained an English-controlled enclave from the fifteenth century, and the other of barely three hours in 1880 when he slipped ashore from a private yacht to attend a service at Christ Church, the other of the two Anglican cathedrals with which Dublin is somewhat over-endowed.

Ireland nevertheless dominated the last phase of Glad-stone's political life, and his two Home Rule Bills, the first foundering in the House of Commons and the second in the House of Lords, offered the last hope of Anglo-Irish recon-ciliation within a common polity. This made the Irish very interested in him, and I gave Gladstone talks both in Trinity, traditionally the bastion of Dublin Anglicanism, a bridgehead on the eastern shore of Ireland with, for four centuries but no longer, its back turned to Catholic Ireland as resolutely as some see New York's back turned on Mid-Western America, and at University College Dublin, the nationalist academy which had, after an interval, sprung up out of the ashes of Newman's Catholic prototype. I also gave the address at the annual Parnell Day celebrations at Avondale, Parnell's County Wicklow squire's house about thirty miles south of Dublin, and was much impressed by the calm objectivity of the subsequent questions and discussion. 'All passion spent' might be an unfair description of the mood of modern Irish historians, but 'all facts and views considered objectively' would be a just label.

There was also a visit which I paid with the other members of my Electoral Reform Commission to study the Irish single transferable vote system. And there were three others for which pleasure was the dominant motive, although they each had a small political handle attached. Among other things these enabled me to see the insides of two of the three British residences which in the last century of the Ascendancy had graced Phoenix Park, one of the largest city parks in the world, even if on the edge rather than in the centre, five times the size of Hyde Park, over twice that of Central Park, New York. These three houses were for the political Chief Secretary, the official permanent under-secretary of the Irish Office and, obviously and already mentioned, the grandest for the Viceroy or Lord Lieutenant.

After 1922 this last become the residence of the Governor-General, the representative of the King–Emperor in London but in fact normally an acceptable Irishman, first Tim Healy QC, wit and long-standing Nationalist MP at Westminster, and then his two successors, more shrouded to English eyes in Irish mists, until in 1937, under De Valera's new constitution, which changed the Irish Free State into Eire, it became the President's House. As such, blazing the trail for a still grander Viceregal Lodge in Delhi which after 1947 became Rashtrapati Bhawan, it was rechristened Áras an Uachtraráin. There we lunched on 17 March 1997 with President Mary Robinson and her architectural-historian husband. Two twists were given to the occasion by the facts that it was St Patrick's Day, when it might be thought that the Robinsons would have wanted to entertain figures more Hibernian than an Anglo-Welsh quartet, for we brought two travelling companions with us, one of whose ancestors, a general of cavalry who lost a leg at Waterloo, had been a (fortunately) liberal viceroy and inhabitant of the house in the 1830s. This illustrated the broad outlook which subsequently made Mrs Robinson such a notable United Nations figure.

The fate of the other two houses was even more interesting, because they perfectly illustrated the foreign policy orientation of the independent Ireland before the rising of the sun of the European Community. The Free State government bestowed the Chief Secretary's Lodge upon the Americans for their ambassador's residence, and the under-secretary's house upon the Vatican for the papal nuncio. Unfortunately the papal authorities allowed the latter to decay even more rapidly than has the absolutism of the Roman Church in southern Ireland, and the nuncio has been forced to move out and seek refuge elsewhere.

Chief Secretary's Lodge, however, sustained by American dollars, has securely survived, and in this house of Morley, Balfour, Birrell and other less distinguished occupants of the office we spent five days in May 1994, accompanied by the Arthur Schlesingers, as the guests of Jean Kennedy Smith, President Kennedy's sister and President Clinton's appointment as ambassador to Ireland. Some in England thought of her almost as a fully paid-up member of the IRA, but in my experience she was a very good emissary of America. Of course she was strongly green rather than orange. Who could expect a Kennedy to be otherwise, and who could believe

that, had this not been so, she could have been a good
ambassador in Dublin? Her strength was not primarily political. She used the prestige of her name and her innate charm
to run a considerable literary and artistic salon. Although her
own writing was not comparable, she emulated in the last
decade of the twentieth century the role of Lady Gregory
approximately a hundred years earlier.

From these various experiences a more or less clear
picture of the shape and superficial characteristics of Dublin
has formed in my mind, although leaving unanswered
two major historical/topographical questions. First, why was
eighteenth-century Dublin so rich, and second what occasioned the move of the fashionable part of the city from the
north to the south sides of the Liffey? That river is far
from being a mighty waterway. It is barely seventy miles from
source to mouth, and even as short a distance upstream as
where it flows down the valley to the south of Phoenix Park
it is little more than a rural stream. Yet it is nonetheless the
indisputable spine of Dublin, which is equally indisputably a
riparian city, as much so as Paris, somewhat more so than
London, for the Thames, although massive compared with
the Liffey, is buttressing rather than bisecting of the main
central area, and incomparably more so than Berlin or
Madrid, where the Spree and the Manzanares have small
impact. The Liffey with its fourteen (soon to be fifteen)
metropolitan bridges is by contrast absolutely central to
Dublin, dividing it psychologically as well as physically, with
the north and south sides having just as separate a character
as do the right and left banks in Paris.

Georgian Dublin is held to have started on the north side.
Henrietta Street, leading to the King's Inns (the Dublin
equivalent of the Inner and Middle Temples, Lincoln's Inn
and Gray's Inn), began in 1720. And two of the finest public
buildings of eighteenth-century Dublin, both by James

Gandon, the Four Courts and the Custom House, flanked
the northern bank of the river. But they both belonged to the
last twenty years of the eighteenth century, with the Four
Courts not completed until 1802. Gandon's Custom House
had been preceded by a south bank one of 1704 by Thomas
Burgh, who with his vast Royal Barracks (later renamed
Collins Barracks and now the National Museum) of 1705,
the Old Library for Trinity College and Dr Steven's Hospital, both the latter two of the 1720s, was as dominant an
architect of early-eighteenth-century Dublin as Gandon was
of the latter part of that century. And Richard Castle with his
Rotunda Lying-in Hospital on the north side and the Printing House in Trinity left an almost equal mid-century stamp.

Mountjoy Square, a splendid name even if somewhat
diluted by sharing it with a prison, was also built late in the
eighteenth century, highly fashionable at the time but now
sadly run down. So was Parnell (formerly Rutland) Square,
which began earlier in about 1760, and, needless to say,
achieved its commemorative name only much later. The
Rotunda Hospital, with its adjacent Assembly Hall, in which
Newman gave his famous lectures on *The Idea of a University*
in 1852, was also quintessentially mid-eighteenth century and
at the time of the lectures ninety-five years old. To complete
(more or less) the north Dublin Georgian pattern, the General Post Office on O'Connell Street, then Sackville Street,
the subsequent focus of so much traumatic Irish history, both
in 1916 and in 1922, was completed in 1818, remarkably
early for such a purpose, over twenty years before Sir Row-
land Hill's penny post made postal services a feature of
English life. Ireland in the eighteenth century and even some
way into the next was immensely lavish in public buildings
and public services.

On the south side there was not much lag in building,
although when, in the late 1740s, the Earl of Kildare built

Kildare House (Lord Kildare soon became Duke of Leinster and Kildare House Leinster House), from the 1920s the seat of the Irish Parliament, he was thought to have chosen an eccentric location. It was rather like Potter Palmer in 1880s Chicago single-handedly moving the fashionable centre two miles from the South Loop to the Gold Coast at the northern end of Michigan Avenue. There, in Chicago, it has remained, and it is equally true that Leinster House, between Merrion Square and St Stephen's Green, has provided the continuing nucleus for offical and fashionable Dublin. The somewhat Harvard Yard-like campus of Trinity is just to the north (although still on the south side of the river). The Government Buildings with the Taoiseach's office are adjacent; until quite recently this quadrangle oddly accommodated the engineering students of University College Dublin – that is the nationalist university as opposed to Trinity. The Ministry of Foreign Affairs is a bare half-mile away. The National Gallery, the Natural History Museum and the National Library are clustered around Leinster House, which, before the new Irish Parliament was installed there after independence, was the headquarters of the Royal Dublin Society. Grafton Street has become the smart shopping street. It connects the two Greens – St Stephen's and College, although the latter has no grass left, and debouches into the curved façade of the Bank of Ireland on the left and faces the front of Trinity on the right. Until 1800 the Bank building was the seat of the two chambers of the Irish Parliament.

Meanwhile north Dublin slid rather than plunged into mild decay. Mountjoy Square is as good an example of Dublin Georgian as anything to be found on the South Side. It was built quite late, starting in 1782, and the developer was Luke Gardiner, who most appropriately became the Viscount Mountjoy, and the present-day O'Connell Street, the main artery of north Dublin, which had started life as Drogheda

Street (with Drogheda given a more phonetic pronunciation in Ireland than its eponymous earldom in England) was rechristened Gardiner's Mall after the future viscount had turned it into a wide boulevard in the late eighteenth century. Then, for less obvious reasons, it became Sackville Street for a hundred years or so, and achieved a certain immortality through Oliver St John Gogarty writing one of those books whose title is more famous than its contents. With an Irish perversity, however, *As I Was Going Down Sackville Street* was published only in 1937, which was thirteen years after that avenue (perhaps the only one in Dublin which could be so described) had made its third change of name to O'Connell Street.

Even without the early decision of the Free State to use it to commemorate O'Connell 'the Liberator', the position of the street in Irish history was by 1924 secure, although not without its ambiguities. The General Post Office on the western side was the core of the 1916 revolt. The rebels held out for a week, until that fine building had been reduced to a smoking shell, and could not be reopened until 1929. Much of that side of the street also went up in flames. The suppression of the revolt was followed by fifteen executions of the 'best and the brightest' which ensured that the dragons' teeth sown in Anglo-Irish relations by the rejections of Gladstone's two Home Rule Bills were doubly or triply fortified. But then, six years later, and, as it were, to preserve a balance against the British being the sole villains, when Michael Collins and others had signed the Irish Treaty in London, De Valera having with deliberate detachment remained in Dublin, and civil war had broken out, the Collins forces shelled the rebels out of the Four Courts, and in a separate operation destroyed much of the other (east) side of Sackville/O'Connell Street.

Nevertheless the street had a degree of renaissance in the

calm of the late 1920s and early 1930s. When, soon after the
turn of the decade a modern semi-luxury hotel, the Gresham,
Dublin's answer to the London Dorchester, was built, it was
in O'Connell Street, which also at that time was the street of
the big shops. But the street had something of Oxford Street's
tendency to tawdriness, and as the tide of fashion moved not
only from north to south but also from big to small shops, so
O'Connell Street suffered much the same fate which has
overtaken not only Oxford Street in London but also, since
reunification, the Kurfürstendamm in Berlin.

O'Connell Street is much richer in statues than either of
those two deteriorating thoroughfares in other capitals.
Apart from O'Connell himself at the Liffey end there are at
least three other commemorations of Irish heroes: William
Smith O'Brien, leader of the mid-nineteenth-century Young
Ireland party, John Gray, proprietor of the *Freeman's Journal*, and Jim Larkin, trades union leader and organizer of
the 1913 general strike – have survived, and by no means all
statues have done so. The most notable destruction was that
of the Nelson column, also in O'Connell Street, as late as
1966. Equestrian statues (mostly of British monarchs and
generals) have also suffered heavily, which is half paradoxical
for modern Ireland remains devoted to the horse and its
attached ceremonies. The Dublin Horse Show at the beginning of August is the peak of the social season. The race-
courses at Leopardstown, the Curragh, Fairyhouse and
Punchestown are relatively more important in Irish life than
are Epsom, Ascot and Newmarket in English life. And it is
impossible to imagine an anti-hunting bill getting anywhere
in the Dáil.

Yet all the equestrian statues have gone. George I was
sold and may have found safe refuge in England. George II
was blown up in 1937; Field Marshal Gough in Phoenix Park
was also shattered in 1957. The Wellington Pillar (not

equestrian, of course) in Phoenix Park has survived, but the duke, although not a great sympathizer with Irish nationalist aspirations, was indisputably born in Ireland, but whether in Upper Merrion Street, the heart of Dublin's south side, or in County Meath, is curiously a matter of continuing dispute. An ill-favoured statue of Queen Victoria was removed from the front of Leinster House in 1947 and languished for thirty-five years in various storehouses or dumps until, in 1982, a public site for it was somewhat surprisingly found in Sydney, New South Wales. Today the sole royal survivor in Dublin is Prince Albert, an attractive statue and monument to whom is on the lawn at the rear (or members' entrance) of Leinster House, which location seems to have given it adequate protection from the attentions of the IRA.

Following the pattern of what is now O'Connell Street, Dublin has been semi-addicted to changing street names, almost as much so as Paris. The port of departure for England has become Dun Laoghaire instead of Kingstown (although it had only been Kingstown since the visit of George IV, having previously been somewhat confusingly known as Dunleary), just as the port of Cork has become Cobh instead of Queenstown. Then in 1966, on the fiftieth anniversary of the Easter Rising, there was a great re-naming of railway stations. Westland Row became (Padraig) Pearse Station and Amiens Street became (James) Connolly Station. Equally the terminus for the west of Ireland, which has an exceptionally fine station façade, has become Heuston rather than Kingsbridge (named after Seán Heuston, one of the youngest of the 'martyrs' of 1916). And the Dublin military airfield, from which I once took off, has been christened Roger Casement.

The unanswered question remains that of Dublin's plunge from the eighteenth-century wealth to relative poverty in the nineteenth century and for three-quarters of the twentieth century. The population of Ireland in the early nineteenth century bore a ratio to that of England totally different from the proportions of today. There was never exactly a time when they were both equal at 8 million, but it was narrowly missed. England at the time of the American War of Independence was no more than that figure, which Ireland reached shortly before the Great Famine of 1845–7. But in 1800 it was about 6 million in Ireland to 9 million in England, an incomparably different proportion to that of the 1960s, when England without either Scotland or Wales was 50 million and the Ireland of the Republic under 3 million. In an agricultural country of limited size and mostly poor land a large rural population could be the key to the wealth of the capital city only on the basis of landowners taking an excessive tribute from their land – as was indeed the case in eighteenth- and nineteenth-century Ireland.

Then there is the view that the Irish Parliament, with its two chambers and its central position on College Green, made Dublin a sophisticated capital with a need for squares and terraces of spacious town houses. It is certainly true that it encouraged the Anglo-Irish aristocracy to build and maintain residences in Dublin. Indeed Peter Somerville-Large in the chapter of his *Dublin* dealing with the period from the Union to the Famine proclaims that the eighty-two peers of the Irish upper house were reputed to have spent between them a total of £624,000 a year in Dublin. There is room for puzzlement as to the method by which it could have been so precisely calculated, but even if approximately true it amounted to the staggeringly lush sum of £7,800 per peer (at least £½ million a head at present-day values), even apart from what they spent on their visits to their estates, let alone, occasionally, to Florence, Rome or Naples. When the peers' patronage was transferred to London the shopkeepers were reported to have become surly, rents dropped by 30 per cent, the profits of the fashionable Rotunda lecture theatre declined by 80 per cent, many of the best houses were converted to public use – Leinster House sold to the Royal Dublin Society, which does not sound too bad a fate, but Moira House went to the Mendicity Institute. That, accompanied by the post-Napoleonic Wars depression which affected the whole of the British Isles, sounds a rational explanation of the decline of Dublin prosperity even before the short-term suffering and long-term reduction of the population by emigration which were the results of the 1845–7 Famine.

There still remains the minor mystery of why the Irish Act of Union of 1800 should have had such a contrasting effect upon Dublin from that which the Act of Union between Scotland and England in 1707 had upon the Scottish capital, which was also then deprived of its parliament. In Edinburgh the new-found wealth, mainly of judges and advocates, had a wholly stimulating effect. They became rich enough to create the urbanity of the New Town. Whatever the exact economic and sociological cause, however, it remains an indisputable fact that the eighteenth century was for Dublin as great a period of building as the nineteenth century (at any rate from about 1830) and the first half of the twentieth century were relatively barren ones.

The end of the twentieth century exhibited a reversion to eighteenth-century exuberance and prosperity, although without, some might be tempted to complain, eighteenth-century taste. Can Dublin, and perhaps even more the surrounding countryside with its uncontrolled spattering of bungaloid growth, sustain its small capital city charm and special quality as the tide of European prosperity and global uniformity sweeps in? No doubt it will take a large chunk of the twenty-first century to resolve that, but the traditionalists can perhaps console themselves with the thought that, even when the elegant glories of the eighteenth century were being created, there were no doubt many who thought that those extravagant peers were being as brash in their taste as they were *nouveaux riches.*

GLASGOW

I never saw Glasgow until I was thirty-eight years old. I then went there, accompanied by William Rodgers, long subsequently my successor as leader of the Liberal Democrat peers, to address a Fabian dinner. In my childhood the nearest that I ever got to 'the second city of the Empire', as it still proclaimed itself, was to gaze at a train in Pontypool Road Station which was on its way there from Bristol and Plymouth. Pontypool Road was then a major junction where trains from the South-West to Manchester and Liverpool as well as to the West of Scotland crossed over with those from Cardiff to Birmingham, sometimes exchanging coaches. Three miles from my home it was a mecca for me at the age of ten or twelve. The train for Glasgow, I remember vividly, had two engines, which made me feel that it must be both a distant and an important destination.

Although important, it also carried for me a slightly sinister connotation. At the end of the 1920s a daughter of some close friends of my parents married a Glaswegian and went off to live in a tenement there. (Most people in Glasgow then lived in four- or occasionally five-storey tenements, as many still do, and some of these apartments can be quite grand, the rough equivalent of a London mansion flat around 1900.) To my childhood imagination, however, that poor girl seemed to be going off to a fate worse than death. She might as well have been going to a Calcutta slum or sold into slavery in Buenos Aires.

In the quarter-century after my first Fabian visit I paid about another ten fairly brief visits to Glasgow. Some but not all were political. On one of them the then Secretary of State for Scotland (Willie Ross) took me, as Chancellor of the Exchequer, to see some of the worst slum tenements. He made his point only too forcefully. I released enough money to knock most of them down and the terrible twenty-storey tower blocks which came in their place were even worse. The old tenements ought to have been rehabilitated, not destroyed. On another occasion the ancient University of Glasgow (founded in 1451, the second oldest in Scotland and the fourth oldest in the United Kingdom) very kindly gave me an honorary degree. And on a third well-remembered occasion I opened a large new printing works on the outskirts for my then publisher, William Collins and Sons, which used a Glasgow business of printing bibles and dictionaries as a solid foundation for becoming a fashionable general London publisher, and which did not then regard Rupert Murdoch as even a remote threat.

Despite these various forays Glasgow was a strange (and in some ways still a slightly sinister) city to me when, in early 1982, I conceived the extraordinry idea of becoming one of its members of Parliament. The presumption was increased by the fact that the Hillhead division on which I set my eye was the most interesting segment, containing (after an enlargement of 1983) at least two-thirds of the famous cultural and educational institutions of a city which was notable for its quality in both these aspects. It was also the only one of the then eleven Glasgow constituencies from which as a candidate of the new and centrist SDP–Liberal Alliance I could possibly have hoped to be elected. The story of the Hillhead campaign I have told elsewhere, and I propose no repetition except insofar as it is relevant to the impact which Glasgow as a metropolis made upon me.

At first apprehension dominated. As I later wrote:

> ... I was nervous of Glasgow, even more as a human organism than as a psephological prospect. On the weekend after I had been adopted we stayed in Scotland but retreated to a country hotel, Gleddoch House, high above the Clyde estuary opposite Dumbarton. On the Sunday morning I went for a walk on the adjacent golf-course, which commanded a fifteen-mile-distant view of the city, with its shipyard cranes, its Victorian spires and turrets, and its 1960s high-rise flats all visible. It had the air of a great city, but also of a place of infinite complication and some menace. Its towers looked as mysterious to me as the minarets of Constantinople must have done to the Russian investing forces in 1878. What insanity has seized me, I thought, to take on this assignment?

Yet over the new few months, aided no doubt by the fact that, after a bumpy passage, I won the bye-election, the sense of menace, although not the elusive romanticism which went with it, almost totally receded. Glasgow, and in particular its West End, which was effectively Hillhead, quickly came to occupy in my affections a qualitatively different place from that which my two previous constituencies, one in London and one in Birmingham, generously though they had both treated me, had occupied. It was a sort of senile love affair, but I experienced no reaction of feeling when, after one successful bye-election and one successful general election, I was rejected by the constituency in 1987, the only occasion over a span of fifteen parliamentary elections when I lost what I had previously held, although on two others I failed to gain what I was seeking. This inevitably meant that I subsequently saw less of Glasgow than I had done over the previous five and a half years. But that was a deprivation rather than a cause of resentment. The miracle was that as an intruder on a new and shaky political base they had ever elected me, let alone twice.

What however I do not find difficult to explain is the reason for the infatuation. Glasgow, like Naples at the other end of Europe, has great problems: a declining economic purpose and consequently heavy social deprivation; a somewhat worn-out infrastructure; and a population a high proportion of which is hardened to the misfortunes of life and perhaps consequently, through its eating and drinking habits, subject to above-average ill-health and below-average length of life. But it also has some almost indestructible advantages. First the site, which is God-given in both the literal and figurative senses of the phrase, and which helps to make it an exceptionally vivid place visually, and one to which its strong painting tradition is peculiarly appropriate. The city itself is finely placed with the hills rising on either side of the Clyde in just the right places. Beyond that the estuary of the river, with its associated inlets, islands and mountains, constitutes the most dramatic piece of seascape at the gates of a major city to be found anywhere in the world, with the possible exception of Vancouver Sound. There are, I believe, equally memorable natural formations among the fjords of Norway, or on the western coast of Greenland, or on the shores of Antarctica. But they are all wastelands so far as human population is concerned.

Glasgow's industry also had a peculiar vividness, which is retained by such of that industry as remains. The cranes of Govan, still to be seen on the drive in from the airport, proclaim that this is Glasgow as emphatically as the Eiffel Tower identifies Paris, or the Statue of Liberty does New York, or the bridge and the Opera House do Sydney.

There is also a powerful base of educational strength in Glasgow. By the measurements of the census the Hillhead constituency within its old (1982) boundaries was indisputably the most highly educated in Scotland, and arguably in the whole of the United Kingdom – the argument lying in whether Scottish Higher Grades can be equated with English A-levels. And Glasgow as a whole is rich in academic institutions of note. It is a remarkable double that just over a century after the narrow strips of flat land along the banks of the Clyde became the greatest shipbuilding and metal-working focus in the world, the hills behind the riverside on the north side should more recently have become one of Britain's most concentrated educational areas. There are three universities: the five-and-a-half-centuries-old eagle of Glasgow perched on its Gilmorehill eyrie (to which mid-Victorian gothic splendour it moved in 1870); the enthusiastic and in several fields remarkably successful young pouter pigeon of Strathclyde, barely a couple of miles to the east and hatched in the early 1960s out of a College of Advanced Technology; and the still more recently emergent (1993) chick of Glasgow Caledonian University, which at least balances its youth by the splendour of its academic dress, so that, when seven universities came together at Buckingham Palace in 1996 to honour Nelson Mandela, Galsgow Caledonian outshone all the rest.

In addition the same strip of ground contains three teaching hospitals; three units of the Medical Research Council; the Jordanhill College of Education, the largest such establishment in Scotland; a number of specialized institutions of which Charles Rennie Mackintosh's Glasgow School of Art is the most famous; and four or five high schools or academies of note, including the only day school in the United Kingdom to have produced more than one Prime Minister – Campbell-Bannerman and Bonar Law were both products of Glasgow High School. It is, however, perhaps unfair by virtue of this coincidence to give the High School priority over Glasgow Academy, which in the year 2000 was responsible for the wider spread of the founder figure of the devolved Scottish Parliament, of the Director of the (London) National Gallery, the permanent under-secretary of the Foreign Office, the last intendant of the Covent Garden Opera House to have escaped before the financial deluge, and a recent past president of the Liberal Democratic party. By any standards the educational concentration is formidable.

The products of these various institutions formed the core of the bourgeoisie of the West End of Glasgow, and therefore of my old constituency of Hillhead. It was for the most part a professional rather than a business middle class, which indeed was the reason that I was able to win the constituency in 1982. A business community of equivalent income and status would have been less likely at that stage to flake away from their traditional Conservative allegiance. Fortunately for me however the business classes, as is their wont, preferred the suburban and detached pastures of Bearsden and Milngavie to the older and often terraced urbanity of the West End. Of course this was subject to a good number of exceptions both ways, as is the equally sweeping but nonetheless essentially true statement that the typical West End professional man (or, increasingly, woman) was educated at one of the schools mentioned above and at Glasgow University. This was particularly so with the almost unbelievably high number of 1,300 doctors of medicine – 3 per cent of the total electorate – who were on the electoral rolls of the old Hillhead constituency.

This might have been expected to produce an inward-looking community. In fact almost the opposite is true. Glasgow University has had an excessively local undergraduate catchment area, although the proportion from Clydeside is now somewhat down, but this has never been the case with either the graduate students or the faculty. Nonetheless it makes a sharp contrast with Edinburgh University, which is almost too much the other way. 'There are more Etonians at Edinburgh than there are at Oxford' has become a catch-phrase which is valid about every other year. But at Glasgow, although the input may be too local for an ideal university community, the output is certainly not narrow-minded. It leaves the typical member of the Glasgow professional class with a distinct but wholly comprehensible (to Sassenach ears) Scottish accent. Indeed, like an educated New England accent, it is rather easier to understand (certainly for foreigners) than is so-called 'standard' southern English, which in a slightly setting-apart way is spoken by almost all members of the Scottish landowning classes.

This Scottish professional accent is in sharp contrast with riparian Clydeside, prevalent in my constituency from Scotstoun through Whiteinch, Partick and Anderston to the Broomielaw, which, together perhaps with 'Geordie', consti-tutes one of the most impenetrable dialects in the British Isles. I resolved, when I presumptuously set out to become the MP of many of those who spoke in this way, that the least I could do was to make sure that, at an advice bureau or in other encounters, I would never have to ask for more than one repetition in order to take in what was being said to me. This aim I nearly always achieved, although I recollect at least one humiliating exception. It was during the bye-election campaign and on a Saturday afternoon in Dumbar-ton Road, when and where an additional touch of inebriated opaqueness was neither unexpected nor objectionable. A man approached me and muttered some words which might have been (but were not) in Gaelic. A reprise appeared to yield 'Will you promise to keep the pork out?' I thought he must have been worried by some earlier form of BSE and weakly replied, 'Yes, if it is diseased.' He looked both mystified and discontented, which was not surprising for it ultimately emerged that what he had actually said (it being a few months before John Paul II's pontifical descent on Bellahouston Park), and in my experience a rare example of religious intolerance even in a city split by Rangers/Celtic rivalry, was 'Will you promise to keep the Pope out?'

The accent of the hill, as opposed to that of the river, was quite different. Its fault, if it had one, was that of 'refainement' rather than of any lack of clarity. 'Kelvinside' was the Glasgow equivalent of Edinburgh's 'Morningside' and the two, despite the very different styles of the two major Scottish cities, had much in common, although a good ear, even if less specialized than that of Shaw's Professor Higgins, can easily tell that Glasgow was not the home of Miss Jean Brodie. 'Sex is what coal comes in' is the standard and self-mocking joke about 'Kelvinside', and 'I met Elestair [Alaster] in the perk [park]' is said to be the phrase which best brings out the carefully articulated precision.

This and adjacent forms of speech do not however go with any narrow prissiness. Glasgow is sometimes acclaimed for its warmth, which is real, but is nonetheless a subject on which it is possible to talk a good deal of sententious nonsense. Glasgow people are capable of being very friendly, and they are almost invariably polite, but they are also capable, as are all people of discrimination, of being appropriately chilling when they think it is deserved. The salient characteristic which most struck me when I suddenly came to know well the West End of Glasgow was not so much the warmth as the quiet self-confidence. It was not a complacent or narrow or inward-looking self-confidence. It was not, happily for me, based on a desire to keep out strangers. What it was based on was consciousness of the contribution which their strip of river and hill had made to the advancement of civilization throughout and beyond Britain, and on a feeling that while it was desirable from time to time to go away from Glasgow, even from its best part, it was as good a place to live as anywhere in the world. This was not based on narrow inwardness, still less on compensating for any defensive sense of inferiority, but, as true self-confidence always is, of a curiosity about outside things accompanied by a contentment within one's own skin.

This self-confidence contributes to the reasons why I firmly put Glasgow among the cities of world class (even after having ceased for a decade and a half to be tempted to flatter for votes) and far higher in that hierarchy than its never huge and recently considerably shrinking population alone would entitle it to be. I would do so also upon grounds of site, metropolitan atmosphere, industrial history, visual impact, educational and cultural resources, and the splendid mixture of early- and late-Victorian exuberance in its architecture. The early Victorian is mainly exhibited in quiet residential terraces, the late Victorian in public buildings: the City Chambers (1882–90), the Kelvingrove Gallery (1899–1901) and the London and North Western Railway (as it then was) Central Station Hotel (1882–4).

In spite of the depredations of that terrible decade of the 1960s, Glasgow remains the finest Victorian city in the world. (I am more than willing to take responsibility, deserved or undeserved, for the 'permissive' legislation of those years but not for this careless destructiveness or for the lowering banality of what was mostly put in its place.) There were heavy losses then, not least of hotels, from the late-gothic magnificence of the St Enoch, fully matching that of St Pancras at the other end of the same railway line, to the more restrained curve of the Grand Hotel, which made a fine carrefour of Glasgow's Charing Cross but which fell victim

to the inner-city motorway, vastly improving access to the
airport but leaving, among other fruits of devastation, the
green dome and grand façade of the Mitchell Library
(1906–11) looking like an east-coast cliff-top hotel which
might soon fall into the sea – or in the Mitchell case on to
the motorway. Nonetheless the extent of what has survived
(as with eighteenth-century Dublin, so in nineteenth-century
Glasgow it is at once possible to be horrified by how much
goes and then, twenty years later, to be agreeably surprised
by how much remains) means that Glasgow's only possible
rival as a Victorian repository is Liverpool.

Glasgow and Liverpool have much in common: their
westward-facing geography, the sectarian and potentially
explosive nature of their populations, the historic direction
and nature of their trade and the eminence of their pre-1914
positions. Glasgow's sobriquet as 'the second city of the
Empire' was almost balanced by the catchphrase 'Liverpool
gentlemen and Manchester men'. In Liverpool the splendour
of the Victorian age is almost all in the public buildings,
from Lime Street Station to the Walker Art Gallery and
St George's Hall, now deprived of its law courts, whereas
in Glasgow there is much more surviving domestic architecture. And in Liverpool the trough and the decay to which
it succumbed in the third quarter of the twentieth century
far exceeded anything to which Glasgow, even before the
renaissance of the early 1980s, with its effective slogan of
'Glasgow's miles better', was subject.

There are quite a lot of other cities in which, like some
shaft of Proustian memory, as when the Marcel of À la
recherche dunks the madeleine and is suddenly set off both on
the evocation of his childhood and on the greatest novel of
the twentieth century, I suddenly catch a flavour of Glasgow.
Among them are New York and Chicago, and, somewhat
more tenuously, Barcelona, Boston, Lisbon and Naples. I

was once, even more clutching at moonbeams, reminded of Glasgow when I stood on the Pont des Invalides in a brilliant winter sunset. Never previously had I thought that Paris had much to do with Glasgow, except perhaps for the Scottish Colourists, and they, unusually for schools of painting, owe at least as much to the east as to the west of Scotland, but then suddenly I thought that the line of the Seine, while utterly dissimlar to that of the Thames, did have a flicker of resemblance to that of the Clyde. The Pont des Arts aroused a thought of the Suspension Bridge, the Institut de France was a grander version of the Custom House and looking in the other direction the slopes above the Palais de Chaillot rose up in a passable imitation of the Glasgow West End.

There are however two cities which never remind me of Glasgow, and they, with singular appropriateness in their different ways, are London and Edinburgh. London is a much less European city than Glasgow. (In this or any other comparison it has to be borne in mind that London is nearly ten times the size of Glasgow.) London is an essentially suburban city. As soon as they can, away from the centre, houses with small gardens take over. Glasgow on the other hand maintains a big-city air quite a long way from the centre. Until 1914 indeed, when the city was at the peak of both its population and its industrial prosperity, this metro-politan quality persisted right up to the edges. There was an abrupt transition from the not very smiling agricultural fields of Lanarkshire and Renfrewshire to the beginning of the strictly non-suburban tenement blocks. Charles McKean, the secretary of the Royal Incorporation of Architects in Scotland, put it memorably in an essay in a 1993 book entitled *Glasgow: The Forming of the City* and published, ironically, by the Edinburgh University Press: 'In 1914, the city had stopped where the tenement-builders had stopped. Huge, four-storey gables, fireplaces seemingly glued to the wall forty feet up, abutted fields, providing a dramatically sudden contrast between town and country.' The inter-war period, he lamented, had produced a fraying of this sharp edge. A bungaloid fringe grew up, with the bungalows in that curious tricycle shape, with a single dormer window above the ground floor, which is a Scottish characteristic. 'The dramatic entrance into the Second City of the Empire through tunnels of tenements' was lost.

The tenemented city suffered much worse damage in the late 1960s and early 1970s. In the 1920s and 1930s it was merely made fuzzy at the edges. In the 1960s a great part of the core, particularly in the working-class areas of the Gorbals and Hutchesontown on the South Side and of Townhead just to the north of the city centre, was obliterated. The replacements were the great concrete tower blocks of Easterhouse, Castlemilk, Pollok and Drumchapel, each developments of 25,000 to 30,000 inhabitants, nominally much better than the damp and sometimes rat-infested lower floors of the inner-city tenements, but in fact lacking in almost every social amenity except a wide view, and distant alike from workplace and from both the bright lights of the city centre and the warm glow of neighbourhood pubs and shops. In the old Gorbals the Citizens Theatre survived, and continued to put on the most sophisticated productions, but had to be approached across acres of derelict wasteland.

The salient fact however is how central the tenement, whether being built or destroyed or partially surviving, has been to the architectural and social history of Glasgow over the past 140 years. Glasgow, like Edinburgh in this respect, was historically a high-built city. Much of its Merchant City of the late eighteenth century was on four storeys, but the characteristic Glasgow tenement, which has given the city so much of its late-nineteenth- and twentieth-century air, came with the great explosions of population and industry from about 1860.

There were two major and very sharply delineated waves of building from 1869 to 1877 and from 1893 to 1904. In the former period the stone used was local and cream-coloured. By the latter period the local quarries had run out and the lighter-coloured stone was replaced by imported red sandstone from Dumfriesshire and Ayrshire, which by 1900 became the dominant shade of the city. The tenements created in the half-century to 1914 broadly absorbed, with a neat symmetry, the increase of half a million in the city's population during this period. The result of this formidable wave of construction was to give the city a singular uniformity of appearance. This was the more remarkable because the building was almost all done by private enterprise and often financed by petty parcels of investment, sometimes by local shopkeepers. (The great juggernaut of Glasgow public housing, which was to create over 50,000 separate dwellings between the two wars, did not begin until the 1920s.) Yet this combination of almost speculative building and devolved financing produced no incongruity of styles. No individual block sought to call itself Mon Repos, or to paint itself a new colour, or to graft on an unsuitable porch. Even the firm leasehold hand of the Grosvenor estate in Belgravia and Mayfair would surely have been satisfied with the unity which was spontaneously achieved.

It was however only an external and architectural unity for, within the broadly common four-storey, often bay-windowed, double-fronted group of flats ('houses' in Scotland, for there the term embraces a flat as much as a free-standing dwelling) grouped around a single entrance doorway and staircase, there were (and are) vast differences in both the size and the quality of the apartments. In the poorer parts of the city they were only one- or two-roomed. But in some other areas, notably but by no means exclusively the big West End middle-class tenement development at Hyndland in the late 1890s, they were often six- or seven-roomed, with drawing rooms, separate dining rooms, and three or four bedrooms, with their high respectability testified to by the approach being through 'whally closes' (elaborately tiled even if not softly carpeted entrance halls).

The net result of this sandstone (whether cream or red) late-Victorian revolution was to leave what was then the outer ring and is now the middle ring of Glasgow much more like the Naples of the Vomero and Posillipo or the Barcelona of the Diagonal area than it is like Brondesbury Park or West Hampstead or any other London suburb. These tenement areas are firmly urban (and quite urbane) rather than suburban or mock-rural, and they are a living testament to Glasgow's ability to leap over both England and the Channel into the heart of Europe.

This continental configuration, however, does not separate it from Edinburgh. Some considerable part of that city is also tenemented. Indeed there was (fairly reliably) said to be a Royal Mile building which about 200 years ago was the tallest in Europe, and therefore maybe in the world. Furthermore 'Auld Reekie' is more obviously the northern terminal of the old alliance with France than is Glasgow. There is nonetheless a vast difference both of appearance and of feel between Edinburgh and Glasgow. It is difficult to think of any other pair of cities in the world, certainly not equally geographically close – only forty-five miles from centre to centre – more set up to be natural rivals. They have approximately equal but different fame. They now have a not very different population size, the latest figures being Glasgow 616,000 and Edinburgh 448,000. But this near equality has been brought about by the movement of two blades of a scissors. Edinburgh as a city of government has got bigger, and Glasgow as a city of industry has shrunk, although remaining the centre of a loose Clydeside conurbation of approximately 2½ million. Three-quarters of a century ago the discrepancy was much greater. An excellent encyclopaedia (Harmsworth's) published in the early 1920s, to the study of which I devoted many childhood hours, gave with complete confidence the exact population of every major city down to the last digit. Glasgow then scored 1,111,428 compared with Edinburgh's 320,318. What is certainly the case however is that Glasgow's early-twentieth-century preponderance of size, uncontradicted even if not fully buttressed by the closer present size relationship, meant that, whether or not it was the 'second city of the Empire', it could not be treated as simply the second city of Scotland. It was rather a New York to America's Washington, or at the very least a Milan to Italy's Rome, a rival capital, more dominant as a commercial, press and communications centre, rather than an unchallenging second-in-command like Birmingham in England or Lyon in France.

Within this near equality there exist a lot of differences, some more obvious than others. The short forty-five-mile connecting link passes through a sharp climatic divide. Glasgow has nearly twice the rainfall of Edinburgh, and an altogether softer, west-windy, more gulfstream-influenced climate. Its average winter temperatures are significantly higher not merely than those of Edinburgh but than those of London too. Glasgow is also a much more Irish and therefore a more Roman Catholic city. Traditionally it was also more Jewish. Glasgow's pre-war Jewish community, with Leeds and Manchester the possible rivals, was the largest outside London. This community has become somewhat attenuated recently, with many of its members, of a range of type and talent varying from Isaac Wolfson to Jeremy Isaacs, being drawn south by success. It is also increasingly concentrated in the south-western suburb of Newton Mearns, although until the 1980s it maintained a small West End outpost in the 1938 St John's Wood-like apartment block of Kelvin Court, at the end of Great Western Road. Newton Mearns itself looks more like an affluent Home Counties suburb than anything else in Glasgow.

There is also a sharp difference in Glasgow and Edinburgh senses of humour. Glasgow's is more downbeat and irreverent. Balloon-pricking one-liners, deflating both the recipient and the speaker, and thereby embracing them both in the common frailty of humanity, is a frequent note. It has much in common with the metropolitan quickness of both Berlin and New York. Edinburgh favours a more stately irony. I was recently assured by a very good speaker who had held positions of high public service eminence in both, that it was a great mistake to use the same jokes in the two cities.

Architecturally they are both indisputably interesting, even distinguished. I must reluctantly admit, even as a late-coming Glaswegian and therefore possessing all the partisan fervour of a convert, that Edinburgh is the more conventionally handsome of the two. I used to think it was a sort of Cary Grant handsomeness, a made-to-measure beauty without idiosyncrasy, and as I once described it, playing for easy cheers and abundantly receiving them from a Glasgow audience, as having all the splendid but unanimated perfection of a dead salmon laid out upon a slab. 'Faultily faultless, icily regular, splendidly null', the lines from Tennyson's *Maud* rise to mind. Glasgow could never be accused of being unanimated. It has more vitality, as well as more squalor, although Edinburgh has its own pockets of the latter. Glasgow is essentially a Victorian city, stemming from the fact that this was the period when it rose fastest to eminence, whereas

Edinburgh did so in the eighteenth century, when, following the Act of Union, the fat fees of advocates and the fine salaries of judges found their way into the calm splendour of the New Town.

Glasgow's culture is the more indigenous. Edinburgh has of course great cultural assets, the Festival, the National Gallery of Scotland, the Portrait Gallery and the copyright library. But they come from outside or by virtue of its capital status rather than arising out of the life and work of the inhabitants of the city itself. Scottish Opera and the Scottish National Orchestra are both naturally based in Glasgow, and there is no school of painting specifically associated with Edinburgh in the way that two generations of 'Glasgow boys' have achieved world fame while sticking very firmly to a collective sense of origin. (The Scottish Colourists, although, as has been stated, not belonging to Glasgow, do not do so to Edinburgh either; the fine new Fergusson gallery – in a water tower – is appropriately in Perth.)

Glasgow's public galleries are also remarkably rich for a non-capital city and, without the benefit of a *National* Gallery or a *National* Portrait Gallery, fully match those of Edinburgh. The Burrell Collection erupted on to the Glasgow scene with great *réclame* in 1983. It is a striking building, Danish-designed, and with fine use of vistas into woodland which its Pollok Park location, five miles or so from the city centre, makes possible. Even that was stretching the terms of Sir William Burrell's bequest, for when he died in 1944, and knowing the condition to which he and his fellow industrialists had reduced the air of his native city, he stipulated that the collection should be protected from pollution by being housed at least sixteen miles from the centre. By the 1970s, when the project was belatedly put in train, it was rightly judged that the effects of the Clean Air Act justified a loose interpretation of this provision.

The result was one of the best modern galleries on a greenfield site in the world, which greatly contributed to the cultural and touristic renaissance of Glasgow in the early 1980s. For me its only known rival in this category is the Krøller-Mueller Gallery in the middle of Holland, but I have never seen the Getty at Bel-Air. The new Guggenheim at Bilbao, more rehabilitating of a dull area than green-field, is on a different scale of architectural adventurousness. The contents, so far at any rate, do not remotely live up to the building. At the Burrell, on the other hand, they do so, but only narrowly. The catalogue opens by saying that 'Sir William Burrell was not just a magpie'. This is a fine example of 'qui s'excuse s'accuse'. He was obviously a very shrewd buyer, as well as ultimately a great benefactor to his city. His collection embraces almost everything from Graeco-Roman objects through medieval arches, Renaissance furniture and sixteenth- and seventeenth-century tapestries to four cen-turies of painting. But it does lack personal sinews of taste, as opposed to a good eye for a bargain. The Frick in New York is a much more individual example of an intimate collec-tion. But Glasgow is lucky, although deservedly so, to have the Burrell.

It is however by no means the only similar asset. Even within Pollok Park itself there is the considerable Pollok House collection, well hung and beautifully encased in what might just have been a William Adam-inspired house but probably was not. On the north bank of the Clyde there is the Hunterian Gallery with its unparalleled Whistler collec-tion within the purlieus of Glasgow University, as well as the grand exuberance of the main city museum and gallery, commonly called the Kelvingrove, which has already been mentioned as one of the manifestations of Glasgow's turn-of-the-century (nineteenth/twentieth) architectural flowering. Its contents are very mixed, although in a different and somehow more sympathetic way than in the Burrell. There are natural-history halls on the ground floor, replete with stuffed and skeletal mammals. There is a magnificent Scottish Colourist corner and there is a good but not spectacular spread of the main European schools, although somewhat thinner since those which belonged to the Burrell bequest were transported across the Clyde in 1983.

It is however the whole design and atmosphere rather than the individual contents which make the Kelvingrove an unusually memorable and exhilarating gallery. I remember John Strachey, a sophisticated socialist intellectual and a somewhat improbable (and unenthusiastic) MP for Dundee from 1945 to 1963 (when he died), telling me that there were really only two pleasures which he got out of his infrequent Scottish expeditions. The first was sinking into his seat as the train from Dundee south gathered speed over the Tay Bridge after a completed constituency visit; and the second was occasionally stopping in Glasgow and visiting the Kelvingrove Gallery. I did not at all share Strachey's repugnance for Scottish constituencies, although maybe I would have had it been Dundee not Hillhead, but I became at one with him on the attractions of the Kelvingrove. As I wrote fairly soon after having severed my parliamentary link with Glasgow: 'If I had to choose a single most evocative vignette it would be of a clear late autumn or winter afternoon in the Kelvingrove Gallery with the organ playing, and then as one came out, the sharp light fading over the silhouettes of Gilmorehill and the other hillocks of the West End.' This was a paradoxical time and season to choose, for in November, December and January the light faded remarkably early. But the memory is nonetheless valid. It was in those 3 o'clock weekend twilights that the special metropolitan quality of the Glasgow West End most vividly expressed itself to me.

An utterly contrasting scene associated with Glasgow's latest public gallery made a fresh imprint on my mind just over ten years later. Revisiting Glasgow after a gap I discovered that the old Royal Exchange building, on the western edge of the Merchant City, after a few decades as the home of Stirling Library, had been converted into a gallery of modern art. Originally built as a private mansion in 1778 it had been remodelled and enlarged for use as the Royal Exchange at the end of the 1820s and gained a particularly fine hall, with a copper barrelled ceiling and two lines of fluted Corinthian columns. It was a newsroom in the Library days, and now makes a magnificent core for exhibiting the contents of the new gallery. About these contents there may be more room for doubt. Some seemed more designed to shock than to illuminate, but they were at least attracting an adequate number of visitors on a brilliantly sunlit May Saturday morning. The Glasgow City Council's firm policy of free admission encourages casual visiting, and that building has particularly easy access from its surrounding piazza which contains no fewer than three open-air cafés, all on that early-summer morning with crowded terraces. It is sad that, responding to them so enthusiastically when they occur, Glasgow does not have more rain- and cloud-free days.

Discovering Glasgow was for me a major 1980s experience. There was undoubtedly something of an infatuation about it. I became adept at diverting conversations towards the city with others whose interest was less concentrated upon Glasgow than was my own and who must have been surprised and sometimes bored. Much though I missed Glasgow when the close contact was severed in 1987, no reaction set in. I felt much more deprived by ceasing to be member for Hillhead than by ceasing to be a member of the House of Commons. I continue to regard Glasgow as one of the outstanding non-capital cities of the world, almost comparable with Chicago or Barcelona, although having to achieve the result on a far narrower basis of both population and wealth.

BARCELONA

BARCELONA RIVALS CHICAGO as the greatest provincial city in the world. But to where and to what is it provincial? To Madrid or to Paris? The first alternative would have aroused total derision (in Barcelona at any rate) during most of the two centuries before the death of Franco in 1975. It would have been like asking New York whether it thought it was provincial in relation to Washington. Madrid has only very recently become a city of world class.

Nor has the Paris link been without its ambiguities. The old kingdom of Aragon, which embraced Barcelona, stretched across the Pyrenees and embraced Roussillon (Perpignan, Narbonne, even extending to Nîmes) on the French side. But Roussillon was a long way short of Paris, and in any event that dominion ended in the seventeenth century. When Barcelona entered its great period of bourgeois prosperity and artistic innovation at the end of the nineteenth century, it looked to Paris in everything except the one art for which it was itself most notable: architecture. Of its trio of memorable architects, Antoni Gaudí (1852–1926), Domènech i Montaner (1849–1919) and Puig i Cadafalch (1867–1957), the latter two were intermittently Catalan politicians as well as designers of buildings, and the third, Gaudí, eventually wrapped himself in a reactionary religiosity. Many of their creations teetered on the brink of vulgarity, but were saved by exceptional élan and ingenuity. They had affinities with Horta in Brussels, with Charles Rennie Mackintosh in Glasgow, with Secessionism in Vienna and with *Jugendstil* in Germany, but not with much in Paris, although the design of those fan-shaped Métro entrances was not far away from Catalan *modernisme*. But in everything else – painting, literature, poetry, music more doubtfully, for after a slow start there Wagner had become the epitome of the Barcelona mode – the Catalan city looked culturally to Paris. It was said to take more easily to the French language than to Castilian. Nevertheless, when we went there with a French friend in 1996, she found the taxi-drivers and the waiters depressingly non-francophone. After a few days in Barcelona she resignedly said that she thought Brussels was now the only city in Europe (outside France) where French was more acceptable than English. Perhaps if we had penetrated into the professional circles of Barcelona, francophonie would have been found still alive.

Barcelona is at once a major Mediterranean port, and as such semi-open to the world, traditionally the richest and most advanced city in Spain, but also the capital of an autonomous region, with its own language and some regressive – inward- and backward-looking – features. It prompts an interesting reflection on what Cardiff at the peak of the coal trade (although Barcelona's essential nineteenth-century industry was textiles not coal) might have been like had it been equally big and rich as London and at the same time predominantly Welsh-speaking – which Cardiff never was. Welsh and English also have the advantage of being such utterly different languages that even the most ignorant when looking at a bilingual notice, or being addressed in one language or the other, cannot have a second's doubt which is which. Catalan and Spanish, on the other hand, while indisputably distinct, are nonetheless both so Latin-based that to the hispanically handicapped it is by no means instantly obvious which is which. The old city or Gothic Quarter is, for instance, Bario Gótico in Spanish and Barri Gòtic in Catalan. Barcelona is in consequence a confusing city in which to try to improve one's Spanish or to acquire Catalan.

The Catalans are, however, like the Welsh in the sense that they have a folklore almost totally detached from their recent pattern of life. In the Catalan case it is based upon the valour of the old count-kings of Barcelona, supported by troubadours, remote damsels, courtly and knightly love and the whole paraphernalia of medieval romanticism. In its more modern form it embraced the theory of the patrial home or *casa pairal* in the Catalonian countryside, to which the most determinedly urban Barcelona town-dwellers looked back with poignant nostalgia, and the reality of the successive Carlist Wars for reactionary causes. In the Welsh case it was a matter of druids and of semi-legendary patriotic chieftains, Owen Glendower and Prince Llewellyn, who smote the English. Their Catalan equivalent was Guiffré el Pelós (Wilfred the Hairy) who, rather as the Knights of King Arthur were immortalized in pre-Raphaelite paintings and the poems of Tennyson, was enshrined in a famous nineteenth-century portrait, now in the Louvre, of Louis the Pious, son of Charlemagne, visiting him on his wounded warrior's bed and creating with his bloodied fingers the stripes of the flag of Catalonia. Many, however, think that the dates of Louis' son, Charles the Bold, make him a more likely sick bed visitor to Guiffré.

The trouble was that neither the South Wales coalowners, nor the burghers of Barcelona, who set the tone of that city for the late nineteenth and early twentieth centuries, were remotely in the image of these folk heroes. Many of these Catalans were almost caricatures of *bons bourgeois*. They were bearded, rather heavy men in thick formal suits, devoted to

eating heavy meals, drinking heavy wine and smoking strong
cigars. They were very male chauvinist even by the standards
of the time. And they were also, unless they were anarcho-
syndicalists, inclined to be very hardline if also Gallican
Catholics. There was about them a touch of Harry Truman's
jibe against some Missouri businessmen that 'the louder they
prayed on Sundays the worse they behaved on Mondays'.
Even Gaudí, the great architect and, in his later life, increasingly illiberal mystic Catholic, wrote of his fellow Catalans:
'We . . . are the middle team, with our qualities that become
defects . . . Our instinctive desire is to trade, to make money;
this often leads us into avarice (though not to usury),' the
latter distinction being perhaps more valid in theology than
in practice.

Gaudí himself, however, could not be accused of either
one or the other. In his period of greatest success, say from
1885 to 1910, he liked charging high fees and living something of the life of a (celibate) boulevardier, but after that he
retreated into an austere and solitary old age, devoting such
limited funds as he could command to trying desperately to
keep at least intermittent work going on his somewhat
hysterical basilica of the Sagrada Família, today Barcelona's
most familiar emblem, but which went out of fashion for
the middle two quarters of the twentieth century. He died in
1926 four days after being run over by a tramcar on the Gran
Via, one of the main avenues of the Eixample, that massive
bourgeois poultice on the neck of the old city, in which
poultice so much of his residential work had been done. It
was a fate reminiscent of that of Matthew Arnold in Liverpool
forty-four years previously, except that Arnold expired only
after running for and catching his tramcar, whereas Gaudí
went under the wheels without even mounting.

This turn-of-the-century architectural innovation and
Catalan renaissance, both of language and of desire for

autonomy from Madrid, did not produce social harmony in Barcelona. The patronage of the three architects and the fostering of Catalan identity marched alongside the flaunting of greatly increased wealth by factory owners and merchants benefiting from the belated industrialization which was swelling Barcelona's population and making it substantially the biggest city in Spain. Many of those who flooded into the Barcelona sweatshops came from the south with little feeling for either historic Catalan nationalism or the commercial spirit which made rich those who paid their low wages. They did however have a propensity to anarcho-syndicalism, which Giuseppe Fanelli, an Italian disciple of Bakunin, introduced to Spain, primarily to Catalonia but secondarily to Andalusia, in 1869.

Partly as a result, Barcelona in the 1890s experienced no equivalent of the Belle Epoque of the Paris to which it looked semi-reverentially. Barcelona has always been a bit out of phase with Paris, which is perhaps mostly the case with disciples to mentors or with children to parents. It had been closely influenced by Haussmann in the building of the Eixample, which started in the 1860s and flowered in the 1870s and 1880s into an even bigger area of bourgeois reconstruction than that which Haussmann had achieved in west central Paris under Napoleon III. But Barcelona had been spared the indignity of defeat by Prussia in 1870 and the horrors of the Commune in 1871. On the other hand the 1890s were less benign in Catalonia. While Madame Swann's carriage was driving through the Bois de Boulogne observed by attendant admirers Barcelona was experiencing anarchist bombings frequent enough to constitute a menacing pattern. In 1896 the bombing of the tail-end of the Corpus Christi Day procession (that is after all the notables had gone) from the soaring gothic church of Santa Maria del Mar, which may have been done by a police *agent provocateur*, led to the rounding up of every possible suspect, to ruthless interrogation with torture and to the notorious Montjuic trials, which produced a wave of protest throughout Europe.

Nor was the first decade of the twentieth century much better. In 1909 came the so-called *semana tràgica* when demonstrations against an ineffective war in Morocco culminated in 116 street deaths. Barcelona (and Spain) kept out of the incomparably greater violence of 1914–18, but it also missed the social cement which the outbreak of war immediately provided for all the belligerent countries, and which victory a little less temporarily sustained for France and Britain. Barcelona's substitute for such patriotic cement took the form of international exhibitions. One, in 1888, led to Philip V's citadel for the intimidation of the city being turned into the public Parc de la Ciutadella, with a zoo and two museums, which stands sentinel to the east of the old city. An Arc del Triomf, which was built in the Moorish style for the entrance to this exhibition, also survives. It is much cheaper in human casualties to create one for the commemoration of an exhibition rather than of military victories, as in most other cities.

The next major Barcelona exhibition was in 1929, which, although it took place under the (relatively benign) dictatorship of Primo de Rivera, helped to redeem the reputation of the hill of Montjuic on the other side of the city. The principal relic of that exhibition is the Palau Nacional, a vast derivative construction dominating the northern slope of Montjuic, but in a most un-Barcelona like way wholly lacking in spirit or originality. It redeems these deficiencies by now containing a truly remarkable and beautifully displayed exhibition of Romanesque frescoes and paintings on wood assembled from the churches and monasteries of Pyrenean Catalonia. A short distance away is the Miró Foundation with which the architect José Lluis Sert in the early 1970s looked forward to the end of Franco (which occurred in November 1975) as well as establishing a fine monument and house for many of the works of Joan Miró, who, unlike his near contemporary Picasso, was a genuine Catalan and not just a bird of (ten-year) passage. Both of them, however, spent much of their lives in Paris.

Much of modern Barcelona stems from the city's being host to the 1992 Olympic Games. These produced a new airport designed by Ricardo Bofil. It has a handsome but too elongated terminal building admirably designed for long-distance walkers. The city also has a transformed waterfront, which for the first time places recreational sailing on an equality with commerce and also opens up fine vistas, although at the price of two huge new towers, one an hotel and the other an office block, which are depressingly reminiscent of what once was the New York World Trade Center. But above all there was an imaginative sense of spending public money for civic improvement. Barcelona is an outstanding example of the advantages both of local initiative and of countervailing political power.

This countervailing balance is splendidly symbolized in the Plaça de Sant Jaume behind the cathedral. There two somewhat Italianate buildings, both of around 1400 origins, although subsequently modified and added to, face each other with an equal gaze. The one is the Generalitat, the seat of the now highly autonomous regional government of Catalonia. The other is the Ajuntament or Town Hall, the headquarters of the city administration and the mayor. Both have historic roots and striking assembly chambers, the Golden Chamber of the Generalitat and the Salo de Cent of the Town Hall, emblems equally of early oligarchic independence. Both have been considerably modified over six centuries and have gone through periods when the traditional liberties out of which they emerged were suppressed by centralizing power from Madrid. Philip V notably did so in the early eighteenth century, as did General Franco in the middle quarters of the twentieth century.

In the post-Franco period, however, they have both had a strong and semi-compatible reflowering. For the 1980s and most of the 1990s the regional government was run by a right-of-centre moderate nationalist, Jordi Pujol i Soley, who had been imprisoned for three years by Franco but who, in spite of being dependent upon rural votes for his majority, was a sufficiently solid urban figure to strike such an acute observer as Robert Hughes as 'the reincarnation of those Catalanist burghers who ran Barcelona in the late nineteenth century'. Born in 1930 he had been a doctor of medicine and a significant local banker as well as a political prisoner. Opposite him in the Ajuntament for nearly the same period was Pasqual Maragall i Mira. Ten years younger than Pujol and the grandson of a famous Catalan poet Joan Maragall, he had in 1982 succeeded Narcis Serra i Serra, a former London School of Economics student, who had become Felipe González's deputy in the Madrid government. Maragall was a moderate socialist mayor just as Pujol was a moderate conservative president of the Generalitat.

To those who believe that power cannot be shared without being dissipated it sounds a classic recipe for feebleness of administration. In fact it has led to one of the strongest civic renaissances in Europe. The Barcelona which sixty-five years ago was torn by a civil war within a civil war (between the Anarchists and the Communists) and which two years after that was to be the epicentre of the Republican débâcle and the flight into France, has become, in the words of my opening sentence in this essay, the greatest provincial city in Europe; and has been heavily dependent for this achievement upon public administration. New parks have been created and old ones transformed. Museums have been refurbished.

Streets have been pedestrianized, and previously decayed squares have achieved cleanliness without sterility, partly through the most extensive public sculpture programme in Europe. And urban transport has been so improved as to make London, by comparison, seem like Calcutta.

This has happened without the regional and the city governments engaging in a zero-sum game. A large part of the reason is that the Madrid government, perhaps with more sense of inevitability than of enthusiasm, had devolved power to an extent that would make Livingstone of London green with envy. Pujol and Maragall have both had enough to do without just stultifying each other. Maragall, having given up the mayoralty in 1997, is currently seeking to move across the square to the Generalitat when Pujol retires before the 2003 provincial elections. Whether Maragall wins and, if so, how the new balance works, remain open questions. Barcelona, partly as a consequence of the Olympic Games extravagances, is now short of money, and again believes it is being unfairly treated by Madrid, giving more than it receives. The old lavishness is over.

The late-1980s and 1990s transformation of Barcelona was much aided by this erstwhile lavishness. The Ajuntament and the Generalitat between them spent nearly £1½ billion on embellishing the city for the 1992 Games. There was a consensus in favour of elevating the special spirit of Barcelona after its suppression by the dead hand of Franco and his long-term mayoral nominee Joseph Maria de Porcioles i Colomer, who held the office from 1957 to 1973. That was an unfortunate period for the destruction of the good and the construction of the bad all over the world. If Porcioles were facing an international urban crimes tribunal he could summon some powerful defence witnesses from London, Glasgow, Brussels and several other cities. Nevertheless his record was even worse than most. He built an appalling extension to the city offices, which is a blot upon the skyline of the core of Barri Gòtic. He cut down the trees and closed one of the Ramblas to pedestrians, turning it into an urban motorway. He was indifferent to Barcelona's monuments of *modernisme* and allowed them to fall into decay (although, luckily, mostly to escape destruction). He presided over a Barcelona in which Catalan newspapers were not allowed to be published, and did his best to turn it into nothing more special than Madrid's Mediterranean seaport. As a result he gave it a rundown and almost nondescript air.

Yet, even had Porcioles thought otherwise, the tide of fashion and the oppresive hand of the Spanish government would have been against him. Gaudí, Domènech and Puig were certainly not names with which to conjure in 1950s and 1960s Barcelona. Work on the basilica of the Sagrada Familia (although it seemed at least as near to completion when I first went there in 1953 as it does today) was suspended. The Parc Güell was neglected and overgrown, while in the Passaig de Gracia, Barcelona's very passable imitation of the Champs-Elysées, Gaudí's Pedrera was dingy apart from a wildly inappropriate accretion of neon signs, while the leather-goods firm of Loewe a little lower down the avenue was allowed to tear out the street-level façade of Domènech's Lleó Morero.

The tide of architectural fashion is a flickering will-o'-the-wisp. I remember when, in 1930s Oxford, the multi-chrome brick of Butterfield's Keble College was thought to be a bad joke. Now it appears to me, as to others, to be a fine example of high-Victorian gothic, and I do not believe that is just because John Betjeman and others have taught me that I ought to think it so, although such influences have no doubt played their part. Just as Butterfield has graduated in Oxford and elsewhere from being a man who could not use a decent single-coloured stone, so in Barcelona Gaudí, Domènech and Puig have advanced from being men who could not draw a straight line into being the magnets of Barcelona tourism. The fantasies of the Parc Güell, 25 per cent a superior Catalan version of Aubrey Beardsley and the Yellow Book, 25 per cent a precursor of Disneyland, but above all an architectural reincarnation of the amazing natural features of the thirty-mile-distant massif in which the monastery of Montserrat is set, are now beautifully maintained. From its dominating site looking over the whole city and out to the Mediterranean the Parc Güell has become a great draw, not only for tourists but for the local population. On an early-spring festival day in 2002 half the Barcelona schoolchildren seemed to be going round in parties. And the extraordinary serpentine seating on the roof of the main structure provides many places, at least as original as but more comfortable than a Charles Rennie Mackintosh chair, for surveying the whole city, spread out from there to the three-mile-distant Mediterranean.

Yet there is room for wondering how artistically innovative is the new, prosperous, apparently contented and Europeanized, certainly peaceful Barcelona compared with the strife-ridden city of most of its history. 'At least as innovative so as is Paris' would be a fair riposte. There were two relevant special exhibitions in 2001–2. The first in London (at the Royal Academy) was of Parisian art of the past century. The almost universal comment (and not I think inspired by anti-French British chauvinism) was that it illustrated how abruptly the French painting genius, which had dominated the world from about 1860, had run into some figurative buffers around a hundred years later.

The second, entitled 'Paris–Barcelona 1888–1937', opened in the Musée d'Orsay in October 2001 and then moved to the Barri Gòtic of Barcelona in February 2002. What this demonstrated is that the Catalan city is living as much on its past as is the French capital. Picasso and Miró are the local heroes, and there has been no one much to replace them. Even more striking is the extent to which the tourist attention of the whole city of Barcelona is organized around homage to that architectural school of *modernisme*.

None of this seemed to mean anything to the Barcelona which I first visited in the cold and cloudy Easter week of 1953. The whole of northern Spain (and maybe southern Spain too, but I did not see that) seemed dark, isolated and cut off from any of the stimuli of post-war Europe. We crossed the western Pyrenees to Pamplona, where at that season there were no bulls running in the streets (and not much spirit of Hemingway either), but mainly sad old men sitting in the corners of quiet cafés and reading pole-fastened newspapers, who might have been in any provincial city of the Europe of 1912, except that the newspapers were then less censored. We proceeded to the Ebro valley, almost as blood-soaked in the Civil War, which was then only fourteen years over, as the Somme had been a generation earlier, to Saragossa, the Aragon capital. There, with northern barbarian insensitivity, I provoked almost the reaction of one of the old Bateman cartoons by trying to order an *entrecôte saignante* on Good Friday evening. Francoist Spain kept alive the spirit of *los reyes catolicòs* (Ferdinand II and Isobel).

We went on through a coldly drizzling Tarragona to several nights in Barcelona. I find it almost impossible to reconcile the city then with the city I have known in the past twenty-five years. It was dingy and it was dull. It seemed to have little even of the bravado triumphing over squalor which I remembered from the Naples of four years earlier. The Civil War had exhausted its spirit more than changing sides in the Second World War had done to that of Naples. No doubt it was also due to the dead and anti-Catalan hand of Franco, working in double harness with the Spanish Church, hardly then in one of its more liberal moods and elevated into its most powerful position for several centuries. Perhaps my most abiding vignette of that visit comes from trying to go up the little hill to the right of the cathedral and being temporarily stopped by the then ubiquitous police while the Cardinal Archbishop came out of his palace in the back of a huge Cadillac, the driver admittedly edging his way gingerly through the scattering of mostly mutilated beggars. Princes of the Church were indeed proud in the Barcelona of those days.

But not much else was. We stayed in an uninspiring superannuated hotel appropriately called the Queen Victoria, and now I think happily pulled down. (Barcelona always had the white and ormolu opulence of a Ritz, but that was beyond our means.) We saw the Sagrada Familia, but the more recherché works of Gaudí and all of those of Domènech and Puig were hidden and disregarded, and we did not have the forward-looking discrimination to seek them out. We went to a second-rate bullfight, but it was not the season for grand *corridas*, and in any event Barcelona has never been much more of a bullfighting city than Dublin has been a cricketing one. It prefers football, and as I write this, sitting on the terrace of the Hotel Colón and facing the cathedral on a sunny early-March morning, the peaceable inhabitants milling gently around the pedestrianized square are threatened with the imminent arrival of both Liverpool FC and the European Council with the attendant entourages of Messrs Chirac, Schroeder, Blair, Berlusconi *et al.*, I am not sure to which event they look forward with more apprehension.

To complete the story of that 1953 visit, we then drove north along a wholly undeveloped Costa Brava to the French frontier. So far from being oppressed by touristic over-development our main difficulty was finding our way along pot-holed rural roads between one quiet fishing village and another while worrying whether we might run out of petrol before we found one of the very few filling stations. Returning to France was both cosseting and liberating.

The transformation of Barcelona (and indeed of Spain as a whole) over the past half-century has been a triumph for a combination of the resilience of the Catalan spirit and of the material prosperity, accompanied by a revival of openness, which Spain's 1986 entry into Europe has brought with it. My main criticism of the present city, as culturally vibrant as it is commercially (and touristically) successful, is that its preoccupation with two competing Iberic languages leads into an unbecoming linguistic provincialism. When, a few years ago, I asked the head waiter of a high-class Catalan restaurant whether he could speak French or English he drew himself to his distinguished full height and said, 'No, but I speak Castilian,' as though that was the most in the way of a second language that anyone could possibly expect of him. My complaint is not about English, which is gaining ground and in a pidgin form is much more to be encountered in Barcelona than in, say, Estremadura, but about the absence of French. The frontier with France is only 150 miles away. Catalan culture claims to span the Pyrenees and to look to Paris as much as Madrid. In that case it might teach its citizens to speak a little more of the language which only two generations ago was the dominant one of civilization. There is far more German spoken in Prague or Budapest than there is French in Barcelona. And it is a pity, to say the least, that in the exhibition called 'Paris–Barcelona', much of it of French painters or of Catalans who have spent most of their productive lives in Paris, the labelling of individual exhibits is confined to Spanish or Catalan, particularly as they must all have had a French version done for the Musée d'Orsay. To make up for this, however, arrival at the exhibition can be by one of the best and cheapest taxi services in Europe, and a competing excess of Catalan and Spanish can be balanced by reading the London newspapers of the same day, available from 8.30 a.m., over breakfast, a degree of journalistic internationalism which cannot be found in any Italian city, or for that matter in Berlin.

In the nearly thirty years since the end of Francoism Barcelona has been riding a mounting wave of success, prosperity and cosmopolitanism. It has created new vistas, new museums to house its artistic treasures, and new hotels to house the visitors who come to see them. It has been self-confident and well governed. It has combined a liberation of its Catalan spirit with a successful exploitation of its cultural heritage. I have a little doubt as to where it goes from here. Like Paris, it has not added much recently to that cultural heritage. Like Berlin it has run through the intoxication of liberation and has begun to suffer from a mild hangover following years of lavish expenditure.

Perhaps cities, like some great intellects, need occasionally to lie fallow. And Barcelona has certainly achieved enough in the past thirty years to entitle it to such a period of repose. But I hope and believe that the period will not go on for too long. There is a Catalan folk dance called the Sardana which is performed twice a week in the large pedestrianized area between the cathedral and the Hotel Colón. To the uninitiated it looks boring. Large circles of participants holding hands just bob up and down. It is neither erotic nor spectacular. But it does go on in a very steady way. Maybe that is all right for Barcelona for the next decade or so; but not indefinitely. To maintain its high world profile a new impulse will then be required.

BERLIN

BERLIN'S HISTORY has been as dramatic as it is relatively short. Of the major European capitals only Madrid, so artifically man-made that Philip II sited it by caliper in 1561, is arguably younger. But Madrid quickly achieved at least some of the appurtenances of being the capital city of the greatest sovereign of his time in Europe, whereas Berlin, until the middle of the seventeenth century, was no more than the recently sacked (by the Swedes) capital of a very minor ruler of an infertile territory (Brandenburg) situated in a sandy plain on the edge of civilized Europe. In 1643, when Friedrich Wilhelm Hohenzollern, who subsequently earned for himself the sobriquet of the 'Great Elector', returned to a broken-down capital and an uninhabitable 'palace', Berlin had only 6,000 inhabitants.

From then on there was no direction for Berlin, Brandenburg (later Prussia) and the Hohenzollerns to go except up, and they did so with considerable buoyancy – for the next 160 years. A century after the Great Elector, Frederick the Great performed the superficially contradictory roles of making Prussia into the power with the most feared army in Europe, 'frenchifying' his court, and providing a notable station on the long line of those who combined military skill with homosexuality. He preferred to live at Potsdam eighteen miles away, but he nonetheless did a lot for Berlin including the construction of the fine central building of what became the Humboldt University, as well as underpinning the city as the capital of a serious power and seeing its population rise to over 150,000.

His successors, Friedrich Wilhelm II and III, did not distinguish themselves in the Napoleonic Wars, but the latter nonetheless came out of the settlement of Vienna with Prussia doubled in size to a state of ten million people, stretching from the borders of France to those of Russia, and embracing the potential industrial wealth of the Ruhr and the Saarland. Freidrich Willhelm III was also the sovereign of the so-called Biedermeier period. Biedermeier was not a man but a made-up satirical name, intended to express a complacent bourgeois respectability, but, thanks largely to Karl Friedrich Schinkel (1781–1841), these years gave Berlin its best neo-classical buildings and the air of a proper capital city, which, if not quite the equal of Paris or St Petersburg or Vienna, could at least be discussed alongside them. No architect since Schinkel has left a comparable impression on Berlin.

It was only in the reign of the next Hohenzollern that Berlin began to take off on its trajectory towards being not only a *Großstadt* (big city, although many other German towns had exceeded it in this respect as late as 1800), but also a *Weltstadt* (world city). That apotheosis occurred at almost exactly the mid-point of the nineteenth century, coinciding as is noted in the essay on New York with a similar emergence to maturity on the other side of the Atlantic. Berlin's maximum of 4½ million, in 1939, made it the third biggest city in Europe and the sixth largest city in the world. A combination of the Kaiser's Second Reich and Hitler's Third Reich decisively achieved *Weltstadt* status for Berlin, although they also produced two phases of degradation for the city, the second much deeper than the first. The years 1918 and 1919 were a violent nervous tremor which destroyed the self-confidence of the Wilhelmine state but also released frenetic cultural energy. In addition it paved the way to a much worse fate for the city, which experienced its nadir in 1945 after twelve years of Hitler's regime. Air Chief Marshal Harris by night and General (of the US Air Force) Spaatz by day had done their best to reduce it to rubble, and then, against Churchill's wishes, Eisenhower held back from racing the Russians to first occupation (as he did in Prague and Vienna) so that Berliners were subject first to Russian artillery bombardment and then to the brutalities (predictable in view of the appalling preceding slaughter on both sides) of unilateral Soviet occupation for nearly three months.

Many people might have said that it served Berlin right. But this would have been a superficial, even an ignorant, reaction. Berlin, in its harsh Prussian plain, had been the least Nazi of the big German cities, just as the apparently *gemütlich* Munich had been the most. The cocky irreverence of the Berlin spirit, with its downbeat humour, mockery of self as well as of the pretensions of others, had long made it unpopular with rulers who liked pomp and circumstance. Frederick the Great, as already noted, preferred to live at Potsdam. Wilhelm II was also suspicious of Berlin and its citizens, and this was one issue on which Bismarck agreed with him. Hitler never had a permanent residence there. And even Konrad Adenauer, the first of the post-1945 German democratic Chancellors and himself a man of simple tastes, except for power and political manipulation, who had at one stage of his life frequently to travel to Berlin by night, said that he always slept badly as soon as his *Schlafwagen* crossed the Elbe out of his preferred Rhineland, into the flat land towards the ungodly sophistication of that modern Babylon amid the northern steppes.

To my great regret I never saw Berlin before its semi-destruction by a combination of British and American bombs and Soviet artillery. It was not so much the six and a half peacetime years of Nazism that I regretted having missed, although there would have been a macabre interest in knowing the city at its most intimidating and with its maximum population size. Nor would such a visit have been chronologically implausible, for my father went there several times in the middle to late 1930s, mainly passing through on journeys to Prague and Danzig, and was quite inclined to take me on his foreign trips, but to what he probably regarded as more agreeable destinations.

It was however more the Berlin of the last years of the Weimar Republic that I most regretted not having seen. The atmosphere of this was vividly captured for English readers of my generation in Christopher Isherwood's *Mr Norris Changes Trains* and *Goodbye to Berlin*. To my undergraduate taste it seemed that fascination with these short novels showed one's cosmopolitanism. But, looking back, it seems more to illustrate inherent insularity in that one saw what were to be the world-shattering death throes of democracy in the centre of Europe primarily through the eyes of a twenty-seven-year-old part-time teacher of English, talented a writer of autobiographical fiction though he was, rather than through those on more indigenous and profound political commentators. (In 2002 this gap was somewhat repaired by the posthumous publication of Sebastian Haffner's *Defying Hitler*, a fascinating tract of his 1933 experience, edited by his son.) What however is indisputable is the Isherwood influence on my imagination, as illustrated by the fact that on visits to the still-damaged and sundered city of the 1950s and early 1960s I remember frequently trying to discover areas which brought back the feel of the rather dowdy middle-class quarters like Nollendorfplatz of which Isherwood had written so memorably.

For all this the reality was that I never saw Berlin until June 1952, three years after the drama of the blockade and the airlift, when the city was firmly divided, with the Western sectors cut off from the surrounding countryside, yet with movement between West and East within the city still reasonably free. Both the S-bahn (mainly overhead) and the U-bahn (mainly underground) were running across the sectors. On the other hand the journey into Berlin from the west was formidable. I came to give a political lecture under the auspices of the British occupying authorities, and arrived, eccentrically, at the end of a more or less continuous rail journey from the far west of France. But I always liked trains. There was a good French express from Rennes to Paris, then a long overnight *wagon-lit* to Hanover, a short day of British Control Commission hospitality there, and finally a second night in a slow-moving and somewhat less comfortable sleeping car of the British military train through the 150 miles of the Soviet zone from Helmstedt to the semi-suburban station at Charlottenburg. This was then the British terminus for the West for all the city-centre termini, in which the railway hub of Berlin was as rich as London or Paris, were in the Soviet sector. That nearly forty-eight-hour journey at least made me feel that a goal had been reached.

There was already an immense superficial difference between the glitter of the Western sectors, and particularly of their 'main street', the Kurfürstendamm, and the sombre austerity of the East. Yet there were some paradoxes. On that first visit I was taken (crossing the sector border by S-bahn) to see a very stylish performance of Offenbach's *La Vie Parisienne* at the Komische Oper on Behrenstrasse, a few hundred yards within the East. This opera house was then under the notable and long-lasting direction of Walter Fellenstein. I never saw as great a contrast between sombre environs and a refulgent stage until thirty years later I went across the bulldozed ruins of the Gorbals to the Glasgow Citizens Theatre to see an equally stylish performance of Wilde's *An Ideal Husband*. And the glamour of the Kurfürstendamm was always somewhat skin-deep. For all its animated cafés and vast neon-lit cinemas, quite smart shops and the dramatic backcloth of the bombed stump of the Kaiser Wilhelm I Memorial Church at the eastern end, it always gave the impression of being the broadwalk of a temporary international exhibition rather than the permanent axis of a great city. And that I suppose was natural, for the Kurfürstendamm never had a closer relationship to the historic centre than, in London terms, does Sloane Street at best or Kensington High Street at worst. After 1990, with the reknitting of the old centre of Berlin, the Ku'damm went sadly downhill and recalled Oxford Street on a Saturday afternoon. Still more recently, however, it may have recovered somewhat, particularly towards the western end, away from the Memorial Church and beyond the Fasanenstrasse, which side street is still quite chic.

Nevertheless West Berlin in the 1950s, so far from remaining the symbol of defeated Nazism, became the eastern spearhead of the free world. This was an uncovenanted outcome of the Soviet blockade and the consequent Anglo-American airlift of 1948–9. At the outset it appeared to be the first of the three or four occasions when the Cold War was in most danger of becoming hot. But in its medium-term effect it forged a solid alliance of interest and sentiment between Berliners and the Western powers, which in turn greatly aided the Adenauer policy of pushing the Federal Republic towards being America's most valued European ally. Without the drama of the airlift and the semi-heroic roles which successive governing mayors of the city – Ernst Reuter and Willy Brandt – were given in Western mythology, it would have been impossible to imagine President Kennedy

in 1962 touching both German and American hearts, even if
not impressing with his knowledge of demotic German, by
proclaiming from the steps of the Schöneberg Rathaus: 'Ich
bin ein Berliner.'

This gave West Berlin a role and a lot of subsidies for a
full decade, and then, just about when there might have been
danger of these flagging, the role was fortified by the East's
brutally defensive erection of the Wall in 1961. Visits in that
preceding decade all had the air of being arrivals at a film
festival. Landings and take-offs at Tempelhof, the airport
much enlarged for the 1936 Olympic Games and barely three
miles from the *Stadtmitte*, had the mild excitements associated
with the old Hong Kong airport, and with practically
nowhere else in the world. One almost went through the
bathroom windows of the surrounding apartment blocks. But,
once arrived, there were bouquets of flowers and messages of
welcome from the Governing Major.

One flight to Berlin I particularly remember from those
years. It was after the 1960 Anglo-German meeting at
Königswinter on the Rhine, and we were encouraged to go
on by a British European Airways Dakota (only the airlines
of the allied powers and not Lufthansa were in those days
allowed to overfly the Soviet zone) to see what was going on
in the Western outpost with the bait of a performance of
Rosenkavalier under Karajan at the Deutsche Oper. My neighbour on the flight was the redoubtable Lady Violet Bonham
Carter, the then seventy-three-year-old daughter of my major
biographical subject of the period, H. H. Asquith. But as she
had not then seen the highly favourable text, to which she
nonetheless took some exception, we were on excellent terms,
even though she was deeply shocked that I had never previously heard *Rosenkavalier*. 'Oh, my dear Roy,' she said in
terms which were a mixture of shock, sympathy and disdain:
'Never heard it? I must have heard it thirty times, beginning

at Dresden in 1911.' Despite my revelation of cultural poverty we got on sufficiently well that when on the approach
the pilot came on the intercom, thanked us for flying with
BEA (we had no option) and hoped that we had had a
pleasant flight, Lady Violet, in her most eloquent and high-
caste speaking voice said, 'And thank you very much, captain,
for flying us so well. I have had a very pleasant flight, thanks
to my conversation with Mr Roy Jenkins.' Fortunately even
her voice reached only a neighbouring couple of rows.

The next Berlin occasion I clearly recollect was in August
1962, when I took my elder son there as a reward for having
survived his first term at Winchester. As ten years before,
the journey was by train – by boat to the Hook of Holland
and then up through the Soviet zone. It was a year after the
erection of the Wall, and a high (or arguably low) point of
the visit was a slow progress through Checkpoint Charlie
to the oppressive East sector. Another aspect of the day
which remains fixed in my mind is that when we wandered
cautiously around the Soviet war memorial (paradoxically just
in the British sector), with Russian soldiers goose-stepping
up and down, my thirteen-year-old son was more shocked
than was I. He thought it demonstrated that the regimes of
Hitler and of Khrushchev were uncomfortably close together.
As a first result he was never, while always firmly left of
centre, tempted, even at the most impressionable ages, by
Communist or fellow-travelling sympathies. That in itself
made the journey well worth while.

Another, much later visit to Berlin was in April 1978
when, as president of the European Commission, I made an
official excursion to the sensitive offshoot of the Bundesrepublik, the most economically important member state of
the Community. But West Berlin was not juridically part
of the Community, although in full sympathy with it. And
the Russians were always watching for anything which could

put the West juridically in the wrong. The two days were
therefore full of potential elephant traps. It also had high-
lights, one of comicality, another of some importance. The
comicality, much to our anglophone discredit, arose on the
morning of the second day when, in the course of a long and
informative discussion of Berlin's problems, the deputy
mayor, who in general spoke the most excellent English,
suddenly announced that a major social issue for Berlin was
the presence of two or three hundred thousand immigrant
'Turkeys', who, apart from anything else, made a great deal
of noise in the streets. I frivolously said, 'What, even after
Christmas as well as before?', and then, such is the English
juvenile sense of humour as well as our capacity for expecting
linguistic perfection from others while not even attempting it
ourselves, we found it difficult not to giggle for the rest of
the meeting.

On the other hand I enjoyed both the friendliness which
the Berlin establishment bestowed upon me and the opportunity for a serious bilateral conversation. This latter encounter remains even more fixed in my mind. We were installed
by the city government in a large suite at the top of the Hotel
Kempinski, which was then the principal establishment in the
West. Kempinski was a great name in Berlin catering. In
the early decades of imperial prosperity the first Kempinski
had opened an emporium of a restaurant – the very approxi-
mate equivalent of the Lyons Corner Houses which came to
London about twenty years later – on the Leipzigerstrasse,
the main shopping street where the almost cathedral-like
Wertheim department store was opened in 1896, which also
had the advantage of being adjacent to the newspaper and
theatrical districts. Assisted by the location and maybe by the
attendance of the Kaiser at the gala opening, Kempinski had
a great success. But the family were less favoured by the next
'emperor' of Germany. Their property expropriated by the

Nazis, they sought refuge in London, but returned to Berlin
after the war, and rebuilt their prosperity and reputation in
the Hotel Kempinski before providing the management for
the new Hotel Adlon when that great caravanserai was rebuilt
on its Wilhemstrasse site (just inside the old East) in the last
years of the twentieth century.

In 1978, however, the Adlon was rubble and there would
in any event have been no question at that time of staying
on the far side of the Wall. So, after an evening lecture to
the Chamber of Commerce followed by a fairly demanding
dinner with thirty or so Berlin notables, I found myself back
at about 10.30 in my Kempinski suite with its panoramic view
of the bright lights of the West fading into the sombre
darkness of the East beyond the Brandenburger Tor, and
more or less ready for my third performance of the evening,
which was a two-hour conversation/argument with Otto Graf
Lamsdorff, then the West German Economic Minister, who
always somewhat reminded me, both physically and in the
working of his mind, of Iain Macleod. Lamsdorff, very much
from the free-market end of the FDP, the junior partner
in the Schmidt coalition, was said to be the minister most
sceptical towards the European Monetary System, which we
were then engaged in putting together. On a more solid basis
than those who today believe the pound, which used to be
worth twelve D-marks, is Britain's finest possession, he did
not want that symbol of German post-war success to be
defiled by mingling with inferior currencies. My objective
was to change his mind, or at least to modify his opposition
to Chancellor Schmidt's new enthusiasm for a European
monetary advance.

Looking back it seems to me to have been a formidable
task to try to achieve at that time of night and after such a
testing day. It did not seem so then. Maybe it showed that
there was something in the view that *Berliner Luft* (Berlin air)

had some peculiarly stimulating quality, rather like that which
Keynes attributed to New York. How far I succeeded I am
not sure, although at least Lamsdorff neither resigned nor
frustrated Schmidt's European monetary enthusiasm. But I
shall never forget that prolonged late-night discussion, with
the Berlin skyline, illuminated by a brilliant April moon, all
around us.

These reminiscences of the divided city are supplemented
by three from the days after the Wall came down. The first
was a weekend in January 1991, which we spent in a house
party assembled by Christopher Mallaby, then British ambassador in Bonn, in the subsidiary embassy residence in Berlin.
This house had been in British hands since the early post-
war days, and ambassadors had always been encouraged to
pay frequent visits to the outpost of the divided city. But the
Mallabys were unique in my experience in running their
embassies – they subsequently did the same in Paris – for
voluntary as well as involuntary hospitality, and thus, happily,
making them more like a private house than an hotel. On
this occasion they had assembled, apart from ourselves, Noël
and Gabriele Annan and Frank Roberts, the last a former
ambassador to Germany and then a retired diplomat whose
capacious memory went back to his presence at the Yalta
Conference in 1945 and contrasted with his tiny size but
relentless energy, which gave him the sobriquet of 'the
electric mouse'. Gabriele Annan's presence added a specially
interesting quirk to the party, for the house had been built
for her father, Louis Ullstein, and she had lived there for a
time as a child. Ullstein, head of the eponymous and famous,
also liberal and Jewish, Berlin publishing firm of newspapers
and books, had decided in 1931 to forsake his former house
in the Tiergarten and move two or three miles to the sandy
soil and sylvan seclusion of Grünewald. By 1933 he was dead
and his family were soon constrained to forsake not only the

Tiergarten but Berlin as a whole as well as the business, and seek refuge in England.

On that 1991 visit the Wall had only been down for thirteen months and the wound in the centre of the city was not remotely healed, barely stitched together. The area just to the east of the Brandenburger Tor, the fulcrum of Wilhelmine and Nazi power, was more chaotic than monumental. My main impression was of a lot of tourists (even in January) milling round intermingled with several hundred souvenir sellers, the latter trying to get rid of everything from fragments of the Wall to Soviet military insignia.

Nevertheless the collapse of the Eastern empire and of its satellite, the so-called German Democratic Republic, had already made a vast difference to the social geography of Berlin. Throughout the forty-four years of the divided city West Berlin had been in one sense lucky that, as a result of the big boundary extension of 1920, the circumference of the city was exceptionally large, and contained within the boroughs of Grünewald and Spandau big tracts of lake and woodland and even farms. If Paris had been confined within the twenty arrondissements or London within the area of the old LCC with its twenty-eight Metropolitan boroughs, life in the French or British capitals would have been still more claustrophobic than it was for Berliners in the third quarter of the twentieth century. But the position was transformed after 1989. Not only was the old Soviet sector of the city open, but one could also drive freely down the 110 miles of ill-maintained autobahn to the half-surviving glory of Dresden, battered almost equally by Anglo-American destruction in 1945 and by insensitive Communist reconstruction in the subsequent forty years.

It was however the new ability to visit Potsdam which made the most impact. I had never previously seen it, except for going through in a sealed train in insignificant imitation of Lenin's journey to the Finland Station of St Petersburg. The Potsdam collection of Hohenzollern monuments is about as big a jumble of architectural styles as is the University of Oxford. They range from the 1745 elegance of Sanssouci (the state of which showed that Communist conservationists could do a single thing reasonably well even if they could not remake the street pattern of Dresden or manufacture decent consumer goods) through the slightly oppresive grandeur of the Neues Palais (1769) to the gabled Eastbourne-villa style of the Cecilienhof, built for the Kaiser's son, somewhat surprisingly in 1914–17, in which the allied victory summit of July 1945 was held. As we went through the inglenook-like rooms of this bathetic building, as undistinguished in architectural style as it is redolent of history, our fellow guest, Frank Roberts, was in an agony of frustration that, although he had been at the earlier Yalta Conference, he had not by ill-chance been at the Potsdam one and could not therefore speak with authority about where Truman sat, how Churchill spoke and whether Stalin dominated.

The second post-Wall visit to Berlin which I remember was in April 1996 when I went as chancellor of Oxford to speak at the fiftieth-anniversary celebrations of the Technische Universität, which had been elevated in 1946 on the foundations of the old Technische Hochschule. It was a rough introduction to the new Berlin, from which had been removed the cement of resistance to the Soviet threat together with the generous subsidies which went with that role. I had been expecting a rather bland affair. I remembered such an occasion about thirty years previously in the 'pregnant oyster', to give that 1950s Kongresshalle its familiar name, when Western platitudes had been received with excessive enthusiasm. The platitudes survived longer than the building, which collapsed rather than giving birth, although it has now been restored.

In 1996 at the Technische Universität there was an audience of at least 5,000, but the mood was sour and rebellious, recalling Paris in 1968 or American campuses at the time of the Vietnam War. The first speech by the governing mayor was mercilessly heckled. He was thought not to be doing nearly enough to keep the students in the financial state to which they had grown accustomed. I began to feel that my reflective comparative speech on universities in different countries would be wildly inappropriate. It is possible to confront a large obstreperous audience, although preferably in one's own country, and to enjoy it, but not with a semi-ironical speech. However my fears were largely misplaced, for when the mayor left, apparently to go to Bonn to plead for some more money, about 40 per cent of the audience left with him, not as a phalanx of support, but as a barracking escort on his way to the airport. I therefore was left with a rump but respectful audience of barely 3,000. Even quantitatively it was not bad by any standards, but it nonetheless felt a little flat. It was however a very good introduction to the new Berlin, unencumbered by excessive enthusiasm for or dependence upon the West.

The third visit in this post-Wall series was in April 2000, when I went half to participate in a conference under the auspices of Helmut Schmidt and half to speak at a surprisingly strongly attended Oxford dinner, with German Oxonians and British temporary expatriates almost equally matched in the audience. The transformation of the city since 1996 had been immense. It had been firmly stitched together, and had assumed a superficial air of unity, quite different from the chaos of ten years earlier, when there was no unity but merely a gap where the Wall had been. But the stitches had not been taken out from the wound, so that there were still many signs of where the incision had run.

Nevertheless the whole orientation of the city had been changed. Even more than by the opening up of the surrounding countryside, this was as a result of Schinkel's 'Prussian-style' old Berlin (and in his day Prussian style meant a cool neo-classical austerity rather than a heavy flamboyance) after a gap of fifty years, again becoming the effective centre of the whole city. Unter den Linden had replaced the Kurfürstendamm as the main street. New hotels had sprung up in the streets off Unter den Linden almost as fast (although fortunately not as high) as they had done in Beijing in the quinquennium before my last (1996) visit there. For the first time we stayed (and automatically stayed) in the old East. This hotel, and the one in which the Oxford dinner was held, as well as the flagship of the Adlon, were all built and furnished to the highest Western standards, but there was at least one significant difference between them and similar establishments a couple of miles away in one of the old Western sectors. Partly because of its dependence upon the Americans and, to a lesser extent, the British, West Berlin had become almost excessively anglophone. English was a strong second language, well taught and avidly learned. East Berlin had been utterly different. Russian was the second language on offer, maybe equally well taught, although perhaps not as avidly learned. By 2000 it had become largely useless, except for students of literature. As a result practically no one in thse grand new hotels – apart from the concierge and maybe the head waiter – could speak anything except German. The hotel staff are also remarkably ethnically pure by British, French or American standards. There are hardly any black faces on the streets of the old East or hispanic employees in the hotels and restaurants.

Another superficial but striking and persistent difference

is that whereas the old West is full of newsstands – Berlin had traditionally been very much a newspaper and magazine city – there are practically none in the old East. There are plenty of the pavement poster pillars (or Litfass-säule, a Berlin invention by Ernst Litfass) in the old East (as in the old West); they were good, apart from anything else, for carrying official instructions. And, maybe in the old East there was not enough variety of newspaper titles allowed, and little foreign press, except for *Pravda*, to justify newstands. How long will this difference persist?

Of much more importance is the great gain of the opening up of the fine perspectives of Unter den Linden, even if the western end became for a time the largest building site in the world – although the cranes are no longer so dominating as they were a couple of years ago – but also making available the vast space and monumentalism of the old Mitte, not merely for a hurried excursion into semi-hostile territory, but for leisurely strolling and gazing. A walk of a mile eastwards from the Adlon Hotel takes one past the Komische Oper, into first the fine balance of the Gendarmenmakt and then, 500 metres to the north into the old Forum Fredericianum, now renamed the Bebelplatz.

The Gendarmenmakt has two small baroque, early-eighteenth-century semi-matching cathedrals at the north and south ends with Schinkel's 1820 Schauspielhaus on the western side. It is one of the best squares of Europe, now giving the impression of being very much designed for living and not merely for show. It has a more friendly mixture of classical architecture and open-air cafés than any Parisian site. The Schauspielhaus, which started life as a theatre, has now become a music auditorium renamed the Konzerthaus and is home to the Berlin Symphony Orchestra. The still more famous Berlin Philharmonic has achieved a hall of spectacular acoustics in an adventurously designed 1960s building near the south-east corner of the Tiergarten.

The Bebelplatz is less friendly, more authoritative, and at least equally monumental. There is nowhere to sit and stare – let alone to drink as well. It is the very heart of capital-city Hohenzollern Berlin, which makes it a peculiar irony that it should now be named after Ferdinand August Bebel (1840–1913), that old Marxist theoretician and Socialist parliamentary leader of the Wilhelmine years. On its south side is a subsidiary building of the Staatsbibliotek and St Hedwig's Roman Catholic Cathedral, which has a fine front and a broad green dome giving it an air of being a more than passable imitation of the Pantheon in Rome. On the left, facing north, are the Alte Bibliotek (1775) and the Altes Palais (1834–7), both originally royal premises, but now taken over as part of the Humboldt University. The main Humboldt Building, which was constructed in 1753, although the University of which it is now the core was not founded until 1810, faces the square from the other side of Unter den Linden. On the right is the massive presence of the Staatsoper. It was in this square, surrounded by institutions symbolic of German culture, that the new Nazi regime instigated the 'burning of the books' on 10 May 1933, when 25,000 volumes went up in flames, provoking the main author of the *Eyewitness Guide to Berlin*, one of the best, to recall the prophetic 1820 remark of Heinrich Heine that 'where books are burned, in the end it is the people who will burn'. And it is now not only the people but the buildings as well which have been semi-destroyed. There is hardly one of these described in the last few paragraphs which has not had to be reconstructed to a greater or lesser extent since 1945. Sometimes it has been done with a utilitarian exterior hiding the original sumptuous interior, as with the Komishce Oper, sometimes the other way round as with the Schauspielhaus, and sometimes with a new but fine exterior concealing an equally new but inappropriate interior as with St Hedwig's Cathedral.

Beyond the Humboldt University lies first the Neue Wache and then the baroque Zeughaus (or Arsenal) of 1706. The Neue Wache is one of a group of small, much admired buildings of indeterminate use which are scattered around the civilized world. The Casino on the edge of Dublin, the Jeu de Paume and the Orangerie in Paris, even the Banqueting Hall in London, spring easily to comparative mind. However the Neue Wache has compensated for its indeterminate use not only by looking elegant for two centuries but by being able to adapt itself to a series of memorial purposes. Designed by Schinkel at the height of his fame in 1816–18 just after the Napoleonic Wars it was designated in 1930–1 as a monument to the German dead of 1914–18. Then in 1960 it was given a wider remit as a memorial to the victims of fascism and militarism. In 1993 it was rededicated to all sufferers from war and dictatorship.

Beyond the Zeughaus over the Schlossbrücke (in GDR days the Marx-Engels Brücke – it is difficult to know why some ideological names survive and other do not) lie the vast treasures of Museum Island. There, between the Spree and the Kupfergraben Kanal, guarded by the fierce mastiff of the Berliner Dome or Protestant Cathedral, built in its present unappealing form from 1894 to 1905, are five separate institutions, the Altes Museum, the Neue Museum, the Alte Nationalgalerie, the Pergamon-museum and, at the tip of the island, the Bodemuseum. The Pergamon is pre-eminent throughout the world for massive antiquities, and takes its name from the Greek Pergamon altar of 160 BC, although the Ishtair gate from Babylon (sixth century BC) and the Market Gate from Miletus (120 AD) are equally famous – sufficiently so that even in the days of the divided city the

East authorities were eager to show all these marvels to
visitors from the West. The other institutions are currently
in some flux (the Bodemuseum indeed being completely
reconstructed) as exhibits are reallocated between these and
the other galleries Dahlem, Charlottenburg and the Neue
Nationalgalerie, which were previously in the West.

The *chef d'oeuvre* of the new Berlin is however Foster's
Reichstag dome. The Reichstag, although not completed
until 1894 (but that was only forty-two years after the Palace
of Westminster), and in spite of Germany rarely being
famous for its parliamentary tradition, nonetheless occupied
a symbolic position in the Germany of the twentieth century.
Its building was paid for out of French reparations money for
1870, its deputies, including the large Social Democratic
contingent, showed a sufficiently convenient willingness to
support the Kaiser in the First World War for the prominent
inscription of *Dem Deutschen Volke*, which was added to the
west front in 1916, to have seemed appropriate. Two years
later however the Weimar Republic was proclaimed from the
balcony beside the motto, and (mostly) solid and respectable-
looking deputies settled into a life of reasonable parliamentary comfort for the next dozen years. The Reichstag dining
rooms, library and writing rooms of these years looked well
up to Westminster standards. Then, in 1932, the arrival of a
uniformed phalanx of 180 Nazi members changed the whole
ethos. Looking in the spring of 2002 at the remarkable
photographs which surround the base of the new dome, a
distinguished German diplomat of aristocratic and famously
combative name remarked to me on the look of twisted
hatred on most of their faces. A year later their leaders
arranged for the building to be destroyed by fire in order to
put the blame on the Communists and to justify the suppression of them and other opponents of the new regime. Thus
ended the first half-century of the Reichstag's history.

In May 1945, the Soviet flag flew symbolically over the ruin. But once the division of the city settled down the ruin was just inside the British sector with its back to the boundary and what in 1961 became the Wall. By then rebuilding had restarted and the West German Bundestag met there occasionally in the 1970s and 1980s. In the 1990s Norman Foster was set to work on the dome, and produced a great German popular success. On a recent Sunday morning of pouring rain there was a queue of nearly half a mile waiting more or less patiently to get in. Once in, and electrically elevated to the base of the dome, the amble up a gentle circular slope provides the great bonus of a slightly different perspective of the Berlin skyline with every twenty yards covered.

Yet, in spite of these splendours, there are major question marks over the future of Berlin. First, can any city go through the trauma which was its fate for nearly fifty years, and emerge normal and untraumatized? We all know of reformed alcoholics who have admirably overcome their central problem, as Berlin has done its sundering, but who nonetheless bear many scars both of their erstwhile experiences and of the admirably determined but half-draining way in which they emerged from it. Is there here a touch of analogy with Berlin? Has the city, in the way it has been sewn back together, lost something of its vitality? Is it cured of its frenzy but left dull and unspontaneous, even a little artificial?

Second, is Berlin's vast current wave of construction becoming top-heavy? Can one imagine circumstances in which the new Potsdamerplatz might become more famous for its 'to let' signs than for the quality of its new buildings? Third, how chronically short of money is the new Berlin? It obviously has big debts and heavy commitments, with a great range of cultural institutions to support, from the museums to its pre-eminent Philharmonic Orchestra, all of them used to generous subsidies. From a purely financial point – there are no other similarities – it suggests the state in which Northern Ireland might find itself if, peace being finally secured, the province were expected to live on its own resources, no more favourably treated than any other group of a million people in the United Kingdom, or for that matter in the Republic of Ireland. Fourth, are the politicians and the officials of the unostentatious Federal Repubic really content with the return to the old Prussian capital? The politicians voted for the move, even if only by a majority of 337 to 320, but may that not have been more an obeisance to the idea of reunification than a spontaneous preference for the Brandenburg plain over the cosy amenity of the provincial Rhineland? There are indications that many of them spend less time in Berlin than their French counterparts do in Paris or the British in London, or even the Americans in Washington.

Fifth, and most important, is the question of whether the size and grandeur, partly traditional and partly, as with the reconstructed Reichstag, very deliberately recreated, likely to change the style of government, modest, cautious, liberal, rational, but strikingly successful, which characterized the Bonn years. It will take at least the whole of the second decade of the reunited Berlin for the questions to be answered. The way in which they are will be fascinating not only for Germany but for the world as a whole.

ROY JENKINS

The Chancellors

PAN BOOKS

In *The Chancellors*, Roy Jenkins employs his political acumen as a former Chancellor of the Exchequer, to write engagingly about the dabblings of nineteen of his predecessors responsible for Britain's finances from 1886 to 1947, six of whom went on to lead the government.

In these illuminating, astute and engaging essays, Roy Jenkins provides us with a gallery of personal and political portraits ranging from Winston Churchill to Robert Horne.

'A perceptive, elegant work'
Anthony Howard, *The Times*

ROY JENKINS

Gladstone

PAN BOOKS

Winner of the Whitbread Biography Prize, 1995

This biography of William Ewart Gladstone charts the political career and personal life of the only man who was elected to four terms as British Prime Minister. Jenkins examines all the controversies of Gladstone's life with affection and insight.

This is the definitive biography of Gladstone, beautifully written by a consummate biographer.

'Perceptive, sympathetic and highly readable'
Robert Blake, *The Times*

ROY JENKINS

Churchill

PAN BOOKS

The most celebrated Prime Minister of the twentieth century and arguably the most renowned British Prime Minister ever, Winston Churchill is an icon of modern history. In this brilliant account of his life, Roy Jenkins analyses Churchill's exceptional character in all its strengths and weaknesses and illuminates his political career through its campaigns, elections, changes of allegiance and its troughs and peaks.

Exceptional in its breadth of knowledge and distinguished in its style, *Churchill* is enlivened with humour and highlighted with a penetrating intelligence.

'A hugely entertaining and instructive read'
John Campbell, *Independent*

'A first-class, well-sustained work of history and a masterpiece of biography'
Andrew Roberts, *Sunday Telegraph*

OTHER BOOKS
AVAILABLE FROM PAN MACMILLAN

ROY JENKINS

CHURCHILL	0 330 48805 8	£9.99
GLADSTONE	0 330 41171 3	£9.99
CHANCELLORS	0 333 73058 5	£12.00
MR BALFOUR'S POODLE	0 333 76681 4	£12.00

MAX HASTINGS

GOING TO THE WARS	0 330 37710 8	£7.99
OVERLORD	0 330 39012 0	£7.99
BOMBER COMMAND	0 330 39204 2	£7.99
THE KOREAN WAR	0 330 39288 3	£7.99

All Pan Macmillan titles can be ordered from our website,
www.panmacmillan.com, or from your local bookshop
and are also available by post from:

Bookpost, PO Box 29, Douglas, Isle of Man IM99 1BQ
Credit cards accepted. For details:
Telephone: 01624 677237
Fax: 01624 670923
E-mail: bookshop@enterprise.net
www.bookpost.co.uk

Free postage and packing in the United Kingdom

Prices shown above were correct at the time of going to press.
Pan Macmillan reserve the right to show new retail prices on covers
which may differ from those previously advertised in the text
or elsewhere.